Project Leadership

Project leadership is a much discussed and written about topic but it suffers from being hard to define and describe in a meaningful way that enables people to reflect on their areas for development. It was therefore refreshing to review Project Leadership 3rd Edition. The authors have tackled head on this challenge and provided materials that both experienced and new-to-the-role project leaders will find of great value across all industry sectors. It contains a number of new models and diagnostics that will help readers to tackle the very real challenges they will face in their role. This book also goes much further than any other: it helps the individual to identify different development opportunities relevant to their own situation to help build their career; it also helps organizations set out excellent project leadership development programmes to support their talent. Every project leader, aspiring project leader and organization with project management communities should own a copy of this book.

Professor Denise Bower, Executive Director of the Major Projects Association and Professor at the University of Leeds, UK

Effective project management is well recognised as paramount to the success of both public and private organisations and there is a myriad of reference material on the subject. What makes Project Leadership 3rd Edition so different is the relevance it brings to the modern day complexities and fresh challenges created by the demanding pace for change and acceleration of returns on investment. This book is a must read for any level of PM who wants to keep ahead of their game; it brings new angles of currency to some fundamentally important areas that have been somewhat glossed over in the past, including emphasis on the emotional intelligence and "softer" sides of the role. This book will strike a chord with those planning for their future and also the more experienced honing their project organisations' skills, knowledge and capability.

Jes Newman, Head of Transformation at Vodafone CHS; previously Program Director for multiple global Blue Chip technology companies

Project Leadership is more than a well-researched guide to this strange, yet essential, value called leadership. It takes the best of the research and explains concepts in straight-forward terms with real-life input from professionals across industries. This book contains helpful and insightful questions and checklists for every element of project execution and organizational/team development making it something you can read through and reference throughout your career.

Dyan L Foss, Global Managing Director Nuclear Sector, CH2M.

This book is excellent. Not only does it address the new realities of project management but it also gives superb guidance as to how to deal with them. Too many textbooks are focussed on the narrow mechanistic and procedural aspects of projects, but this one gives broad and refreshing insights on how to really excel in an increasingly complex world. Read this and join the new generation of project leaders!

Stephen Carver, Honorary Fellow Association for Project Management; Consultant in Project & Programme Management; and Lecturer at Cranfield School of Management, UK

For Andrew, Matt and Josh. Because we can. Sarah Coleman

For Saira, Leena and Haris. Because you were there. Donnie MacNicol

Project Leadership

Third Edition

SARAH COLEMAN

and

DONNIE MACNICOL

GOWER

Published by
Gower Publishing Limited
Wey Court East
Union Road
Farnham
Surrey, GU9 7PT
England

Gower Publishing Company
Suite 420
101 Cherry Street
Burlington
VT 05401-4405
USA

www.gowerpublishing.com

Sarah Coleman and Donnie MacNicol have asserted their right under the Copyright, Designs and Patents Act, 1988, to be identified as the authors of this work.

British Library Cataloguing in Publication Data
A catalogue record for this book is available from the British Library.

ISBN: 978-1-4724-5280-1 (pbk)
978-1-4724-5281-8 (ebk)
978-1-4724-5282-5 (ePub)

The Library of Congress has cataloged the printed edition as follows:
Coleman, Sarah, 1961-
  Project leadership / by Sarah Coleman and Donnie MacNicol. -- Third edition.
    pages cm
  Earlier editions authored by Wendy Briner.
  Includes bibliographical references and index.
  ISBN 978-1-4724-5280-1 (hardback) -- ISBN 978-1-4724-5281-8 (ebook) -- ISBN 978-1-4724-5282-5 (epub) 1. Project management. 2. Leadership. I. MacNicol, Donnie. II. Briner, Wendy. Project leadership. III. Title.
  HD69.P75B75 2015
  658.4'092--dc23
                                                                  2015018111

Printed in the United Kingdom by Henry Ling Limited, at the Dorset Press, Dorchester, DT1 1HD

Contents

List of Figures

List of Tables

About the Authors

Sarah Coleman leads and supports the shaping, design and implementation of business critical projects in the UK and internationally in order to help organizations deliver better outcomes and value. She brings with her an entrepreneurial mindset and a wide range of diverse perspectives.  She draws on over 25 years' practical experience of leading and supporting multi-million GBP strategic projects, programmes and change across sectors with multi-nationals, corporates and medium-sized enterprises. She says that an early lesson was that culture, behaviour and a focus on 'soft' people skills are as relevant as the focus on the technical 'hard' skills.

Sarah's early career was spent in software development and telecoms, so beginning a profound interest in the management and leadership of projects, programmes and change in organizations. Having founded Business Evolution Ltd (www.businessevolution.co) in 2007, she now provides her clients with a range of consultancy, interim, training and development, facilitation, coaching and mentoring. Typically, she helps shape, develop and deliver improvements in change, project and programme management and leadership capability within organizations. Her career has given her the opportunity to work across many industry sectors and she has worked in government, healthcare, financial services, technology, telecoms, engineering and professional services. Her clients say they value her ability to challenge positively and constructively, her ability to provide clarity and focus, and her excellent communication skills.

Sarah is a Fellow of, and Non-Executive Director for, the Association for Project Management. She holds an MBA from Cranfield School of Management and is a Mentor at Judge Business School, University of Cambridge. She is Visiting Senior Fellow at Lincoln University and is regularly invited to speak at business schools, events and conferences.

Sarah contributed *"Dealing with Power and Politics"* to "Business Analysis and Leadership" (Kogan Page, 2013), and blogs and tweets on all things project and programme. A qualified and experienced coach, Sarah provides support to managers and leaders who want to move their performance to the next level.

Donnie MacNicol is an experienced project and programme leader who is passionate about developing the leadership capabilities of individuals, teams and organisations to deliver success. He is at his best when working with senior management teams, challenged by complex situations and inspiring individuals and teams to perform.

He leads consultancy and training assignments, specializing in developing leadership capability, details of which can be found at www.teamanimation.co.uk. Donnie is currently working with infrastructure, defence, technology, aerospace and public sector organisations to improve delivery and leadership capability.

Widely recognized as contributing to the 'people and organizational side' of project management thinking, he is much in demand as a lecturer, speaker and writer. He is passionate about delivering value by incorporating the latest organisational, cultural and behavioural thinking.

Donnie is chair of the PMI UK Chapter Organisational Project Management (OPM) Forum and previously the APM's People SIG for 10 years. He is also a Visiting Teaching Fellow at Warwick Manufacturing Group (WMG) and has strong relationships with other prestigious academic bodies. Donnie is a member of the Acumen7 network of business leaders and has established an enviable network of leaders across the projects world. He has had over 30 articles published and contributed to 5 books including Programme and Portfolio Management Demystified and MSP® Survival Guide for SROs. He has presented at over 100 events and conferences including for the MPA, Defence Academy, IOD, APM, PMI, RICS and ICE and a host of private and public sector organisations.

"I first connected with Donnie MacNicol in mid 2014, during the first few months of moving into my new, and current, role as Head of Project Management for BAE Systems. I was seeking advice in writing a business case to support the introduction of a high level Project Management Development Programme and very much appreciated the discussions with Donnie, which helped me to clarify my thinking on this subject. Since then, through other enjoyable and stimulating discussions and through reading this book in order to write the Foreword, I have come to value Donnie's high level of expertise in the subject of project leadership capability development."

Stuart Forsyth, Head of Project Management, BAE Systems

Acknowledgements

Firstly we want to acknowledge the authors of the first and second editions of *Project Leadership*, Wendy Briner, Colin Hastings and Michael Geddes, with whom we share a passion for improving project outcomes. Their agreement paved the way for us to write the third edition, and we are delighted to be able to build on their cumulative experience of helping organizations make projects and project leadership work.

In undertaking this book, we recognized early on it would be a collaborative process therefore we reached out to our own networks and to the project management community at large. Thank you to all those who responded. Particular thanks must go to Alastair Godbold, Stephen Carver, David Beare, Kevin Parry, Philip Smelt, John Rowley, Ian Gambles, Dyan Foss, Judy Payne, Charles Smith, Owen Gadeken, Harvey Maylor, Liz Lee-Kelley, Paul Mansell, Rod Sowden, Ron Rosenhead and Mark Winter for their ideas, comments, experiences and research.

We are grateful to leading academics and practitioners who were kind enough to allow us to include their material, including Daniel Goleman, Eddie Obeng, Dov Dvir, Aaron Shenhar, Rodney Turner and Ralf Muller.

We are particularly indebited to Stuart Forsyth for providing the Foreword and to the four reviewers Denise Bower, Dyan Foss, Jes Newman and Stephen Carver. Also to Dr Penny Pullan who brokered the original meeting between the co-authors and without who, truly, this book would not have been written.

Special mention should be given to James Knight from iMA Strategies who allowed us to extensively use the iMA materials. Also to Jacqui Grey from The Neuroleadership Institute (NLI) who contributed a piece on the new realm of neuroleadership.

Finally, our greatest thanks goes to Jonathan Norman at Gower for his incredible patience and support.

Foreword

Project Leadership, Third Edition captures three of the current important trends in the project management profession: the need to evolve project management skills and competencies from 'technical' to 'leadership'; growth in the use of projects in non-traditional industries and therefore the need for organizations to invest in talent management to support recruitment and retention in an increasingly competitive environment; and the growing expectations that project management practitioners embrace professional standards and qualifications. It synthesizes these highly topical subjects and presents their significance for practitioners and for organizations in a clear and structured manner, providing useful and practical advice and tools for on the job application.

The company I work for, BAE Systems, is a global defence, aerospace and security company that consists of many thousands of complex projects, varying in size and scale from a few thousand to multi-billion pound prime contracts for military aircraft, Royal Navy destroyers and aircraft carriers, submarines, combat vehicles as well as through life, support and maintenance services. In my role I have the responsibility for developing project management capability across the company. My previous roles, spanning 25 years, have been in project leadership, of which 15 years have been at project director level across a range of major projects. Hence, I have great sympathy with the project leadership practitioner community and a great desire to use my new role to help this community understand the need for improvement and to help provide the mechanisms within BAE Systems to support this improvement. Coincidentally, this is also the underlying purpose of this book: the authors have written it to help project management practitioners responsible for leading the delivery of a project ('project leaders') and also for those responsible for developing the organizational capability necessary for the project leaders to do their jobs effectively.

Like most project-based organizations, BAE Systems is on a continuous improvement journey: we manage complex projects well but are always looking to improve. Our current improvement plans already embrace many of the initiatives contained in this book. However, reading this book has provided me with confidence that we are on the right improvement path, along with some ideas for fine tuning our initiatives. At a personal level it has also helped me to clarify my own career development thinking (even at this late stage!).

One of the features of project management is that project leaders have tended to learn by experience (I am an example of this), and indeed this has been self-perpetuating to the point that many senior practitioners have the view that only hard-won experience qualifies people for senior project leadership positions. Whilst this is largely true, modern research emphasizes that the development of project leaders can be accelerated through learning and development. The concepts and tools provided in this book help to move this debate forward and should also help individuals to plan and navigate a career route map and organizations to make the necessary culture shift.

I particularly like the questions at the end of each chapter, which I found helpful in challenging my current assumptions and forced a bit of reflective thinking.

The authors describe the role of a project 'leader' vs a project 'manager' (lead vs manage) and provide insight into the practical reality of the skills, competencies and styles required to lead in a project environment, as opposed to a business line leader or functional leader. This is very important, as leading projects to achieve agreed objectives is a specialist leadership application and should never get mixed up with general leadership development. The 'Eight Lookings' model is a helpful reminder that project leaders need to engage with multiple stakeholders and in doing so will have to apply high-level relationship and behavioural competencies. From my personal experience of leading projects in different environments, I very much relate to the point that good project leaders need to be able to change their styles to suit the situation, for example, type of project, phase of the project, culture of partner organization, style and behaviour of stakeholders. The ability to analyse and reflect on complex situations and change behaviours accordingly is introduced in the context of the need to develop 'reflective practitioners'. This is a highly topical subject and I believe fundamental to achieving a step improvement in individual and organizational leadership capability.

The authors describe three project leadership competencies that they consider are critical for project success. This is a very thought-provoking part of the book: there may be other relevant competencies, but for sure, if project leaders master the three identified, they will be well on their way towards leading successful projects. The common thread running through the 'Vision and Big Picture', 'Building Key Relationships' and 'Communication and Engagement' competencies is the importance of building meaningful, sustainable and mutually beneficial personal relationships with stakeholders, that is, people who can influence the outcome of a project. This aspect of project management is at the heart of the evolution from project management as a technical discipline to project management as a leadership discipline.

The structure of the book emphasizes the clear distinction between the responsibility for capability development among the individual and the organization. Advice is provided for practitioners on how to plan, organize and manage personal and career development, by creating a Personal Development Plan and treating it like a personal project with emphasis on personal responsibility. Project-based organizations are encouraged to provide the infrastructure (standards, expectations, advice, tools, training and development opportunities) necessary to support the individuals and to align their development with the needs of the project(s)/business. A comprehensive list of development interventions is provided and a blended approach is suggested. A useful development framework for the organization is also provided along with a diagnostic tool. These tools are very useful for organizations to compare against their own development activities as either confirmation that they are on the right path or to identify improvement ideas.

The issue of this book is at a point in time when the subject matter is being much discussed within the profession, and it helps to synthesize topical information from a wide range of sources to provide a coherent narrative that supports the discussions. I view this book as being beneficial for me and for BAE Systems to help confirm that we are on the appropriate continuous improvement path and also for the wider project programme and portfolio community to help move forward and stabilize the debates around project leadership capability development.

I recommend it to project leadership practitioners and project-based organizations who wish to improve their project leadership capability.

Stuart Forsyth
Head of Project Management, BAE Systems

Introduction

What we have already learnt is that Britain is actually rather better at organising big projects than we often gave ourselves credit for – on budget, on time and without the unwelcome discipline of dictatorship.

Vince Cable on the London Olympics 2012

Leaders are made, they are not born. They are made by hard effort, which is the price which all of us must pay to achieve any goal that is worthwhile.

Vince Lombardi

Organizations across industry sectors are operating against a background of constant and major change both globally and competitively. In 2002, Harris (2002) wrote, 'Organizations used to have stable industries, predictable customers, and five and ten year strategic plans. Today whole industries are being turned completely upside down in two years. Seemingly healthy companies that can't recognize and respond quickly to change may be dead but just don't know it yet.'

Driven by this, organizations are increasingly using projects as ways to manage innovation and change, and to make things happen fast, as well as for generating revenue. The media seems to take great delight in headlining high-profile project failures, highlighting issues and problems which often boil down to a lack of clear and competent leadership and accountability rather than project technical skills. Sadly, success typically does not make such a good story. Set against this backdrop, human capital has become increasingly important for competitive advantage in a global market where technology, innovation and commercialization increasingly drive the agenda. In 2012 and on its 40th anniversary, the Association for Project Management (www.apm.org.uk) launched its bold vision of 'a world in which all projects succeed'. This challenging and aspirational vision is a wake-up call to organizations to design, develop and deliver robust project capabilities.

Recent literature suggests a continued shift in focus and concern amongst many organizations and project professionals, from projects themselves to project management. The traditional view of project management continues to evolve in two fundamental ways.

First, it is moving away from a preoccupation with project planning and control tools as the keys to success and towards the management and leadership of people and their performance. There is a growing awareness of the human factors behind projects; a sense that projects are essentially human endeavours and it is our communication, management and leadership of people that helps secure success. This is complemented by the continuing research into and literature about leadership and its role within business and society. And many of us as project managers do struggle with the concept and practice of leadership. We have often come up through the ranks as technical specialists by learning, using and becoming expert in project technical skills. We are now being asked to move into project leader roles with little or no preparation of running a cross-organizational team and with little understanding of leadership and the spectrum of capabilities needed to do it justice. Technical knowledge can never be neglected, but it is the people skills that hold the key to successfully leading projects in the context of the wider organization. Organizations employing or contracting project leaders understand that their value is not simply a function of the sum of their experience or knowledge, but is in how well they work with a team and with diverse stakeholders, how they problem-solve and share their know-how to the benefit of the project team and the organization.

Effective leadership ability is now an important part of the project manager's toolkit. David Pitchford, then at the UK's Major Projects Authority, talked about 'leadership, not management' and the ideas surrounding leadership in business, politics and society continue to change and evolve, never so fast as during the past few decades. Smith (2014) remarked that the credibility of the project manager '... is built not on their knowledge of mechanised practices and administrative procedures, but on how they handle the complexities and challenges of the real project world'. *Project Leadership, Third Edition* is essentially about the human factors and skills that underpin project success at a time when project leadership is becoming a strategic issue for organizations, and for 'mega-projects' commissioned by government.

Second, project management is increasingly being used as a management tool across all industry sectors for diverse types of non-business-as-usual activities. It supports organizations in the design, development and delivery of products and services for external clients; it supports organizations in their need for technically complex products and processes, ever-shortening design-to-market windows for new products, the need for cross-functional expertise and the implementation of outsourcing agreements. Most of all, it is used to boost the performance of the organization both by in-house investment projects and by revenue-generating external client projects. With the economic downturn over the last several years, we are in a much less predictable business environment and organizations have to be more opportunistic and more agile.

Project management had traditionally been perceived as being the preserve of the construction and heavy engineering industries. It now supports projects worldwide ranging from software development and new product launches, to business change initiatives, and to major sporting and entertainment events. These projects can range from the small and discrete to the large, complex multi-currency projects involving tiered supply chain, multicultural and multi-located virtual teams in multiple time zones, and responsible to a wide range of stakeholders all focused on their particular idea of 'success'. The project management community currently talks about P3M (that is, project, programme and portfolio management). For simplicity we will simply talk about projects, understanding that there will be common elements within the programme and portfolio arena.

Increasingly, projects are typically not deliverable from within a single organization but need collaboration and partnership, often from organizations in different countries and cultures resulting in global project teams. Some of these are 'long-haul' projects: those that not only take years to conclude, but whose outcomes and deliverables extend beyond a lifetime. During this timeframe, the external environment often changes and can have significant implications for the project so that the ability to respond quickly and flexibly is crucial. The trend has been to place a project leader at the head of such projects. This means they are often in a high-profile and exposed position. Why would an individual seek out or want to take such a role and what does it take to make it a success?

As an *individual*, how can you make project leadership work for you and your project to successfully support the strategic aims of the organization? It is worth differentiating here between 'project leadership' and 'project leader', the latter being the title given to someone who undertakes the former functional role. But we also know that leadership capability is not only found at senior levels of organizations but is dispersed across hierarchy and function. Providing leadership capability is not just left to 'leaders', as the project community is discovering, and every project manager needs elements of leadership capability to be effective. What do you need to do to develop your own project leadership capability and step up to the mark? Technical competence in project management is the hygiene factor here: this is the professional skill base that you have had to learn and experience in order to get you as far as you have. But these are only the 'entry-level' requirements for more senior positions. Understanding project management techniques and methodologies are certainly important, but the next step up to a leadership role is fundamentally different. How do successful project leaders make things happen, often in situations of great uncertainty, complexity, ambiguity and change?

Within *organizations* there is a greater strategic focus on change and delivering through projects. The phrase 'right projects, done right' is now a familiar refrain and means that projects should be aligned with organizational strategy, and carried out correctly. Gareis (2010) describes how organizations are going through 'projectification', that is the process of change by the organization towards management by projects. As projects become an increasingly used vehicle in organizations to deliver products and services internally and externally, questions are rightly being asked about their relevance to the strategic direction of the organization, how they align with the organizational strategy and how they help to move the organization towards its particular vision. Driver (2014) also reflected these themes by stating, 'Organizations run projects which produce results which people use to create benefits (PRUB).'

As an organization, how can you develop in-house project capability? More specifically, how can you develop in-house project leadership capability and support the role of the project leader in order to achieve clear and persistent value not just for external client projects but also for significant in-house projects? Michaels, Handfield-Jones and Axelrod (2001) recognized an increasingly competitive landscape for recruiting and retaining talented employees, and emphasized the importance of talent to the success of organizations. In the same way that organizations plan for the development of functional and general management and leadership capability, they also need to have in place a strategy for indentifying, developing and supporting project leaders.

As an organization, how can you match a project leader to a project to increase the chances of success? Because situations in the project environment may vary, leadership requirements will differ so how can you be sure you have a 'well-matched' project leader?

These are all important and varied questions, and this book aims to provide answers, ideas and reflection as well as signposts for further information.

Projects in the Modern World

Since the turn of the millennium, one of the biggest themes in business has been the explosion in growth in the emerging markets. This isn't limited to the BRIC countries but includes developing economies across South

America, Eastern Europe, Asia and Africa. Project management is the engine for growth in infrastructure, business development and change. Whilst the recent economic crisis has significantly slowed growth across the world, it is returning and with it the need for an extensive community of capable and effective project managers and leaders to help economies and organizations compete again. Project Management International (www.pmi.org) estimates over a million new project management roles will need to be created globally between now and 2020 just to keep up with demand. Now is the time for organizations to be thinking of increasing their project management and leadership capability.

In the globalized economy, there is an increasing demand for experienced project managers across industry sectors. Arnold (2009) suggests that as major infrastructure projects around the world get bigger and technically more complex, more volatile, multifaceted and interconnected, the pool of people with the experience needed to lead them seems to be getting smaller. So what skills do aspiring project leaders need to acquire and how can organizations develop their in-house project leadership capability?

It is true to say that project management is still not recognized as a discrete profession and as such anybody can give themselves titles such as 'Project Manager' or even 'Project Leader'. The move in recent years has been towards the professionalism of project management, and the recognition that professionalism is more than just the sum of 'knowledge', the use of project methodologies and approaches, and the use of software systems available. David Pitchford, then at the UK Major Projects Authority, explained this as 'mindset, not methodology'.

Simcock (2011) recognized that leadership is a required part of projects: 'Leaders in the field of project management share many of the same characteristics as leaders in operational or functional roles ... the demand for leadership within the profession becomes more pressing as projects become more complex.' Project leadership, whether client or contractor, is often about influencing stakeholders and team members to align activities for a focus. Inevitably, most of the skill is in dealing with the dynamics and interpersonal aspects of groups whilst recognizing that stakeholders and project teams are often now global as well as local. In dealing with multiple cultures, good project leaders also need to define, establish and exemplify a culture that supports the project and the personnel for success.

Commercial and public sector organizations worldwide adopt project management because it provides benefits across all disciplines and industry sectors. It is a way to get businesses and organizations to react quickly but in a structured and controlled manner to rapidly changing business environments and constantly evolving strategies. And in the modern economy, organizations are continually under pressure to deliver more for less. As a result, they are increasingly looking to become 'innovative', 'lean', 'agile', 'flexible' and 'learning', and to continually improve in order to increase productivity and efficiency.

Projects are well documented as disruptors and drivers of change within organizations and the wider community. Of course introducing change at almost any level creates a range of behavioural responses in the people impacted by it, not by any means all positive. It takes particular leadership capability to lead and handle people when they are expressing open or subtle resistance especially in an often intense and pressured environment of balancing time, cost and quality parameters.

Project leaders must be 'organizationally intelligent': that is, able to capture hearts and minds, understand where the key influencers and power-brokers are, who makes the decisions and how to have the difficult conversations. They are being asked to exceed expectations when expectations are already high; they are given high levels of delegated executive power and then expected to hand it back at the conclusion of the project; they lead multicultural, multidisciplinary, multi-geographic, multi-time zone virtual teams and are asked to be visible to team members.

Project leaders share many of the characteristics, attributes and competencies as leaders in other fields. Leaders define, establish and live the culture of an organization. In the same way, project leaders define, establish and exemplify the culture of the project, creating the environment within which the project and project team works and thrives for that specific period of time. Various individual facets of leadership are regularly discussed: focus, vision, team building, communication, clear direction. The overarching theme is about designing and establishing the climate for success within and around the environs of the project.

Two of the most striking differences between the world of *Project Leadership, Second Edition* and the world of *Project Leadership, Third Edition* are the increased rate of globalization, and the introduction and phenomenal rate of adoption of social media and digital technology. These two trends have had marked impacts on aspects of project leadership, especially in relation to project teams working across countries and time zones, and in relation to communication and engagement.

About This Book

This revised edition of *Project Leadership* covers little of current project management techniques, methodologies or approaches since there are many publications already available for the reader covering these.

Instead, the contents and structure of *Project Leadership, Third Edition* focus on the skills, awareness and understanding used by project leaders who operate successfully in a diverse range of organizations and projects to present a comprehensive picture of successful project leadership. We have tried to distil their experience, make sense of it and present it in a form easily read and referenced by the growing number of people who find themselves permanently or occasionally in project leadership roles whether in the developed or majority world, whether in public services, the private sector or not-for-profit sector. It is a book intended to give the reader inspiration, ideas and practical tips to apply straight away to their project leadership role, and to reflect on and practise.

It is aimed at the 'full-time, part-time, some-time' professional and experienced project leaders, and at junior and aspiring project leaders. It is also aimed at project managers since every project manager should have a degree of leadership ability. It is aimed at the 'accidental' project leaders: those experienced professionals who, because of their business acumen and proven experience, have been handed projects but who have had no previous direct project or leadership experience or development to support them in their role. It is aimed at those who do not have the title 'Project Leader' at all, and this might also include project sponsors, project Board members and third-party project stakeholders. It is also the person evaluating and preparing for a new acquisition, or the person appointed to coordinate a move to new offices, as well as the person responsible for the new multimillion currency capital expenditure project. The common theme across all these is that they are involved in changing what organizations do or provide, and how they function.

This book is also aimed at organizations, regardless of industry sector or geographic location. Increasing 'projectification' means that organizations need to understand how they can develop and support in-house project and project leadership capability, and match appropriate projects to a project leader to increase the chances of success.

The world of project management can be very introverted. The focus on technical methodologies and the emphasis on various bodies of knowledge have meant that to date relatively little of the training, development and literature that is around seems to draw from available knowledge outside the pure project arena. Project leaders need a wide range of skills and competence from the technical, through business knowledge, through engagement to building strong robust relationships. There still seems to be an assumption that you can 'do' project leadership without needing to be developed or to learn how to, that it is something which should come naturally once the title of 'Project Leader' is bestowed upon you. Our view is that project leadership doesn't come naturally to everyone and that some of us need a little help to understand it and develop it. *Project Leadership, Third Edition* seeks to rebalance that focus and to bridge that gap.

Throughout the book we will highlight project leadership in the real world, including vignettes and the hands-on experience and 'war stories' of those who have been there, done it and made it happen. We will give some pointers as to how you can develop your project leadership skills and how the organization can improve their project leadership capability. We'll also look at how project leaders have moved on and the future of the project leader role.

This book is divided into four parts (see Figures I.1 and I.2), each designed to be read independently of the others. We're conscious that many people want to 'pick and flick' through a book, particularly when they have specific issues they would like addressing and need to see some relevant and immediate information.

Part 1 looks at leadership, project leadership and the breadth of competencies and skills required for the project leader to undertake the project leadership role, and to drive the project to its successful conclusion.

Part 2 looks at the project itself: how the lifecycle of the project is divided into logical phases and activities to ensure it is shaped, scoped, started, delivered and closed effectively and efficiently. Attention here is on the role of the project leader during these phases, not on the mechanics and technical detail of these phases. As such, we explore how the focus of the project leaders changes with various stages of the project lifecycle.

Part 3 looks at three core competencies for the project leader. These are the things over and above technical abilities that make the difference. They rely strongly on business acumen, interpersonal skills and organizational intelligence and are Vision and the Big Picture, Building Key Relationships, and Communication and Engagement.

Part 4 looks at how to build personal and organizational capability for effective project leadership, and is written from these two different perspectives. It focuses on the individual and how they can take control of their own development and the course of their career. From the point of view

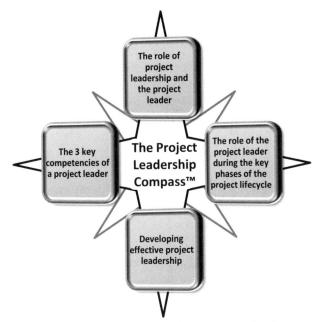

The role of
project
leadership and
the project
leader

The 3 key
competencies of
a project leader

**The Project
Leadership
Compass™**

The role of the
project leader
during the key
phases of the
project lifecycle

Developing
effective project
leadership

**What individuals and organizations need to know
about developing their project leadership capacity and
capability to deliver in challenging times.**

Figure I.1   The Project Leadership Compass™

of organizational learning and development professionals, it also identifies the many ways that organizations can assist the individual to develop project leadership capability. Finally, it describes an ideal project leadership development programme that can be modified and customized for use by a variety of organizations, and that can be used to start the conversation around the type and scale of commitment required for the development of project leadership within the organization.

Project leadership is increasingly important as projects become more complex and challenging for organizations which cannot afford to be blindsided, and understand that they need to continue to move forward in a world where markets and economies are constantly changing. The project leader role is both demanding and rewarding at an individual level; more importantly, the range of competencies, skills and knowledge to undertake this role successfully needs to be understood and supported at an organizational level. It is not in anyone's interest to nominate individuals to the role who are unprepared and lack the necessary project leadership skills to lead a project

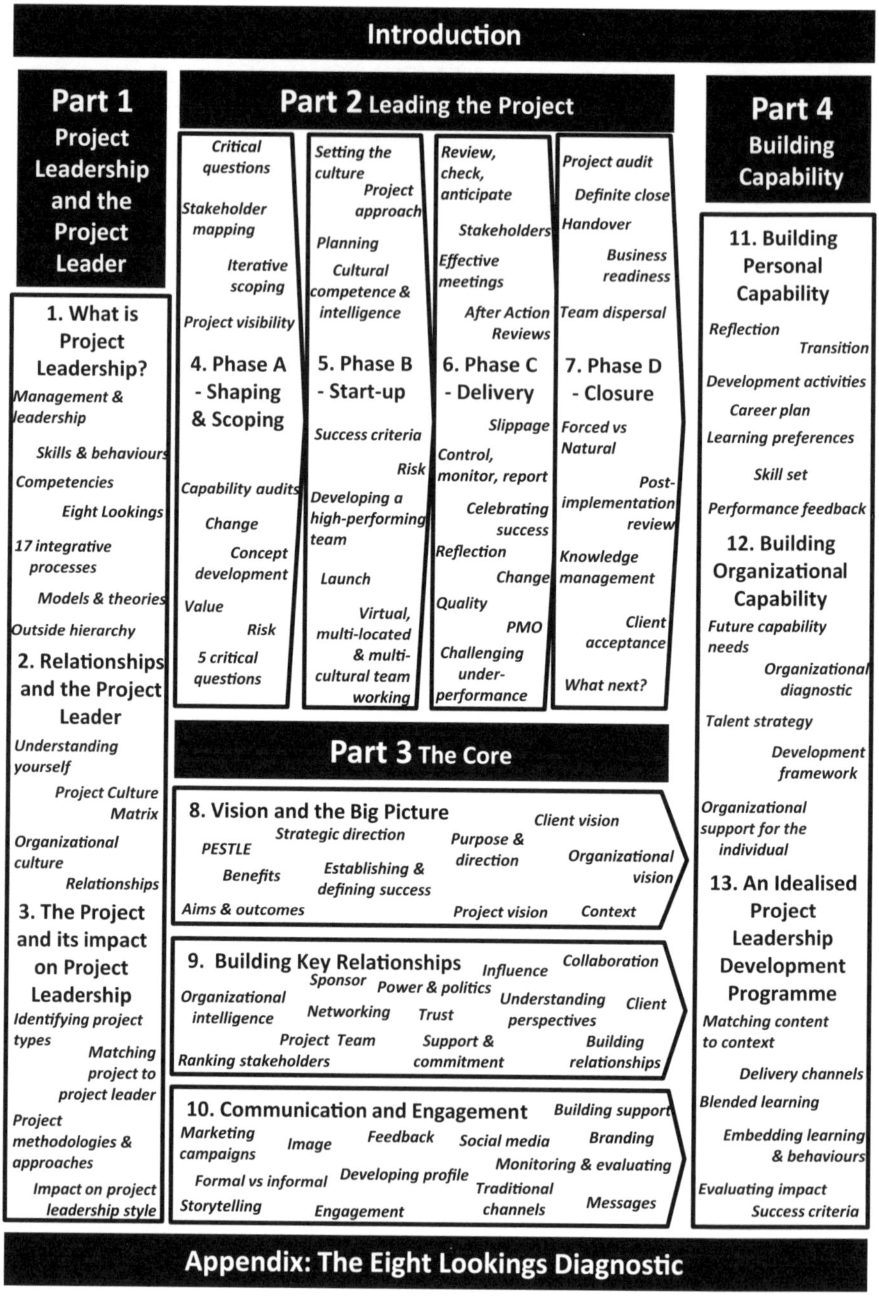

Introduction

Part 1
Project Leadership and the Project Leader

1. What is Project Leadership?

Management & leadership

Skills & behaviours

Competencies

Eight Lookings

17 integrative processes

Models & theories

Outside hierarchy

2. Relationships and the Project Leader

Understanding yourself

Project Culture Matrix

Organizational culture

Relationships

3. The Project and its impact on Project Leadership

Identifying project types

Matching project to project leader

Project methodologies & approaches

Impact on project leadership style

Part 2 Leading the Project

Critical questions

Stakeholder mapping

Project visibility

4. Phase A - Shaping & Scoping

Capability audits

Change

Concept development

Value

Risk

5 critical questions

Setting the culture

Project approach

Planning

Iterative scoping

Cultural competence & intelligence

5. Phase B - Start-up

Success criteria

Risk

Developing a high-performing team

Launch

Virtual, multi-located & multi-cultural team working

Review, check, anticipate

Effective meetings

After Action Reviews

6. Phase C - Delivery

Slippage

Control, monitor, report

Celebrating success

Reflection

Change

Quality

PMO

Challenging under-performance

Project audit

Definite close

Handover

Business readiness

Team dispersal

7. Phase D - Closure

Forced vs Natural

Post-implementation review

Knowledge management

Client acceptance

What next?

Stakeholders

Part 3 The Core

8. Vision and the Big Picture

PESTLE

Benefits

Aims & outcomes

Strategic direction

Establishing & defining success

Purpose & direction

Project vision

Client vision

Organizational vision

Context

9. Building Key Relationships

Organizational intelligence

Ranking stakeholders

Sponsor

Networking

Project Team

Power & politics

Trust

Support & commitment

Influence

Understanding perspectives

Collaboration

Client

Building relationships

10. Communication and Engagement

Marketing campaigns

Formal vs informal

Storytelling

Image

Developing profile

Engagement

Feedback

Social media

Traditional channels

Building support

Monitoring & evaluating

Branding

Messages

Part 4
Building Capability

11. Building Personal Capability

Reflection

Transition

Development activities

Career plan

Learning preferences

Skill set

Performance feedback

12. Building Organizational Capability

Future capability needs

Organizational diagnostic

Talent strategy

Development framework

Organizational support for the individual

13. An Idealised Project Leadership Development Programme

Matching content to context

Delivery channels

Blended learning

Embedding learning & behaviours

Evaluating impact

Success criteria

Appendix: The Eight Lookings Diagnostic

Figure I.2   *Project Leadership, Third Edition* structure and themes

to a successful outcome. This book will go some way to providing potential, new and existing project leaders and their organizations with the knowledge to develop these skills.

We are delighted to have been asked to write *Project Leadership, Third Edition* and are very aware of the shoes we need to fill of Wendy Briner, Colin Hastings and Michael Geddes. We hope you enjoy reading *Project Leadership, Third Edition*, but above all we hope you find the content useful and thought-provoking.

References

Arnold D. (2009) 'Billion dollar brains', *New Civil Engineer*, 29 November 2009.

Driver, P. (2014) *Validating Strategies: Linking Projects and Results to Uses and Benefits* Gower Publishing Limited, Farnham, UK.

Gareis, R. (2010) 'Designing changes of permanent organizations by processes and projects', *International Journal of Project Management*, 28 (4), 314–327.

Harris J. (2002) *Blindsided* Capstone Publishing Ltd, Oxford, UK.

Michaels E., Handfield-Jones H. and Axelrod B. (2001) *The War for Talent* Harvard Business Review Press, Boston, MA.

Simcock J. (2011) 'Time to lead', *Project,* March 2011.

Smith, C. (2014) *Playing the Project Manager* Self-published.

Additional Resources

Association for Project Management (APM) (www.apm.org.uk).

Global Accreditation Center for Project Management Education Programs (GAC) (www.pmi.org/Learning/Professional-Development/global-accreditation-center.aspx)

Global Alliance for Project Performance Standards (GAPPS) (www.globalpmstandards.org)

International Centre for Complex Project Management (ICCPM) (www.iccpm.com).

International Centre for Programme Management (ICPM) (www.som.cranfield.ac.uk/som/p13510/Research/Research-Centres/ICPM-Home).

International Project Management Association (IPMA) (www.ipma.ch).

Major Projects Association (MPA) (www.majorprojects.org).

Major Projects Authority (MPA) (www.gov.uk/government/groups/major-projects-authority).

National Centre for Project Management (NCPM) (www.herts.ac.uk/business-services/access-our-expertise/centres-of-expertise/ncpm).

Project Management Institute (PMI) (www.pmi.org).

Many of the above organizations are UK centric. If you want to find your in-country professional project management body, do look at www.ipma.ch/membership/member-associations and www.pmi.org/membership/chapters-pmi-chapters.aspx.

PART 1
PROJECT LEADERSHIP AND THE PROJECT LEADER

Courage is the first of human qualities because it is the quality that guarantees all others.

Winston Churchill

In Part 1 we look at a key area separating successful from unsuccessful organizations, that of leadership and the person who takes the role as leader. Much of the recent research into leadership looks at the role it has in helping secure organizational success – both in defining and delivering. We will look at the concept of leadership and how the research, models, techniques and ideas about mainstream organizational leadership are helping to shape current thoughts about effective project leadership. We look at how taking the next steps towards senior and leadership positions will typically take you away from your technical skill base to focus more on people and results. What, then, are the differences that make the difference for project leaders, whether they are on the client or the contractor side?

As one project leader told us, 'We need more understanding around the facets of leadership and the way leadership can work in projects and organizations to enhance or suppress achievement, particularly with regard to projects.'

In Part 1:

- Chapter 1 looks at what defines project leadership and the role of the project leader. We focus on the skills and competence needed by the modern project leader: how do they differ from those involved in being a line manager or specialist, and what does a 'good' project leader look like?
- Chapter 2 concentrates on your individual style as a project leader, the relationship you have with – and the impact you have on – other individuals, and finally the relationship you have with the type of organization you work with.

- Chapter 3 recognizes the importance of the relationship between the project leader and the project, and that each impacts the other. As such, this relationship ultimately impacts the performance and success of the undertaking. We also look at the nature of the approach adopted to manage/lead the project and that ultimately defines the tools you have at your disposal to coordinate, manage and report.

CHAPTER 1
What is Project Leadership?

Management is efficiency in climbing the ladder of success; leadership determines whether the ladder is leaning against the right wall.

Stephen R. Covey

Introduction

Chapter 1 looks at what defines project leadership and the role of the project leader. We focus on the skills and competence needed by the modern project leader: how do they differ from those involved in being a line manager or specialist, and what does a 'good' project leader look like? There are no absolute answers but there are guidelines and concepts, tools and techniques, which can support project leaders in understanding the critical capabilities to allow them to actively develop. We introduce the 'Eight Lookings' for the project leader, each of these 'lookings' being developed in later chapters.

1.1   From Management to Leadership

Tempted as we were, we do not explore the difference between management and leadership since this has been researched and covered extensively by others. However, it is worth very briefly considering what makes the notion of 'management' different from 'leadership'. Watkins (2012) described what he calls the 'seven seismic shifts' from management to leadership, see Figure 1.1.

In our discussions with organizations, they typically describe the move from management to leadership as shown in Figure 1.2.

In short, then, leadership is setting the Big Picture, direction or Vision for a group to follow while management is controlling the resources necessary to achieve this. In reality, in organizations the line between management and leadership is more blurred than these stark definitions suggest, especially around the middle management layers of organizational hierarchy. Perhaps

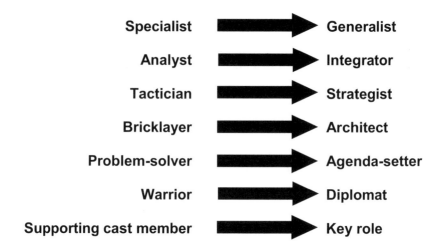

Figure 1.1   Seven seismic shifts from management to leadership
Source: Watkins 2012

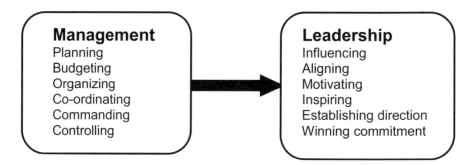

Figure 1.2   Change in focus from management to leadership

confusingly, project managers are not only expected to manage (that is, control) the resources of the project but increasingly they are also expected to provide leadership within the role. A real challenge when you often have no hierarchical power. Welcome to the wonderful world of the project leader.

1.2   Leadership Models and Competencies

We all know people who seem to be natural leaders, whether in the workplace or outside. Those who have 'it' stand out and inspire all around them. These are the people who build strong relationships even when events are undermining them, and who are able to retain a strategic perspective even as day to day problems try to engulf them. Project leaders share many of the same characteristics as leaders in operational or functional roles. The notion of leadership in mainstream organizations has moved on from command and control into the context of organizational strategy and delivery; the ability to provide clarity, focus and alignment to a Vision that supports where the organization is headed. Much of the recent literature and research into mainstream leadership can also help to educate and develop project leaders.

Notions of leadership do evolve over time and are affected by changes in economic, political, social and other factors. These in turn influence academia and professional bodies, which have a key part in shaping expectations of individuals and organizations. This concept is discussed further in Chapter 12 when we consider how organizations identify the critical future capability of project leaders. Many of the modern notions about organizational leadership, rather than leadership in politics or the armed services, noticeably started in the mid-1800s with Max Weber, Henry Fayol and Frederick Taylor amongst others. These ideas have been progressively refined and developed by Peter Drucker, John Adair, Henry Mintzberg, Warren Bennis, Charles Handy and John Kotter to name but a few.

The personal heroic and sometimes maverick models of leadership popular in the 1980s and 1990s reflected the cult of the personality. These have since evolved into newer models which value leadership as a social process. We all know of 'guts or glory' war stories about project leaders adamant at meeting deadlines and expectations, working all hours over extended periods of time, of adrenaline-pumping chaos management. These are remembered stories of past successes as well as monumental cock-ups that pass into organizational and project folklore.

One of our colleagues tells a particular success war story:

'At the height of the North Sea oil boom in the 1980s the design team in London were working flat out to get the drawing to the construction site in Scotland. We were led by a charismatic six-foot Texan project manager who was renowned for "getting the job done". One Monday morning we arrived at the Scottish office to find that all the engineers' offices facing out onto the drafting area had been locked up by an overenthusiastic security guard.

Needless to say as typical Brits we were sitting around drinking tea waiting for the man to arrive to unlock the offices when the Texan arrived. Upon hearing of this small delay he disappeared muttering about timescales and reappeared five minutes later with a fireman's axe with which he proceeded to smash down the 15 doors, pointing out loudly that doors were cheap but oil production was expensive. At that moment the security guard arrived but he decided not to intervene – good call!'

These types of stories often involve what is often called 'natural charisma', but for those of us who don't have this, we need to be able to understand what makes the difference and work to fulfil our leadership obligations in a style that is congruent with who we are.

The current view of leadership emphasizes the social and ethical behaviour of leaders (for example, 'servant leadership', 'authentic leadership', 'collaborative leadership'), which do not commonly appear in connection with management. There are also many different aspects of leadership, but looking at leaders from current business and political arenas we can identify key characteristics for success including courage, exemplar interpersonal and communication skills, the ability to argue the case, personal authority, cultural sensitivity and Vision. None of these, of course, is exclusive to leadership.

Goleman (1996, 2001) in particular has extensively shaped and focused our understanding of leadership through his work on Emotional Intelligence. In his research, he found that while the qualities traditionally associated with leadership (for example, intelligence, toughness, determination and Vision) are required for success, truly effective leaders are also distinguished by a high degree of what he termed 'Emotional Intelligence' (EI) which includes self-awareness, self-regulation, motivation, empathy and social skill, as described in Table 1.1 opposite. Goleman also identified direct ties between EI and measurable business results, although this correlation continues to be debated. The concept of EI has been expanded and continues to be developed.

Many models exist which aim to describe leadership. These can include a description of the practices, competencies, characteristics, traits and behaviours. Each looks at leadership through a different lens. An excellent example is Kouzes and Posner's (2007) Five Practices of Exemplary Leadership. This model identifies the five practices common to personal-best leadership experiences (see Table 1.2, p. 20). We have adapted this for the leadership of projects and added an additional practice, Deliver Value, and two commitments. As part of each practice there are behaviours or commitments that can serve as a basis for learning to lead, an ongoing requirement for each leader as they change and the context within which they lead changes. It is a generic leadership model but can be applied to the role of the project leader, as described below using the original commitments as a basis. Below each Practice title we have also identified the chapter in the book which expands best on this thinking.

Many organizations have developed their own set of leadership competencies that reflect their own circumstances and what they are trying to achieve. This is critical, since although the competencies are broadly similar between organizations and industries, the specific context and areas of focus

Table 1.1 The five facets of Emotional Intelligence (EI)

	Definition	Demonstrated by
Self-awareness	The ability to recognize and understand your moods, emotions and drives as well as their effect on others	Self-confidence, realistic self-assessment, self-depreciating sense of humour
Self-regulation	The ability to control or redirect disruptive impulses and moods The propensity to suspend judgement: to think before acting	Trustworthiness and integrity Comfort with ambiguity Openness to change
Motivation	A passion to work for reasons that go beyond money or status A propensity to pursue goals with energy and persistence	Strong drive to achieve Optimism, even in the face of failure Organizational commitment
Empathy	The ability to understand the emotional makeup of other people Skill in treating people according to their emotional reactions	Expertise in building and retaining talent Cross-cultural sensitivity Service to clients and customers
Social Skill	Proficiency in managing relationships and building networks An ability to find common ground and build rapport	Effectiveness in leading change Persuasiveness Expertise in building and leading teams

Source: Daniel Goleman

must be captured and built in to the set of competencies. This is described further in Part 4.

No self-respecting leadership development book published after 2010 could fail to include reference to the work being done around 'brain sciences' and in particular the field of neuroleadership. This is an emerging field of study connecting neuroscientific knowledge with the fields of leadership development, management training, change management, consulting and coaching. See Table 1.3 for Six insights into the brain aligned to these themes.

1.3   The Role of the Project Leader

So what exactly is the role of the project leader and how can we link project leadership to project performance? Project leadership is about leading the project in the context of the wider business and aligned with organizational strategy. It is creating the culture and working environment within the project that contributes to its success and performance. It is about decision making and

Table 1.2 Commitments as a project leader

Practice	Commitment
Model the Way (Parts 1, 2 and 3)	1. Find your natural style and personal values as a project leader and work with the team to identify a set of shared values to which you can work on the project 2. Lead by example by modelling the behaviours that align with the shared values
Inspire a Shared Vision (Chapter 8)	3. Develop a Vision of the project, aligned to the Vision of the organization and client, which describes a future which is exciting and full of possibility 4. Engage the project team, organization and client in the project Vision by appealing to their shared aspirations
Challenge the Process (Part 2)	5. Actively seek better and innovative ways of working to improve team and project performance 6. Adapt and modify your own approach and that of the project, taking calculated risks and learning from the outcome
Enable Others to Act (Chapter 9)	7. Build a culture of collaboration within the project through building trust across the team 8. Develop the team by distributing responsibility and decision making as appropriate to the person and context
Deliver Value (Part 2)	9. Back up your words with actions and deliver what is required 10. Demonstrate the value that the team has achieved and the link to the Vision
Encourage the Heart (Chapter 10)	11. Recognize individual team members' expertise and contribution to the projects by showing appreciation in a way appropriate to the person 12. Build a community spirit based on your shared values and celebrate success of individuals and the team

Source: Adapted from The Five Practices of Exemplary Leadership® model, Kouzes and Posner, 2007

judgement calls and aligning and motivating others through communicating the Big Picture and the part they play in success. All these areas indicate how the project leader's behaviour can influence success.

Fundamental questions for a project leader to address are: 'Do I understand who are 'those that matter'?' 'Am I clear what my responsibilities and accountabilities are, and the authority or delegated power I have to make things happen and make decisions?'

From our own experience, it is rare to find a project leader who has more than a bullet list of generic responsibilities. The role is influenced by many factors including the project's complexity and the context within which it must be delivered; all these facets should be taken into account when identifying the responsibilities of the project leader.

WHY NEUROSCIENCE IS USEFUL TO PROJECT LEADERSHIP

A contribution by Dr Jacqui Grey, Managing Director, The Neuroleadership Institute, EMEA provided in December 2014

The pressures of twenty-first century project leadership are increasing. Constant communication, 24/7 cultures, increasingly complex global projects and over reliance on technical devices are leading to cognitive overload in our leaders. *Neuroleadership* is the application of findings from Neuroscience to the field of Leadership. It gives us vital clues to why leaders 'burn out' and implications for leading teams, making complex decisions and emotional regulation. Particularly when the pressure is on and people are struggling, both for the leaders themselves, but also in leading and managing others.

Leaders today are expected to do a lot of things in addition to their day job. They are expected to have strategic direction, lead, motivate, engage, measure and reward their people. Neuroleadership gives us the evidence for why good practice in terms of Project, Performance and Talent Management, Breaking Bias, and Learning work. It also explains why poor practice is *worse than doing nothing at all* because it creates 'threat states' in the brain. For peak performance we must create 'Toward or Reward' states. (See 'SCARF: A brain based model for collaborating with and influencing others' by David Rock, published in *The Neuroleadership Journal* in 2008 and widely used in organizations today, reference included below (Rock, 2008).

Table 1.3 Six insights into the brain

1 **The brain is a connection machine.** The brain creates millions of connections each second. When we make useful connections 'happy hormones' like adrenaline and dopamine are released and we want to take action. New ideas and novelty are energizing. If people are really *thinking* and having insights, learning will occur and performance and behaviour will improve.

2 **Up close, no two brains are alike.** Everyone has a unique set of connections for how they think about things. Basic physical functions like breathing and moving have similar circuitry, but thoughts about more subtle issues, like motivation, involve more complex individual sets of circuits. Thus, it is not possible to motivate everyone in the same way.

3 **The brain hardwires everything it can.** New ideas or behaviours use what is called 'working memory', a very limited resource in the brain controlled by a very small area called the pre frontal cortex (PFC). Actions and behaviours that are repeated become 'hardwired' so we don't need to think about what we are doing or utilize the limited resources of the PFC (for example, breathing or digesting food). The PFC is a critical part of the brain for thinking, memory, decision making and emotional regulation. It is easy to shut down through stress (known as an amygdala hijack) where the limbic system takes over. The limbic system is a much older part of the brain which is responsible for the well known 'fight or flight' response. When the limbic system is in control, we are likely to either have an emotional response or run away!

4   **Hardwiring drives automatic perception**. Our perceptions are driven by deeper hardwired circuits and old habits, much more than by receiving data fresh from the world. As a result, people perceive the world through their own set of perceptual filters, according to their beliefs and attitudes, rather than seeing things as they are or as they could be. It is here that the effects of bias occur because we are not able to see the world as it really is, but rather as an extension of what we already believe. This is why it is so important to get different perspectives on any important decision-making activity, and to mitigate against bias with improved systems and processes.

5   **It's practically impossible to deconstruct old wiring**. Attention itself creates change in the brain. Quantum mechanics provides an explanation of the idea that where we focus attention, new circuits can be created in the brain, through the Quantum Zero effect. This means that trying to deconstruct unhelpful wiring requires focus, which unhelpfully tends to deepen the wiring because we are paying it attention. This explains why focus on solutions is more helpful than focus on problems. Feedback is an overrated pastime as it depends not just on the ability of the person delivering it, but also whether the person receiving it has what Carol Dweck describes as a 'fixed' or 'growth' mindset. This is why performance management is fraught with difficulty. Brain scans in laboratory work have shown that people with fixed mindsets literally cannot hear what is being said to them because they are only focused on the fact that they are being criticized – there is literally no activity recorded. By contrast, people with growth mindsets desire feedback in order to learn. Very few people are totally fixed or growth, but other people's approach can affect which way we go. It is therefore vital to create 'toward states' in our people before even starting to give feedback. Our ongoing research into performance management shows that regular quality conversations not linked to bonus calculations work much better than performance management interviews. The formalization of the process, together with feelings of being judged, will create 'threat/away' responses and fixed mindset in the recipient.

6   **It's easy to create new wiring**. The brain creates new connections all the time. Every time we travel to a new part of a city we create a map of the area, or meet a new person or understand a new idea. Creating new more helpful circuitry can be quite easy. The key, if we want to create a long-term circuit, is to pay it lots of attention. Attention, in the form of quality and quantity of focus, is what changes our brains and the way we think over time. This is known as neuroplasticity. This is why coaching works. By asking the questions that bring people to an insight, it is relatively easy to engage them in taking action and focusing on their growth. The taking of repeated actions creates new habits and ultimately new wiring that leads to performance improvement.

Source: © The Neuroleadership Institute

Understanding how the brain works and what it needs for optimal performance is helpful to everybody. It can make us make better decisions, have more insights, manage our emotional responses and lead our people more effectively. Read more about the SCARF model, Insights, Fixed and Growth Mindset and The Healthy Mind Platter and you will be well on course for applying the principles that will help you. Project managers are often good at 'toughing it out' in high-pressure situations and expect their people to do the same. Sometimes the counter-intuitive approach can work too – go for a walk, take a break, let the limbic system calm down and integrate learning. Celebrate successes and focus on solutions.

Sources: Rock, 2008; Rock and Cox, 2012, Dweck, 2008; Rock et al., 2012

One suggestion to resolve this situation is to play the 'project responsibilities game' (developed through working with sponsors and programme leaders across a government department). The game involves taking a job description framework that has been created to meet the objectives of the business and then reviewing and negotiating individual colour-coded responsibilities between each of the key roles. This allows a realistic balance to be sought across all of the key leadership roles – with the colours highlighting where responsibilities have been taken on by others in additional to their normal scope of responsibilities. As projects and the context within which they are delivered are unique, so the roles within the project team should be uniquely defined. The output of the exercise facilitates (in some cases forces) an important discussion between the key players regarding roles and responsibilities which influence information flow, decision making and governance. Another approach is to ask key stakeholders, primarily your sponsor, to describe your role (hopefully more than sending you a generic list of responsibilities) and what they would see as success when congratulating you at the end of the project for a job well done.

Increasingly in the project management community, there is a view gaining traction that if projects are done well they should be uneventful and seemingly effortless. If you start a project badly, it is very difficult to recover and the chances of you delivering it well are reduced. In practice, of course, we all know that projects are not easy: the implementation phase in particular is fraught with difficulties, and there is a danger that the project leader's role becomes one of firefighting to cope with the latest crisis instead of providing far-sighted guidance. And firefighting can be more fun and adrenaline fuelled than the 'boring', planned and smooth-running project. We want to be a hero, and what better way than to impress by firefighting a drama and a crisis? As one of our colleagues once put so succinctly, 'Chaos management is, after all, the best fun you can have with your clothes on.' Often projects are compared to synchronized swimming teams: all aligned to achieve, collaborative teamworking, smiles on the faces and at the same time frantic movements under the surface to try to keep them upright, working to the common goal within the timeframe allowed. Perhaps we need to be more open about how hard it is to make successful projects look easy.

1.3.1 WORKING OUTSIDE LINE HIERARCHY

A project is outside 'business-as-usual' and is typically outside the normal line hierarchy. There are unusual and temporary links to senior management, the

Board or the C-suite often by virtue of the governance structure for the project. Moreover, the project team includes cross-functional experts and multi-located virtual teams; the project leader is given a particular set of responsibilities and authority specifically for the duration of the project. Projects create a temporary organization within the permanent organization; they are deliberately 'silo busters', spanning functional boundaries and collaborating across permanent teams.

Even working within particular project methodologies or approaches, the reality is that many project leaders find they have to establish their own lines of contact and develop their own informal network to get things done. They need to build relationships, recognize and use their bases of power, use influence, and collaborate and build alliances with others to achieve results.

Outside the 'normal' organizational hierarchy project leaders have some freedom to determine their own destiny just because they are out of the ordinary and day-to-day running of the business. On the other hand, they may meet considerable opposition to their demands and initiatives because they are seen by colleagues to be rocking the boat or undermining the status quo. The project leader, however, typically has the delegated responsibility for the success or failure of the project. This makes it easier to insist on the provision of resources, but it also means having to deal with the numerous and often conflicting interests which are at play. This reinforces the need for the project leader to develop their power base and supportive networks, and to build strong channels of influence. These are all based on an individual's personal credibility and the ability to ensure that their expertise has an impact on the project performance and so on business performance.

So, what are the main features of the project leader role, and how do these differ from a project manager, a line manager or specialist? The key distinction within projects is generally the rate of change and the complexity of relationships involved in delivery. We have picked a few of the unique project complexities that we recognize are important to the project leader and included in Table 1.4 opposite.

1.4   The Characteristics and Competencies of a Project Leader's Role

There are many ways of distinguishing and listing the characteristics and competencies of a project leader's role. Generic characteristics and competencies are certainly useful, but what is more useful is that these should be unique to the organization and its context and situation. A further consideration is that these characteristics and competencies should not just reflect the current

Table 1.4 Complexities faced by a project leader

	Complexities faced by a project leader
Organizational context	• Need to understand many organizational models and the cultures that underlie them • Complex nature of 'success' not defined as a single entity but as a diverse range of transitory perceptions held by the broader stakeholder group • Need to have a focus and understanding on the business context to ensure decisions are made from an outcome and benefits perspective • Expectation by all those involved in the change process for high levels of openness and engagement whether from those working directly on projects or those being impacted by the eventual change
Managing up	• Difficulty of uncovering what drives the opinions/decisions of stakeholders and figuring out their relative levels of power/influence • Need to sell the Vision via the stakeholders to ensure the necessary level of direct and indirect support • Recognizing, valuing and marshalling the subjective views of customers and stakeholders • Translating the political into a reality – understanding and then transforming organizational strategies and expectations into not only technical but also politically feasible solutions that are supported by stakeholders
Managing down	• Influencing teams without traditional positional or hierarchical authority by developing and leveraging stakeholder relationships • Need to lead teams such that they become greater than the sum of their parts to offset resource shortages and the need to meet challenging objectives • Ability to deal with high levels of uncertainty and often relentless change which can be disconcerting and challenging to deal with for many • Accept and work with the inevitable resistance to change • Ultimately the need to constantly model what you say in the behaviours you exhibit – a critical requirement as a leader of change

Source: Lock, Scott and Harrington (2013). Reproduced with permission

situation of the organization, but also try to future-proof these characteristics and competencies by taking into account the ambitions and aspirations of the organization. This is discussed in more detail in Part 4.

Although projects are unique, there are common characteristics found in the roles of project leaders across organizations and multinationally which are not necessarily found in other managerial roles. We recognize that every project manager has to have some leadership ability to successfully run their projects. Technical and management skills are strong, robust building blocks but project leadership is not about technical or managerial superiority and new skills are needed for a new role. The difference is that leadership skills and competence are more often found at the strategic level, which outweighs the need for the more operational and technical skills around planning, monitoring and controlling.

Crowe (2006) found that particularly successful project managers made a strong distinction between leading and managing. They understood that being a strong leader did not necessarily equate with popularity, and that being liked on a project was secondary to being respected. As one project leader we have worked with remarked, 'One of the best pieces of advice I was given early on was that project leadership is not a popularity contest.'

Gadeken (2005) reports that the Defense Acquisition University's extensive research since the 1980s has identified that top-performing project managers also exhibit eight key leadership behaviours as listed below. The two behaviours which differentiated exceptional performers were numbers 1 and 7.

1.   *Are strongly committed to a clear mission.*
2.   Focus on external stakeholders.
3.   Have a long term and Big Picture perspective.
4.   Are both systematic and innovative thinkers.
5.   Find and empower the best people for their teams.
6.   Are selective in their involvement in project issues.
7.   *Thrive on relationships and influence.*
8.   Proactively gather information and insist on results.

1.4.1   CHARACTERISTICS OF PROJECT LEADERS WE HAVE WORKED WITH

From our own experience, a successful project leader has many of the following characteristics, which make the role so challenging and ultimately rewarding:

- More than a specialist.
- Responsible for the achievement of project goals, which are defined but require very visible and dynamic activity. In relation to the project, the role is similar to that of a managing director of a division or business unit
- Unable to hide. It is clearly apparent who is in charge. It is therefore a high-profile role which carries with it some risk to the project leader's own reputation.
- Limited in direct authority. This varies according to the project leader's position, but it is usually necessary to negotiate for resources and support from a wide network of people inside and outside the organization.

- Expected to cut across normal organizational boundaries and customs and needs to be unconventional in approach. Dealing with resistance or opposition is not unusual and can be very demanding.
- Leads the project in the context of the wider organization and its commercial requirements. Not only does the project leader need to understand how the project fits with the organizational strategy to help the organization realize its ambitions, but the project leader also needs to create the appropriate environment for a successful project and that means creating the environment for the project team to thrive and prosper.
- Often works in areas new to the organization. This might be assessing or introducing new technology or capital equipment, mergers and acquisitions, opening up new markets or new approaches to existing situations. The unknown and unpredictable are often feared by many in the mainstream organization. Credibility may be low to start with and needs to be built up.

1.4.2   COMPETENCIES OF A PROJECT LEADER

We were asked by a multinational information and communications technology (ICT) organization to help them decide the core competencies required of their project leaders. So we asked a range of project leaders, their sponsors and team members what makes the difference, in their experience, between an average or poor project leader and those who do well. They told us that the competencies in Table 1.5 make the difference.

The lists provided can easily be extended and in Part 3 we look at three core competencies for the project leader. The realization is the leader's role is one which integrates, orchestrates, energizes and coordinates people and processes. The project leader should give as much emphasis to managing the organizational context as to managing the technical delivery. Interestingly the people we talk to about the project leader role assume technical abilities to be a given and do not see technical superiority as making the difference. However, we have found that without the technical capabilities to fully understand the project, the role may not be taken seriously. Being able to interact and communicate well while managing the project's tasks seems to be the key. We can cut the lists of characteristics and competencies in a lot of different ways but we believe that the Eight Lookings is a model that illustrates extremely well the key distinctions of the role.

Table 1.5 Competencies of a project leader

Excellent communication	The ability to connect with people and explain complicated things simply, in understandable language and in an informal conversational tone. Let people know what's happening all the time and that includes your team members, senior managers and customers. Don't default to mushroom management because everybody then expects the worst and the grapevine has a habit of filling in the gaps in communication. Knowing the good and the bad news are equally important
Collegiality	That ability to build collaborative relationships and recognize the strengths that others in the team bring. The leadership role is not about the cult of the personality and 'it doesn't all reside in the number one'
Staying calm	Don't panic and become hyperactive or alternatively become paralysed into inactivity. Stay calm and find a step-by-step way forward with the team
Face up to problems	Be courageous, it is better to make a decision and act on it than to do nothing (although that could be the best thing to do once you have made the decision!). Don't bury or ignore problems but find out the causes and make proposals to management and customers. Understand that 'unknown unknowns' will surface and that how you handle these will reflect on you directly
Developing physical and mental resilience	Most projects are a marathon, not a sprint, so it takes tenacity, commitment and persistence. Attend to your physical health as actively as you manage your stress levels
Model what you want to see in others	You should walk the talk and always do what you say you are going to do in the way you tell others they should act. If you need to go back on what you said, which will happen, be honest and open with people. Be someone who is worth following
Having a 'matrix mind'	Keep an eye on the Vision or the Big Picture whilst having a finger on the pulse of the project's progress
Acknowledging that the success of the project is all about the people	Understand the strengths and key skills of the project team and make use of them; identify the leadership style that suits particular team members best; recognize different motivators and perspectives
Asking the questions and making the decisions	The ability to navigate through. Often asking questions is the least developed skill in leadership
Showing humility	Understand that it isn't a sign of weakness to accept you don't know everything. A degree of humility is necessary – if you are too arrogant you stop listening, and you need to be able to listen to those people who will impact on your success. You need to be clever, but only just clever enough
Having the blend of commercial skills as well as technical skills	To be able to understand the context and the landscape as well as the process
Being adaptable	Recognize that the project leader role requires many different things at different times: collaborator, coach and mentor, knowledge manager, politician, facilitator, cheerleader, cat herder

1.5   The Project Leader's Eight Lookings

Given the apparent complexity and multiple expectations on the project leader role, it is often helpful to categorize and consolidate these into a model. Figure 1.3 illustrates the idea that a project leader must look in eight directions in order to identify and understand the whole picture: upwards, outwards, internally, externally, backwards, forwards, inwards and downwards. These directions can be paired up as they focus primarily on stakeholders, delivering the Vision, keeping on the ball and focusing on results respectively. Each of the eight facets is described below in Table 1.6.

Projects, as we will discuss, come in many shapes and forms. The Eight Lookings assume that the project is being delivered by your organization for an external client. If the project is internal to the organization then the client referred to in Looking outwards* (part of 'Wiring into stakeholders') and Looking externally** (part of 'Delivering the Vision') will also be internal to the organization.

You can reflect further on your own Eight Lookings profile by completing the Diagnostic in the Appendix. See Figure 1.4 for an example of the Diagnostic output we use when working with project leaders and teams. This will provide you with valuable insight into where your focus is and, more importantly, is not, presenting you with the opportunity to consider how this may be impacting your own and the performance of the project. We suggest you complete this once you have completed Chapter 1, certainly before reading Part 4, as it will provide an insight into the areas for your development.

We have used the Eight Lookings in different ways with project leaders. Some suggestions are included below for you to consider how you might use it and obtain value:

- individual insights into development areas that would support delivery;
- as part of a feedback process such as 360 degree;
- with your project sponsor to understand how aligned your focus is to theirs;
- with a project team who wish to understand their collective focus and the impact that this may be having on the performance of the project (as shown in Figure 1.3);
- with an organizational function aiming to understand the culture and way of working that had evolved and how these might be modified to meet new opportunities.

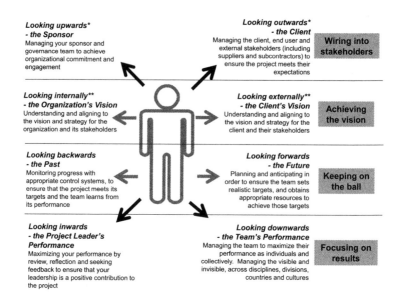

Figure 1.3   The project leader's direction finder – the Eight Lookings

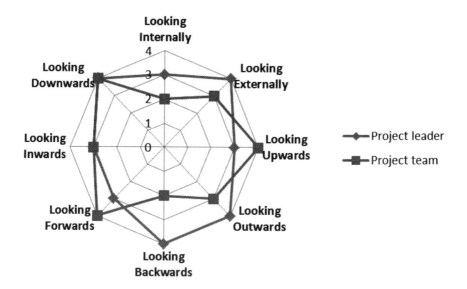

Figure 1.4   The Eight Lookings example diagnostic output

Table 1.6 The Eight Lookings descriptions

Wiring into Stakeholders

Engaging with *stakeholders* within your direct influence or control (if you can ever say that you directly control anyone). This involves networking, building credibility and marketing the project: all these aspects work towards securing stakeholders' agreement and towards generating support for the project:

[Aligned to Part 3, Chapter 9 – Building Key Relationships, Chapter 10 – Communication and Engagement]

Looking upwards – the Sponsor

Looking upwards and managing internal stakeholders, primarily the project sponsor and governance group, is an essential part of the project leader's role. The make-up of your project governance team is dependent on the project methodology, the size and sophistication of your organization, or it may simply be the organization's leadership team. In any event, ensure you identify and develop a close relationship with your project sponsor.

Looking outwards – the Client

All projects have a client, an end user (who might be different from the client) and possibly a number of other external stakeholders (such as investors, partners and others who indirectly benefit from the project outcomes and deliverables). Identifying all these external stakeholders, their perceptions and expectations, as well as managing and meeting their expectations, and securing their agreement, are also a key part of the project leader's role.

Achieving the Vision

Projects deliver outcomes to achieve objectives that may ultimately lead to an organization achieving its Vision. A Vision, something that people can be motivated by and orientate towards, is critical to success. It can be helpful to distinguish between three potentially separate Visions that must ideally align to deliver success: the project Vision, the organization's Vision and the client's Vision. Projects are not delivered in isolation: they exist only to serve a need and must be delivered alongside other changes and the day-to-day operations of all organizations involved.

[Aligned to Part 3, Chapter 8 – Vision and the Big Picture]

Looking internally – the Organization's Vision

The project leader must understand why the organization has chosen to deliver the project: how the Vision for the project aligns with the Vision for the organization; how the project's outcomes align with the organization's strategy.

Looking externally – the Client's Vision

The project leader must understand why the client has chosen to make the changes that will result from the project. Also how the Vision for the project aligns with the Vision for the client and their strategy.

Keeping on the Ball

Leading through the project lifecycle or, to use a football or rugby analogy, keeping on the ball and therefore maintaining control. This also involves anticipating by stepping back from the immediate pressures of the day and looking at the Big Picture, keeping the whole team informed so that their focus is maintained and aligned, and finally on continuous planning and review. These perspectives are to do with time.

[Aligned to Part 2, Leading the Project]

Looking backwards – the Past

Learning from the past but not focusing on it to the detriment of spotting what is approaching, thus the importance of planning and risk management. Many projects often seem as if they are driving using the rear view mirror, the results being obvious. Learning from the past is crucial if you are to avoid making similar mistakes.

Looking forwards – the Future

You can only get a true appreciation of the project by first looking forwards – establishing realistic plans and raising the necessary resources to ensure you can deliver success. Looking forwards is also about horizon scanning – not just being focused on the end of the project, but surveying its impact on the organization's strategy. Also, anticipating trends inside and outside the organization and how they might impact the project is a crucial skill for any project leader.

Table 1.6 The Eight Lookings descriptions (*concluded*)

Focusing on Results

Managing performance: maximizing both your own performance and that of your team by actively seeking feedback to help improve your performance as well as that of the project. As a project leader you will need appropriate measuring, monitoring and control systems to ensure that you meet targets and learn from your mistakes. This can only be achieved if you have in parallel provided purpose and direction for the project team, celebrating successes to help maintain momentum and motivation, clarifying individual success criteria to provide focus, creating a supportive culture and being tough on quality.

[Aligned to Part 2, Leading the Project]

Looking inwards – My Performance	*Looking downwards* – the Team's Performance
It is all too easy to become too involved in the day-to-day tasks of a project and forget that your own performance has a big impact on the overall progress of the project. You must therefore take time to reflect and seek feedback from others.	As the leader of a team, you have a responsibility to ensure that they perform well, both individually and collectively, including suppliers and subcontractors.

> *We have suggested at different points through the book where the Eight Lookings would provide insight. They are highlighted in a similar way to this text.*

1.6   The Project Leader's 17 Integrative Processes

Undoubtedly, the project leader has a multitude of responsibilities to the project team, the sponsor and key stakeholders, to their organization and to the client. With a long list of responsibilities and things to consider, many project leaders feel that they would need to be super-human and omnipotent to do everything which is expected of them. So how do successful project leaders become successful? The answer lies in not holding on to every activity and task, and in understanding that you don't have to know everything and do everything yourself. The project leader role is not about working harder, it is about working smarter. The project leader role integrates, orchestrates, energizes and coordinates people and processes. A project leader understands that success depends on coordinating and unifying effort across the team regardless of functional expertise or geographic location. In the words of one architect client of ours, 'I used to see my leadership role as being like rowing alone through treacle. If there were problems, I rowed harder and put more effort into the architecture. Now I realize that my role is actually to work on making the treacle thinner and on building up a team of different kinds of rowers with me as the cox! If I get the organizational context going with me and the teamworking right, the rest is easy!'

So one key to working smarter is to recognize that you need others to help. Another is to let go of your image of yourself as a particular technical specialist and instead recognize that your new specialism is that of identifying your own and others' strengths and capabilities and then integrating them into a high-performing team for the project. Project leaders usually manage specialists in areas other than their own, who have to be brought together to produce effective results. So the project leader's own expertise may be important in commanding respect and credibility, but be of limited use in actually ensuring that the job is done. A good example of this is the paediatrician who heads a child care unit in which his own abilities are combined with the specialisms of psychologists, physiotherapists, social workers and educationalists to provide a complete service to disadvantaged children.

As an integrator, the project leader ensures all the activities of the project are pulled together and that any links missing or broken are identified. The project leader should also give as much emphasis to the organizational context as to the technical delivery. Since the project leader role often extends across the organization they work for, and the client organization that the project is delivering into, the project leader can often find it necessary to manage both organizational contexts.

From the project leader's Eight Lookings you will begin to understand there are core integrating processes that you, together with your team, will need in order to deal with the dynamic complexity of project leadership. We are not going to inundate you with lists of competencies, skills and behaviours but we will indicate what needs your attention and give you some practical ideas.

The integrative processes illustrated in Figure 1.5 are interrelated, so don't treat them in isolation. They apply across all four project leadership dimensions we described above in the Eight Lookings. The integrative processes are described briefly below (and in Figure 1.5), then described in more detail in the following chapters.

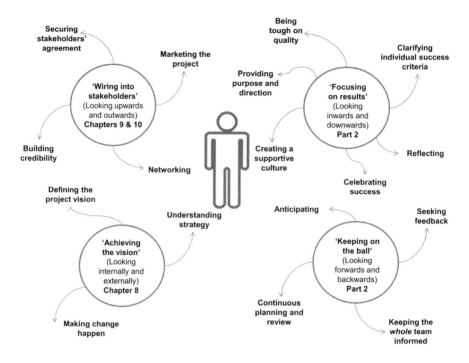

Figure 1.5   17 Integrative Project Leader Processes

1.6.1   WIRING IN TO STAKEHOLDERS: LOOKING UPWARDS AND OUTWARDS

This is essential to building strong, durable links with key stakeholders. 'Wiring in' suggests making contact. The metaphor is intended to remind you that electrical wires are only useful if the current is flowing:

- Securing stakeholders' agreement: projects can have a bewildering number of stakeholders and they often have different, and sometimes competing, expectations of the project.
- Building credibility: an often undervalued resource you and your team can have is the positive support of your organization, but you have to earn this.
- Networking: there are formal and informal ways of ensuring things get done, of finding things out and of getting decisions made.
- Marketing the project: the merits of your project are not self-evident to everyone. If you do not help to communicate and market the project, it may not be understood within the organization. This, in

turn, may mean it is not sufficiently valued especially when you are in need of support.

- Networking: successful project leaders build networks of relationships to help them get things done. Spend time networking: talk to people informally to trade information and find out what is going on. Project leaders who are not properly plugged into their organization and that of their client often find themselves wrong-footed, surprised and left in an exposed position. Successful project leaders learn from what they hear and see. They learn that there are formal and informal ways of getting things done, of finding things out and of getting decisions made.

1.6.2   ACHIEVING THE VISION: LOOKING INTERNALLY AND EXTERNALLY

To provide the team with direction and a purpose it is critical that the project is articulated in the context of the organization's own strategy as well as that of the client. This helps to link and frame the external context with the internal project and to answer the typical questions: 'Why should I put my energies in to this?' 'Why is this important?'. The project leader will be expected to answer these questions and many more during the life of the project.

- Communicating the organization and client Vision: As we will describe in Chapter 8, the organization, client and project can each have a Vision. Ensuring people are aware of the organization's and client's Vision will help them understand the context and ways in which their decisions on the project could cascade upwards and impact these Visions. Working with a bank carrying out a major refurbishment, what appeared to be tactical decisions had to be made regarding the IT infrastructure within the building. Only by realizing that the organization's Vision was to be highly networked and adaptable given the new markets it was planning to move into, was it possible to make an informed decision about what appeared to be an unjustified expense.
- Understanding the strategy: If the Vision is the 'what', the strategy is the 'how'. All organizations have a strategy, articulated in different ways, to varying levels of detail and clarity. Taking time to understand how the organization intends to achieve its Vision and strategy, and the mechanisms it has in place to achieve it, will help the project leader and the team to understand why certain decisions are being made that may impact the project.

- Making change happen: Projects are about delivering change of some form and therefore the leader must identify how the changes will actually be made, delivering the benefits against which the project was originally justified. The field of change management is a growing area of knowledge and practice, elements of which we will cover throughout the book. As an example, on a major programme which we worked on within a bank, a large number of mainly property and IT projects were delivered but what had not been focused on was the unfortunate resulting reduction in staff against which the programme had been approved. This was complex and challenging, especially for those impacted, but should have been faced up earlier and more openly.

1.6.3   KEEPING ON THE BALL: LOOKING FORWARDS AND BACKWARDS

The project leader needs to think like a footballer in possession of the ball, constantly aware of the opposition's threats, of his own team's support and of the need to maintain the initiative:

- Anticipating: As the project leader, you need to be able to step back from the immediate pressures of the day and look at the whole situation. Disasters rarely occur out of the blue; there are nearly always early warning signs if you look for them. Find short periods of time to run through any worrying situations, preferably with somebody else off whom you can bounce ideas. Just think through implications and contingencies.
- Continuous planning and reviewing: We still find many project leaders who think that planning is something that needs to be done just once, at the beginning! This approach assumes that everything can be predicted in advance. Continuous cycles of planning, doing and reviewing must take place throughout the project, and the greater the uncertainty and innovation, the more important this process is.
- Keeping the whole team informed: Are you keeping your team, your sponsor and other key stakeholders up to date? Not everyone has the same understanding and grasp of current progress as the project leader. Project leaders need to maintain interest and enthusiasm for the project. A regular dialogue with key stakeholders should ensure that they are never taken by surprise.

- Seeking feedback: Asking for feedback is so much more effective than waiting for it. It provides invaluable early warnings of any problems. The request itself, and any necessary follow-up action, builds a project team's credits within the organization. You don't need to have anything as structured as a questionnaire – there are several other ways, such as review meetings and informal conversations. Of course, it's no good asking for feedback and then ignoring it when it comes. We know of a case in which clients were asked how they saw the company. The answer came back, 'You are arrogant.' The company's response was, 'Yes we know; that's what they said last time we asked!'

1.6.4 FOCUSING ON RESULTS: LOOKING INWARDS AND DOWNWARDS

As project leader, it's up to you to maintain motivation, momentum and direction:

- Providing purpose and direction: You can help create a sense of purpose amongst your team in a number of ways:
  - help their understanding to go beyond the project specification to the underlying reasons *why* the project is important to the organization as a whole. We worked with a project team developing a major new piece of software in a financial service company. The technical specification was clear and the project complex, but somehow the systems analysts and programmers involved weren't fired up about it. The turning point came when the team spent an hour with the chief executive and the marketing director, who explained how the new system was a crucial part of the company's aggressive expansion strategy. This appreciation of the project's wider purpose triggered a new and real sense of motivation in the team;
  - tease out of the team how the project could be used to achieve some of their own personal Visions and aspirations;
  - communicate your own excitement, conviction and sense of mission about the project. If *you* are not very enthusiastic about it, it's very difficult to expect others to be motivated.
- Clarifying individual success criteria: The project as a whole must have clear objectives, defined in terms of time and cost. But these must be translated into clear work goals agreed with each individual, specifying what work will be done, by when and within what constraints. Always

make sure that the different jobs are coordinated with each other. In projects with high levels of uncertainty, team members are given considerable scope in terms of how they reach their objectives, but you need to demonstrate through your attitudes and behaviour what is acceptable and what is not.

- Being tough on quality: Having set individual success criteria, you have to follow up to ensure that they are met. For example, ensuring that even seemingly insignificant changes follow the process of registration, impact analysis and client agreement. Build the expectation of quality into the project culture and ensure that team members understand why this is important.

- Creating a supportive culture: To maintain high performance in the team, you need to give support in every way possible. This might include developing a particular culture within the organization, honest and frank discussion, positive and constructive criticism without focusing on the shortcomings of any individual.

- Reflecting: Introspection, self-analysis and quiet reflection do not come naturally to people of action. Being busy and doing things are ways of being validated but it is surprising how frequently issues come into perspective in the most unusual of places: walking the dog, jogging, in the shower.

- Celebrating success: Effective project teams and leaders help themselves to maintain momentum by celebrating their collective and individual achievements and successes along the way. Interim targets are important markers of success. Project leaders are always looking for ways of recognizing and celebrating achievements and contributions.

1.7   Leadership and the Leader

Adair (2009) identified that leadership exists on three levels within organizations: the team level, the operational level and the strategic level. This means that leadership doesn't start and stop only at senior and Board levels. Instead, leadership is viewed as a process that is diffuse throughout an organization rather than lying solely with the formally designated leader. This requires a distinction to be made between leadership and leader, one we will come back to a number of times through the book. The emphasis therefore shifts from developing leaders to developing organizations with a collective responsibility for leadership. Both of these topics are covered in Part 4 of the book. Other terms used to describe this concept of dispersed or distributed leadership include informal or emergent.

Leadership is neither a unique capability nor the sole responsibility of a named leader. Leadership does not come from just one person in most cases; instead, it is dispersed across a team with each person, in different ways and with different outcomes, doing their part to ensure that the objectives are achieved. We can think of the single leader who takes on sole responsibility for defining, articulating and ensuring that the Vision is achieved by singlehandedly bringing the team together and motivating them. These situations rarely, if ever, occur on projects

Considering your own role for a moment, you may wish to reflect on whether you solely bear this burden or gift, depending on your perspective. Leading anything is rarely down to one person, and that is certainly true for projects. Ideally you want to look to disperse leadership. The benefits of this approach include making the team more resilient, providing you with the time to reflect and also gaining value from multiple perspectives and capabilities.

Adopting this approach also has a positive impact on those individuals you trust to share the leadership role (both developmental and motivational). This will in turn positively impact the broader team. In our experience people are often doing a role below which they have been employed to deliver, frustrating all those involved. This is not harnessing the proper energy and capabilities of these individuals and often impacts negatively on engagement and productivity across the organization.

Dispersed leadership is one way to negate this. This approach requires an investment of time and energy (including developing team members to take on additional responsibilities) but the payback can be considerable. If you are looking for potential leaders, we can suggest the following simple test. Attend a typical team meeting in which you normally play a leading role, but do not contribute when it comes to key decisions or identification of next steps. Identify who steps up. After the meeting observe if they follow through on their commitments competently. You have hopefully identified a new leader in the team.

1.8   The Future of the Project Leader Role

Business leaders and organizations are now seeking to employ and develop leaders who will overcome the many challenges that exist in successful delivery within, or for, organizations. There has, and will continue to be, challenges which include the increasing complexity of business relationships, extended supply chains, need for flexibility to meet changing customer demand and market needs, demand for constant innovation, among others. Organizational commentators suggest that these challenges and complexity will only increase rather than diminish with time. Add to this the challenges within organizations themselves: the changing nature of governance and management, and the increasing need to demonstrate value for any investment. All this will change the nature of the role and expectations on the project leader.

This book will focus on the growing mix of existing and new capabilities expected of project leaders. What is the future and how does it translate into capabilities? Table 1.7 looks at this further.

Table 1.7 The capabilities of the future project leader

From	To
From communication planning	**To** expert engagement of disparate stakeholder groups
From delivering outputs and outcomes	**To** delivering value, both explicit such as defined benefits but also implicit such as enhanced relationships and trust
From focusing on time, cost and quality as the definitive success criteria	**To** identifying the range of 'hard' and 'soft' success criteria, recognizing the life-time value
From focusing on the control of change	**To** actively seeking ways of improving value by identifying opportunities and actively advocating their acceptance
From viewing projects as stand-alone entities and trying to manage as such	**To** accepting their place within organizations and therefore the complex relationships that exist with the many stakeholders critical to ensure success including other functions and networks, informal as well as formal
From rigorously applying standardized P3M (project, programme and portfolio management) approaches	**To** applying in a flexible and agile way to deal with an increasingly fast-moving world where customer requirements are expected to change
From working in static hierarchical organizations	**To** delivering change continuously in dynamic and innovative organizational frameworks
From being a master of process	**To** a reflective practitioner with the capabilities and emotional intelligence to learn and apply what is most appropriate from the arsenal of materials available.

The demand will therefore grow for those with leadership capability and potential. As an existing or prospective project leader the questions are: how well placed are you to benefit from the opportunities presented? What do you need to do to maximize your chances of being the inspiration for a case study in a future edition of this book? The book will help inform as well as prompt you to reflect on what it takes to be a successful project leader. Part 4 in particular provides guidance on how to improve your capabilities. In particular you should consider completing the Eight Lookings Diagnostic.

Conclusion

The project leader's role is broad, challenging and rewarding. It requires a myriad of different skills and abilities to be successful in different situations. The project leader must therefore treat their time and energy like any other resource. Only you can judge what proportion of your time you should allocate to 'looking' in any particular direction or working on any of the multiple integrating processes. Whatever the decision, conscious or not, there will be a need to change as the project progresses. Many project leaders are too reactive – they revel in firefighting and crisis management, instead of balancing these skills with the more productive, strategic approach. One thing is clear: you should always create small but significant periods of reflection time. Without these you will never even realize if your priorities are upside down. As the world changes the leader and the leadership role must adapt. It is therefore important that you identify what type of leader you are and wish, or need, to be in the future to be successful.

Key Questions

- What proportion of your current role is focused on project management? On project leadership?
- What are your primary characteristics as a project leader?
- How would you describe your own strengths in your project leader role? How would others describe your strengths?
- How much of your time is spent on each of the Eight Lookings? What insights have you gained?
- Is the leadership of the project solely down to you? Will the project stop tomorrow if you disappear for a month?

References

Adair, J. (2009) *How to Grow Leaders: The Seven Key Principles of Effective Leadership Development* Kogan Page Limited, London, UK.

Crowe, A. (2006) *Alpha Project Managers: What the Top 2% Know That Everyone Else Does Not: What the Top 2 Per Cent Know That Everyone Else Does Not* Velociteach, Kennesaw, GA.

Dweck. C. (2008) *Mindset: How You Can Fulfil Your Potential* Ballantine Books, New York.

Gadeken, O.C. (2005) 'PM leadership: Seven keys to success', *Defense AT&L*, 34 (1), 10–12.

Goleman, D. (1996) *Emotional Intelligence: Why it Can Matter More than IQ* Bloomsbury Publishing plc.

Goleman, D. (2001) 'An EI-based theory of performance', in *The Emotionally Intelligent Workplace*, Cherniss, G. and Goleman, D. (eds), Jossey-Bass, San Francisco, CA.

Lock, D., Scott, L. and Harrington, P. (2013) *Gower Handbook of People in Project Management Gower Publishing Ltd*, Farnham, UK.

Rock, D. (2008) 'SCARF ©: A brain based model for collaborating with and influencing others' *Neuroleadership*, 1.

Rock, D. and Cox, C. (2012) 'SCARF © in 2012: updating the social neuroscience of collaborating with others' *Neuroleadership*, 1.

Rock, D., Siegel, D., Poelmans, S. and Payne, J. (2012) 'The healthy mind platter' *Neuroleadership*, 4.

Watkins, M. (2012) 'How managers become leaders' *Harvard Business Review*, June.

Relationships and the Project Leader

Leadership defines what the future should look like, aligns people with that vision and inspires them to make it happen despite the obstacles.

John Kotter

Introduction

Chapter 2 focuses on three particular areas (Figure 2.1):

- your individual style as a project leader;
- the relationship you have with and the impact you have on other individuals;
- the relationship you have with the organization you work with.

2.1   The Project Leader – Understanding Yourself

Understanding your own individual strengths and preferences will help you understand your role as project leader and your effectiveness in taking on this role. To support you in this there are a number of widely used psychometric profiling tools in the market place that enable individuals and teams to define personal styles and explore the position others may take. Some of the most popular tools to provide such insights include Myers Briggs, Thomas International, Highlands Ability Battery, iMA, StrengthsFinder, BELBIN® Team Roles and DiSC.

Many individuals who make use of these psychometric profiling tools come away with the idea that they are being pigeon-holed into a particular type of behaviour, but such tools only indicate a preference. The reality is that as individuals we typically have a range of responses to a situation and that we

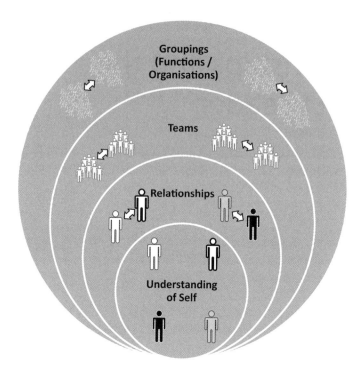

Figure 2.1   The layers of understanding and relationship

work across a spectrum, often depending on the context. Being able to flex your leadership style as the situation and context requires is one of the key attributes of successful leaders, project or otherwise.

The insights that this range of tools provides help to develop our self-awareness: that ability to recognize and understand our moods, emotions and drivers as well as our impact on others. We often work with organizations that elect to provide all their project team members with the opportunity to take these psychometric profiles. The additional insight these tools provide is not just at an individual level, but also helps team members to explore their relationships with each other and to understand the diversity of approach, strengths and weaknesses within the team. They provide an objective and impersonal way for team members to discuss their different motivations, and the impact these have on relationships and project performance.

One such example is iMA, which provides a simple way to understand the communication and engagement preferences of others and therefore not a psychometric in the true sense. iMA stands for Identify, Modify and Adapt – the process that we would encourage everyone to follow when interacting and collaborating with others. We talk in Part 3 about core areas of a project leader's role including communication, engagement and managing key players. Few would argue that building awareness of different personal styles provides useful insights to improve relationships and understand how your key stakeholders most likely want to be engaged. The challenge is often how you go about gathering and sharing these insights. The iMA Colour Styles tool provides a framework to interpret the style of your key stakeholders and build engagement strategies using two distinctions that distinguish between assertiveness and openness. By defining preferred style along these axes, iMA segments four 'types', each with their own typical characteristics, behaviours and preferences. You can complete this at www.ima-pm.co.uk. This is represented visually below in Figure 2.2 and a description of each colour style is provided in Table 2.1.

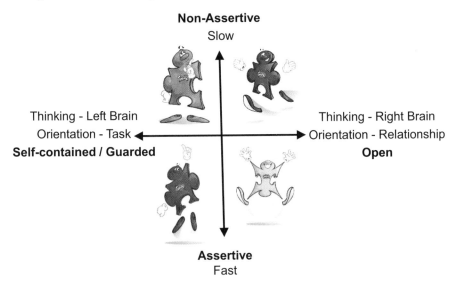

Figure 2.2   Description of iMA colour types
Source: Reproduced with permission by Team Animation Ltd and iMA Strategies

Understanding the preferred style of different personnel within the project is important both in terms of what is delivered and in the way it is achieved. For example, if the project leader is a High Red and the project sponsor a High Blue, it would be important for the project leader to understand that they may appear pushy and insensitive to the sponsor if delivery of outcomes is all that is focused on during their discussions.

Table 2.1 iMA colour styles associated characteristics and tips to get to know them better

	Description	Tips on how to work with them more effectively
iMA High Blue 	... are warm, supportive and nurturing individuals who develop strong networks of people who are willing to be mutually supportive and reliable. They are excellent team players, courteous, friendly and good planners. They are also persistent workers and good with follow through.	• be pleasant • be non-assertive • be consistent • be selfless • be supportive of my feelings • be sincere
iMA High Green 	... are serious, analytical, persistent, systematic and task-oriented people who enjoy problem solving, perfecting processes and working towards tangible results. They do research, make comparisons, determine risk, calculate margins of error and then take action.	• be time disciplined • be logical and prepared • be respectful of rules • be supportive of my thoughts • be structured and well organized • be precise
iMA High Red 	... are goal-oriented go-getters who are most comfortable when they are in charge of people and situations. They focus on a no-nonsense approach to bottom-line results. They are fast-paced, task-oriented and work quickly by themselves.	• be practical • be brief • be assertive • be to the point • be supportive of my goals • be respectful of my time
iMA High Yellow 	... are outgoing, friendly and enthusiastic idea people who excel in getting others excited about their vision. They are fast paced, high energy and deal with people in a positive upbeat way. They are also eternal optimists who can influence people and build alliances to accomplish their goals.	• be flexible • be quick paced • be positive • be open • be generous with your praise • be supportive of my ideas

Source: Reproduced with permission of Team Animation Ltd and iMA Strategies

For example, when faced with High Greens other colours can feel that they cannot provide sufficient information or engage with them easily to influence their opinion or decision.

Many of these profiling tools use self-assessment so that effectively there is a single view, that is your view, which is represented. What is often more valuable is a collection of positive critical views and feedback (known as '360-degree feedback') from colleagues and peers that help to build up a more detailed picture of an individual and by extension the team, and provides a more objective view.

2.2   The Project Leader and Relationships

At the most basic level, the essence of leadership is the ability to create a willing and sustained following: to create in others the desire to want to share the same journey and purpose. This view of leadership is about creating connections, engaging hearts and minds, and building trusted relationships, so relationship-building is one of the key elements of the project leader's role. Strong relationships built on trust and respect help to generate support for the project outside the project team, as well as enabling collaboration inside the project team. From assembling the team in the initial stages of the project through coordinating effort, developing expertise and monitoring performance of the team as well as the project, the project leader has a critical role in ensuring that the maximum value is achieved from and for those involved in the project.

Being able to identify those relationships that you need to build with the client, the sponsor and with others, and being able to identify their respective interest in the project, will help to pinpoint how to hook their support and keep it. Just like personal relationships, these relationships are not static: they need attention and nurturing. They are dynamic; therefore just because you have built trust and understanding in the past, it does not mean to say that you can take the continued relationship for granted.

The previous section provides insights into how to build successful relationships through understanding the other person, modifying your behaviour and then adapting when required. Ultimately, if you are the project leader and you are committed to delivering success, it is up to you to find ways to improve understanding, minimize conflict and build motivatation.

Formal position and hierarchy confers specific authority, but working across organizational barriers, in a temporary team, outside normal hierarchy, means that project leaders need to be aware of a different set of challenges. Often the majority, if not all, of your team will come under the direct management of another for the purposes of line management, appraisals, salary and promotion.

As a project leader you will spend a lot of time trying to make things happen and get things done either for yourself, in order to meet expectations and deadlines, or on behalf of the project team. Working outside the formal hierarchy of an organization means that, although you have the accountability and responsibility to produce results, delegated or otherwise, you cannot rely on a formal position or a place in the hierarchy to get things done. It also means you need to be 'organizationally intelligent' and make sense of the power bases, politics, networks and relationships within your own organization, as well as the client's organization. Being able to move and work easily and confidently across all areas of the organization, and to build influence and support at all levels of the organization from the C-suite to operational levels demonstrates a professional and personal maturity (Coleman, 2013).

Bargaining, negotiating and persuading holders of resources leads back to the idea of building good working relationships, especially if there is the opportunity to create some reciprocity or obligation on their part.

We talk further in Part 3 about building relationships with key players and about effective communication and engagement, and in Part 4 we will identify how the organization can support the project leader to develop.

2.3   The Project Leader and Organizational Culture

All project activity takes place within the influence and context of the organization's culture. Culture is a notoriously difficult term to define although many anthropologists, researchers and authors have spent an inordinate amount of time trying to do so. Spencer-Oatey (2008) suggested that culture is 'a fuzzy set of basic assumptions and values, orientations to life, beliefs, policies, procedures and behavioural conventions that are shared by a group of people, and that influence (but do not determine) each member's behaviour and his/her interpretations of the "meaning" of other people's behaviour'. However, organizational culture has been most famously described as 'the way we do things around here' (variously ascribed). Our particular focus here is the dynamic relationship between the project leader, the culture of the organization for which they work and the way that each plays on the other to ultimately impact the success of the project. Identifying organizational culture allows us to reflect and consider what requirements there may be on a project leader or the style of leadership they deploy. So, for example, what might happen if a hard-nosed and assertive project leader is asked to deliver a challenging project in an organization with a harmonious and consensual culture?

This raises the interesting question of whether a project leader should adapt their style to suit the organization, or whether the organization should adapt to the experience and behaviours of a project leader. We would lean much more towards the former, since ultimately projects are there to serve the organization. However, we've encountered situations where part of the project leader's role was to introduce and embed project structures within the organization; in these cases, organizations have needed to adapt themselves to becoming project-oriented and to the project leader.

Engwall (2003) looked at history and context for projects. We suggest that organizational culture is part of the context for projects, and is certainly pertinent to the project leader in providing some level of distinction to allow them to consider the impact on the role they are being asked to undertake. As an example, if the organization has a high level of centralization and collaboration, this will inform and shape what the project leader must do to ensure success. We have identified these two indicators as important to help differentiate the types of organizational culture within which project leaders must deliver:

- *Level of Centralization*
  Centralization refers to the degree of concentration of power and authority, and activities such as planning and decision making within the organizational structure. The level of centralization within an organization is often visible and easily discernible.

  A high degree of centralization is evidenced by strong, robust and established governance and decision making concentrated within a particular location (for example, at headquarters) and/or at the very senior level. The Vision identifying the future state is typically developed and held centrally by a few people and communicated out.

  A low degree of centralization is evidenced by responsibility for governance and decision making delegated to local levels geographically and/or functionally and/or departmentally. This may similarly impact innovation and how it is viewed and supported within the organization. The Vision identifying the future state is developed and owned by the broader organization.
- *Level of Collaboration*
  Collaboration refers to individuals working together to achieve a *defined* and common *business* purpose and, as such, is critical to project success.

Organizations can encourage or even actively discourage collaboration through the culture that has evolved. The kind of indicators may include:
- the ease with which you can build your relationships and networks within the organization, and so obtain the support necessary;
- the ease with which you can identify those people who will important to the project;
- how cross-functional support for the project is encouraged and facilitated.

In Figure 2.3, Project Culture Matrix™, we have identified the type of project leader and also the style of leadership that thrives in this culture, as distinguished by the level of centralization and collaboration.

The Project Culture Matrix™ can be used in a number of ways:

- an individual project leader wishing to identify the type of culture they are best suited to or to better understand the culture within which they currently work and how they may be able to adapt their approach and behaviour to suit this;
- those tasking the project leader and considering the best person for the job;
- for an organization to consider the culture within which their project leaders must work and therefore how to recruit and develop people with talent to thrive.

Any model which helps you and your organization to reflect on the reasons for challenges or successes as you deliver your project is of value. Without this you cannot identify the learning or consider how it can be applied to future projects in the same or different organizational cultures.

Conclusion

Just as there is not one 'best' style of leadership for functional directors and executives, there is not a single 'best' style of project leadership. Leadership styles may have to change during the life of a project and for different groups of stakeholders: good leaders know when to and how to flex and change their style to suit the context and circumstances.

The project leader role has recognized core competencies; outside this it is dependent on the context and situation. It is also unique to the person, project, organization – as we will explain in next chapter.

Process rules	**Community rules**
Low level of collaboration and high level of centralization. Organization has:	High level of collaboration and high level of centralization. Organization has:
• Defined structure and hierarchy for decision-making	• Defined structure and hierarchy for decision-making
• Low cross-functional working or organizational networking opportunities or facilitation.	• High incidence of cross-functional working or organizational networking opportunities or facilitation.
What type of Project Leader / Leadership thrives in this culture?	**What type of Project Leader / Leadership thrives in this culture?**
• Highly structured and organised, process driven	• Able to insert self easily into established processes and structures, and work well within these parameters
• Recognizes project governance team and sponsor critical to success	• Flexibiliy and adaptability
• Feeds up, waits for and accepts decisions from more senior level	• Organizationally intelligent: understanding power bases, influencers, able to build strong relationships and networks to own advantage and the advantage of the project
• Recognizes his/her power may come from the size and status of the project	
• Works well with influence and power based on position, role or title	
• Networking and relationship building not as important as formalized authority	
iMA colour that would thrive: Green	**iMA colour that would thrive**: Blue
Individual rules	**Relationships Rule**
Low level of collaboration and low level of centralization. Organization has:	High level of collaboration and low level of centralization. Organization has:
• Delegated authority and decision-making to appropriate levels and/or locations	• Delegated authority and decision-making to appropriate levels and/or locations
• Low cross-functional working or organizational networking opportunities or facilitation.	• High incidence of cross-functional working or organizational networking opportunities or facilitation.
What type of Project Leader / Leadership thrives in this culture?	**What type of Project Leader / Leadership thrives in this culture?**
• High self-reliance and can develop support networks and relationships for self, team and project	• Organizationally intelligent: understanding power bases, influencers, able to build strong relationships and networks to own advantage and the advantage of the project
• Can work with ambiguity and uncertainty	
iMA colour that would thrive: Red	**iMA colour that would thrive**: Yellow

Left axis: **Level of Centralization** (High / Low)

Bottom axis: Low — **Level of Collaboration** — High

Figure 2.3   Project Culture Matrix™

Key Questions

The project leader and project leadership

- What does leadership comprise?
- How would you characterize yourself as a leader?
- How does this impact the way in which you lead a project: the direction you provide, way you engage, and so on?
- How would others characterize you as a leader?
- Is there a 'best' style of leadership?

Organization and culture

- What type of organization are you most comfortable delivering within and why?
- How can you adapt to working in other types of organizational culture? What would the challenges be and how would you deal with these in a way that would not impact the success of the project?
- How should the project leader adapt to the style of the organization within which they are working? Should the project leader impact the culture of the organization in any way?

References

Belbin (www.belbin.com).

Coleman, S. (2013) 'Dealing with power and politics', in *Business Analysis and Leadership: Influencing Change*, Pullen, P. and Archer, J. (eds) Kogan Page.

DiSC (www.thediscpersonalitytest.com).

Engwall, M. (2003) 'No project is an island: linking projects to history and context', *Research Policy*, 32 (5), 789–808.

Highlands Ability Battery (www.highlandsco.com).

iMA (www.imahigh.com).

Myers Briggs (www.myersbriggs.org).

Spencer-Oatey, H. (2008) *Culturally Speaking: Culture, Communication and Politeness Theory, 2nd Edition* Continuum, London and New York.

StrengthsFinder (www.strengthstest.com).

Thomas International (www.thomasinternational.net).

The Project and its Impact on Project Leadership

No man will make a great leader who wants to do it all himself, or to get all the credit for doing it.

Andrew Carnegie

Introduction

Chapter 3 recognizes the importance of the relationship between the project leader and the project, understanding that each impacts the other. As such, this relationship ultimately impacts the performance and success of the undertaking.

Projects cover a hugely diverse range of activities. There are projects to move offices, warehouses and manufacturing plants; to develop a new airline booking system; to re-engineer a purchasing process; to change the organization's culture; to develop computer technicians' competencies; to develop a joint venture with a business partner to deliver a new service.

Do all project leaders need a comprehensive skill range in order to meet this diverse range of project types, or are some project leaders much better suited to particular types of projects than others?

3.1   Importance of Identifying Project Types

We find it helpful to be able to describe different project types in order to understand the characteristics of the project, and to understand what type of project leadership approach might be most suitable.

Don't assume that because projects use a basic set of phases and activities that they are the same. They differ in scope, geography, impact, risk and governance. They differ in the experience and expertise of the project team, the governance body and the client organization. For established types of projects there are the 'known knowns'. However, the more innovative a project is the greater the probability of occurrence of unforeseeable uncertainties. Increasingly, organizations are developing a mixed portfolio of projects so that at any one time they may be running very different types of projects. This can create confusion not only because of the number of projects, but also because each type of project should be approached and led differently. Particular projects demand a greater emphasis on particular competencies of the project leader.

Projects can be viewed in a variety of different ways. Below we look at projects viewed from two particular criteria or 'dimensions', from three and then from four, giving you the choice as to which you might find particularly useful according to your level of interest. Regardless of which you use, each model provides a continuum of project types each requiring different project leadership strategies and skills. There are other models that involve further dimensions for consideration, but we tend to find that the choice of model typically depends on two aspects:

- the level of maturity of the use of project management by the organization;
- the experience and expertise of the individual project leader.

3.2   Project Types: A Three-dimension Model

Briner, Hastings and Geddes (1990) developed a three-dimensional model to help project leaders distinguish between projects. Subsequently Obeng (1996, 1997) developed a two-dimensional model using 'What to do' and 'How to do it' (see Figure 3.1).

Briner, Hastings and Geddes recognized that projects can be classified along a continuum that consists of the extent to which the deliverables can be defined at the outset, the level of structure and formality needed to run a project, and the amount of learning the project team and the organization is undertaking. There are, broadly speaking, three types of project: 'concrete', 'occasional' and 'open'. Each type of project has different characteristics, advantages and disadvantages (Figure 3.2) which need to be understood by project leaders so that they can adjust their leadership role to the project, and use appropriate project structures and tools to manage it.

More detailed descriptions of each of these project types are provided in Table 3.1, p. 59.

Unclear	**Semi-Open or Making a Movie** • Stakeholders are very sure about how the project is to be done • Stakeholders are unsure of what is to be done • The organisation is clear about the method to be used and has the expertise • It needs to spend time defining what	**Open or Lost in the Fog** • Stakeholders are unsure what is to be done • Stakeholders are unsure how the project is to be done • The organisation is attempting to do something not been done before • The organisation needs to spend time defining what and how
What To Do	**Closed or Painting by Numbers** • Stakeholders are sure about what is to be done • Stakeholders are very sure about how the project is to be done • The organisation is going through a repetitive project and knows the skills needed • Written procedures, methods and systems are available to replicate what has been done in the past	**Ideal Case** • Stakeholders are sure about what is to be done • Stakeholders are unsure how the project is to be done • The organisation needs to spend time on defining how
Clear		
	Clear	**How To Do It** **Unclear**

Figure 3.1   Project types
Source: Adapted from Obeng (1995)

It is worth drawing attention to the range of the project leader's preferences described for the concrete, occasional and open projects below. The range of project leader's preferences described may imply what many project leaders have always believed, that they are supposed to be super-heroes. Alternatively it may imply that some project leaders are better suited to some types of project than others, even if they are well trained and experienced in the generic project management techniques, methodologies and approaches. Both project leaders and their organizations need to think about the types of projects they have in their portfolio, and where possible, to match a project to the project leader's preferences. As illustrated here, these preferences will involve more than previous experience or technical capability.

3.2.1   CONCRETE PROJECTS

Examples of concrete projects range across construction and aerospace. They include the naval base refit team responsible for overhauling and refurbishing

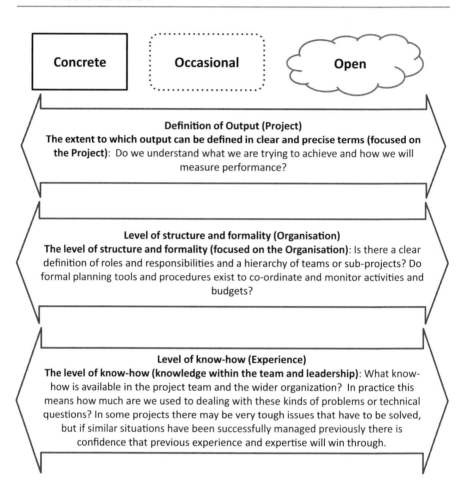

Concrete   **Occasional**   **Open**

Definition of Output (Project)
The extent to which output can be defined in clear and precise terms (focused on the Project): Do we understand what we are trying to achieve and how we will measure performance?

Level of structure and formality (Organisation)
The level of structure and formality (focused on the Organisation): Is there a clear definition of roles and responsibilities and a hierarchy of teams or sub-projects? Do formal planning tools and procedures exist to co-ordinate and monitor activities and budgets?

Level of know-how (Experience)
The level of know-how (knowledge within the team and leadership): What know-how is available in the project team and the wider organization? In practice this means how much are we used to dealing with these kinds of problems or technical questions? In some projects there may be very tough issues that have to be solved, but if similar situations have been successfully managed previously there is confidence that previous experience and expertise will win through.

Figure 3.2   Distinctions between the Concrete, Occasional and Open (COO) three project types

all classes of naval vessels within tight time schedules and even tighter budgets. They use many specialist subcontractors and combine civilian and naval staff. Estimating techniques are based on solid historical practice. The specialists needed are determined by tried and tested systems. See Table 3.2 for concrete project type characteristics, advantages, disadvantages and specifics on successful leadership.

Other familiar examples are office moves or facilities installations, systems development (especially centralized systems), logistics, exhibition organizing, theatrical/film production and new product launches. In all these examples, for many years projects have been an effective way of organizing work. Each

Table 3.1   Description of the Concrete, Occasional and Open (COO) three project types

	Definition of output	Level of structure and formality	Level of know how
Concrete	Precise, clear concrete outputs or deliverables from the outset	Clear roles, systems and procedures consistent with those used elsewhere in the organization. Often the project leader and team members are exclusive to the project while their skills are required	Benefits from existing technical skills and organizational intelligence. There will be some ambiguity and new things to be learnt, but probably not in many critical areas at the same time
Occasional	Are typically used as vehicles for organizational change or to tackle one-off projects. As such, outputs may be ambiguous and a little obscure requiring revisiting after each phase of activity	Often do not have existing or proven structures and procedures so these projects have to create and develop their own. Often the project leader and team members have other line management jobs as well	Are more frequently troubled by the range of ambiguous aspects. Inexperience, in terms of technical issues and how to do things, is high. These projects are often internal to the organization, and may be cutting new paths across the company culture as well as trying to accomplish something new. Existing know-how may be limiting or even unhelpful, holding back changes
Open	Are not clear in the early stages about what outputs are to be obtained. There are many possibilities that need to be investigated. The main aim is to clarify the potential outputs systematically and choose which is most relevant so may use iterative scoping to investigate the options and agree the overall success criteria	May not see the need for any roles or systems. They rely upon the energy and interest of the project team to organize themselves as required and are very informal	Are characterized by experimentation. Innovations are often spawned in this way by finding out what is possible and how to do it. Little is known inside the organization, and sometimes outside it, so much has to be learnt through a planned process of trial and review when past experience is unlikely to help

job will be significantly different in content, but well-tried methods have been developed for tendering, writing specifications, estimating, planning and controlling. The skills and specialist know-how needed are clear, the particular constellation will be different, but everybody can easily identify what will be required. Formal, documented procedures exist, and there is historical experience of what typically goes wrong and how long tasks take. People will be used to working in project teams and will rapidly fit into a new project.

Table 3.2   Characteristics of the concrete project type

Characteristics	• Full-time leader • Full-time visible team members with clear roles, responsibilities, specialisms, hierarchy • Project owner and sponsor are named and active • Resources allocated and formal decision making • Project team and organization very experienced in this sort of project: know what to expect • Well-established systems for estimating, planning and controlling
Advantages	• High levels of relevant experience • Project type is accepted. Individuals and organizations are comfortable with concrete projects. Well understood relationships, structures and risks • Methods, systems and tools are tried and tested
Disadvantages	• The invisible team more likely to be ignored • Potentially combative relationships with subcontractors or external agents • Systems dominate and become rituals of their own, leading to surprises and unaddressed problems which lead to unproductive time • Technical dominance of one discipline closes out other considerations

Leadership	The project leader responsible for a concrete project is like the conductor of an orchestra bringing different parts together using a known score. The situation can be very complex, with different highly qualified instrumentalists to be harmonized, playing to their own highest standards, but in harmony with others. The score is known and each knows his or her part. Nevertheless, there is enormous difference in interpretation and success of the end result: from the original and creative to the mundane or even shambolic. Keeping a sensitive finger on the pulse and taking immediate action based on good judgment, experience and intuition make the difference.
	Successful leaders of concrete projects prefer:
	   • to work within a backbone of a structure provided by a given set of processes
	   • to build a team with people whose expertise they understand, based on their education and experience
	   • to solve problems actively, doing what it takes to get the job done: a trouble shooter
	   • to take a high profile, be the visible integrator of communication and activity: the person with whom the buck stops

3.2.2 OCCASIONAL PROJECTS

As we move across the project type continuum, the projects become less formal, less durable, less familiar and less established within the organization than the concrete type. Frequently they are internally focused vehicles to achieve change in the way things are done, combining people from across organizational, geographical or professional boundaries who do not normally work together. Examples drawn from a wide range are:

- designing a new industrial relations negotiating structure;
- introducing total quality or customer-focused initiatives;
- defining and implementing a new product development process;
- introducing automation to the shop floor;
- creating a new strategic process;
- defining how to enter a new market, perhaps in another culture;
- investigating a corporate policy for service 'standards'.

See Table 3.3 for occasional project type characteristics, advantages, disadvantages and specifics on successful leadership.

The main feature of an occasional project is that the purpose, and therefore the deliverables, is less easily defined at the outset. A direction or theme will have been set, but the precise impact and benefits to the organization will not be specific. As a result resources, budgets and outcomes may need to be planned and renegotiated at particular quality or end-of-phase gates. Who should be involved along the life of the project may be unclear, and the commitment from team members and even the project leader is usually part time. Often these people have not carried out this particular activity before so they may not be confident in their abilities and will find it hard to anticipate problems. So much has to be learnt, individually and collectively, about what the project entails, how to do it and how to work together. Planning will tend to be in short cycles, building rapidly on what has been learned in practice. Simple planning tools will be all that is needed, and decision-making processes have to be defined and agreed between the project leader and the sponsor.

One example of an occasional project is the task of developing a new strategic direction for a company. Here there may be many options; project teams may be asked to investigate, to examine, to pull together and finally to secure agreement to a preferred option. A company making simulators revised its after-sales service using a project team to identify what existed, what should exist and therefore what the new service package might look like. This project

Table 3.3   Characteristics of the occasional project type

Characteristics	• Specific purpose and deliverables less defined at the outset • Often a part-time leader • Part-time team members with conflicting priorities of time and interest with day job or other projects • Unclear roles and relationships across team • Unclear roles for sponsor and client: what they want emerges and evolves • Planning and control methods unfamiliar • Resources including budget and equipment are 'guesstimated'
Advantages	• Flexibility: project leader and team members are nominated because of their interest in the project. The project leader has a wider choice of team members from which to build their team. • Less precedents to restrict process, and many innovative opportunities • Chance to gain wider experience • Controlled: internal projects cross normal organizational communication lines, break boundaries and gain the ear of senior people • Often have the sponsor's interest and positive attention, so a way for the project leader to build profile and credibility
Disadvantages	• Priority conflicts: project work competes with normal day job, so is seen as rewarding and extra • Emerging direction: often frustration results from the time and iterative discussions necessary to clarify and agree options. Pressure of ambiguity in method and/or output • Cultural resistance: suspicion and awkwardness at working across unfamiliar boundaries. The 'not-invented-here' attitude of those left out of the project
Leadership	The project leader responsible for an occasional project is likened to a sculptor. They start with a design, maybe a commission, a sketch or a model. So they need to develop a sense of what their output should look like in the context where it will be placed. Their task is to shape, mould, modify as they go along, often according to the nature of the material they are using: the grain of the wood, the structure of the stone or the properties of the metal. Successful leaders of occasional projects prefer: • to act as alliance-builders and facilitate collaboration in order to integrate a range of different people's perspectives into an evolving output • to keep a focus on the output, but be flexible about the steps necessary to achieve it: they tolerate ambiguity • to question the established ways of doing things, and modify or select to suit the situation so are often seen as pathfinders • to shape ideas, to develop the form and structure of the project, and to manage the environment for all this to happen

was potentially huge. The team had to agree what to include and what to leave out and, perhaps more important, the basis for these decisions.

We have seen a considerable growth in occasional projects being used to define and implement organizational change. Taking people from across the depth and breadth of the organization means that problems can be understood from the many perspectives that exist, and widespread commitment can be generated to the solutions that are agreed. The solutions themselves are likely to be more easily implemented, and therefore more effective, because the implications of the problem are widely understood, options have been generated and people have been involved in the decision making.

3.2.3   OPEN PROJECTS

At the far end of the continuum are those projects whose objectives are unclear and where there is uncertainty about the direction or viability of what is being attempted. An open project sounds like a non-project because its objectives will often be fuzzy and may change frequently. There is accumulating evidence that small, unofficial projects produce significant innovations and are effective vehicles for change. Lockheed Martin uses their in-house developed Skunk Works® to create breakthrough technologies and develop new aircraft that redefine flight, working with the mantra 'quick, quiet and quality' and their 14 rules and practices. These reflect an attitude that encourages unique solutions, disruptive technology and a tolerance of failure, understanding that if you have the opportunity to fail you have the opportunity to learn. See Table 3.4 for open project type characteristics, advantages, disadvantages and specifics on success leadership.

Increasingly, organizations are concerned about overly bureaucratic systems that stifle innovation and new ways of working, and hinder progress. They want to rapidly harness the ideas and opportunities that present themselves at all levels, and this encourages the use of informal projects and identifying new ways of working.

Often open projects start as a small group of interested people gathered together by an enthusiastic individual. Their purpose is to test and develop new ideas for business improvement. The belief is that business improvements can be made not only by large schemes, carefully planned and handled by specialists, but also by pulling together and putting into practice a thousand small ideas. This type of project is more useful than may at first appear. An increasing number of companies are encouraging people to form spontaneous

Table 3.4   Characteristics of the open project type

Characteristics	• No formal leader. The most interested people will be the focal point • Team members select themselves, attracted by the idea or opportunity • Self-organizing activities and monitoring • Try out low-key experiments until something works
Advantages	• Motivation: individual spontaneity or energy can be harnessed without any strings • Creativity: embryonic ideas have a chance to be tested and enhanced into viable innovations, or dropped • Low risk: low-resource investments, low visibility in the organization, so minimal consequences if it fails
Disadvantages	• Slow: low-priority, low-resource levels so can remain as a 'good intention' but interest in the project can fade • Failure: encourages unique solutions, but needs an organizational tolerance for failure and an organizational culture that supports the idea that if you have an opportunity to fail, you have an opportunity to learn • Subversive: low visibility can mean that success goes against mainstream activities and hijacks traditional wisdom. Friends need to be won at the right time
Leadership	Typically, leaders of open projects are good at much less obvious means of getting things done. They tend to work behind the scenes to facilitate, and they have a low visibility. The project leader for open projects tends to prefer: • to work outside the bright light of the mainstream, pulling resources from wherever, finding space and time where it does not officially exist: an underground operator • to find new ways and means to test ideas, break the mould: an innovator • to build continued support with a few influencers to maintain the momentum of early successes: an informal influencer or entrepreneur

groups to resolve problems that they see as hindering their work. Quality drives, customer-focused drives, innovation drives, performance improvement drives: all these promote more open projects. For every open project that makes the grade and emerges with substantial results, there are many that fold or remain invisible.

Open projects start small and invisible, but through their demonstrated success and the energy of the team involved in gaining support step-by-step, their potential impact becomes clear, and wider organizational commitment becomes mobilized. Many open projects transform, as they become more formal, into either occasional or concrete projects. As they become more defined, with anticipatable benefits, they gain a sponsor, a more formal team and customer expectations. However, they have to put effort into building their 'market' or reason for existing in order to win internal support for the allocation of the resources necessary to grow.

The main feature of open projects is that they enable limited experimentation because there is always limited time and even more limited resources. So open projects usually involve developing the first steps of embryonic innovations. Examples are:

- research laboratories with small-scale experiments to investigate new substances;
- developing new management development programmes;
- applying more participative and empowering working practices;
- identifying applications for untried technology.

3.3 Project Types: A Four-dimensional Model

A final model we believe is of value for the project leader is the project classification framework (Shenhar and Dvir, 2007). This aims to connect the world of project management with the tumultuous world of strategy by helping both parties to better understand and discuss at a conceptual level the project that is being delivered.

The Diamond model identifies four dimensions that link executive and project leaders together in a discussion that helps them address what needs to be considered before a project is launched, or gain an insight into why a project is not performing. This helps ensure correct resources are assigned to the project as well as a shared understanding of the expected results and why the project is important. The Diamond model identifies levels of Novelty, Technology, Complexity and Pace (NTCP) along four orthogonal dimensions with a common origin as shown below. Each is split into three or four further criteria. When a project is plotted on, as shown, a diamond is created (Figure 3.3).

Two different projects are shown, each requiring a different strategy and leadership style. The important issue is for the sponsor and project leader to see the project in the same light to allow them to identify the optimum approach to delivery of the project. These dimensions and levels are what the authors argue must be considered before a project is launched. By understanding these dimensions or the diamond pattern, the executive and project leader can plan for and share common expectations of performance and impact.

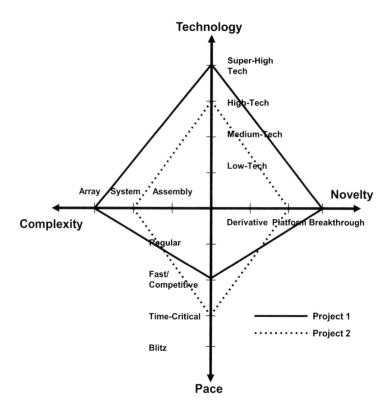

Figure 3.3   Shenhar and Dvir Diamond model
Source: Reproduced with permission

We will use the Diamond model to discuss the particular challenges for the project leader and project leadership as described in Table 3.5 opposite.

Table 3.5 identifies the impact on the style of project leadership for each individual dimension. In reality projects are a combination of dimensions and therefore a complex impact on the leader and their style of leadership. Consider the two absolute extremes:

- If the project were positioned at the lowest level for each dimension, it would be relatively undemanding and not challenging for an experienced and capable project leader.
- If the project were positioned at the highest level for each dimension, it would require a unique individual who not only demonstrates leadership qualities but has had them tested, is resilient and an exceptional role model for others.

Table 3.5   Implications on the project leader and leadership of the different characteristics of the Diamond model

		Variation within projects and impact on the project leader
Novelty	**Represents the uncertainty of the project's goal, the uncertainty in the market, or both. It measures how new the project's product is to customers, users or to the market in general**	*From*: Extensions and improvements to existing services or products (for example, streamlining organizational procedures) *To*: A product or concept that is new to the customer or public (for example, Google Glass) • Comfort of working with a high level of uncertainty (breakthrough) which will impact the project delivery strategy, the method of planning and the plan itself, for example, product is based on intuition, many changes, prototyping and lack of clarity with the customer • Consideration by the project leader of when project requirements must be frozen, either early or late respectively (and ensuring the team is clear as to the reasons)
Technology	**Represents the project's level of technological uncertainty. It is determined by how much new technology is required to complete the project**	*From*: Existing and well-established technologies (for example, most construction projects) *To*: Technologies that do not exist at project initiation. Mission is clear, solution is not (for example, moon landing) • Approach can range from a no-nonsense, formal, tightly planned, fixed-price delivery for low-tech to a flexible, phased overlaps, cost-plus type of strategy – the extremes being favoured by different project leaders • Need to plan for and ensure that informed decisions are made – the project leader ensuring that the correct people are involved and that they have sufficient understanding to facilitate this process. It should not be the project leader making technical decisions
Complexity	**Measures the complexity of the product, the task and the project organization**	*From*: Assembly – creating a collection of elements, components and modules combined into a single unit or entity that performs a single function (for example, CD player or vehicle transmission) *To*: Array – widely dispersed collection of systems that function together to achieve a common purpose (for example, a corporation, national comms network) • At Assembly, the approach may be for simple, informal control and reporting with a low risk of missing requirements • At Array, may require master or central control by a project office; separate additional control for subprojects: many reports and meetings with contractors. High risk caused by weak coordination between the systems that make up the array meaning missing objectives or extensive spending of resources in case of overruns • At Array the project leader must have the experience necessary and temperament to provide leadership when the team may not always be clear

Table 3.5   Implications on the project leader and leadership of the different characteristics of the Diamond model (*concluded*)

		Variation within projects and impact on the project leader
Pace	Represents the urgency of the project – namely, how much time there is to complete the job	*From*: Time is not critical to immediate organizational success *To*: Most urgent, time-critical. Solving a crisis as fast as possible is the criterion for success • Varies in the amount of energy required • Immediate and special task force; team has great autonomy • No bureaucracy; work goes on around the clock; can benefit from prepared contingency plans but must be ready to improvise • Available at all times; constantly providing support, resources, and needed decisions • From Regular with no unique structure, no specific attention and management by exception to Blitz requiring immediate team intervention, likely with considerable autonomy. • For the project leader in Blitz, they may have to be available at all times; constantly providing support, resources, and needed decisions

Source: Adapted from the Shenhar and Dvir Diamond Model © Shenhar and Dvir

The model can be used in three ways:

- by the individual project leader or sponsor to identify the type of project and then reflect on their style of leadership and strategy for delivery;
- by those responsible for sourcing, appointing and monitoring the project leader to reflect on the type of leader required, using the insight gained regarding the nature of the project;
- by those responsible for leading the different aspects of the project to compare their potential differing perceptions of the project and the impact this may have on how it is run, people involved and so on.

The model described above is a practical tool that can help the project leader and others to have a discussion in a high-level way without having to look at the detail and therefore miss key issues.

We consider it important to return to this and remap the project on an infrequent basis. Projects inevitably change and therefore the project leader may have to adjust what is done and how; for example, a project may have to become more innovative given changes in the market.

We used this model in a government department as part of a developmental programme of the project sponsor community. We were fortunate in some workshops to have both the sponsor and project leader. We therefore had an opportunity to have both key team members to independently complete the model using pre-prepared templates.

In a number of projects there were more than two criteria significantly different on one or more axis. This instigated initially a challenging discussion around the projects that were already underway and provided clues as to the issues being faced. On one occasion the project leader and sponsor were in the initiation phase and therefore had an opportunity to shape the project strategy after collectively agreeing on the shape of the project and the implications for its resourcing and delivery.

3.4   The Importance of Matching the Project Leader to the Project

The message is clear. If you know what type of project you are running, and consciously lead it as that type, you are much more likely to develop appropriate structure and processes. If there is incompatibility between the type of project, the way it is being structured and the expectation of key players, there will be severe difficulties in delivery. Especially where projects are not well defined, structured or supported by experience and know-how, the project leader needs to exercise a great degree of judgment in the face of uncertainty.

Context is a critical component of successful project leadership. Just as there is no single type of project, there is no single type of project leader. A project leader who is successful and effective in one type of project with one set of circumstances will not necessarily perform as expertly in another type of project with a different set of circumstances. This has ramifications for both the project manager looking to move into a project leadership role and for the organization itself.

Müller and Turner (2010) identified leadership competency profiles of successful project managers of engineering and construction, IT (not shown) and organizational change projects (Figure 3.4), concluding that the leadership competencies and personalities of successful project managers differ by project type:

- the intellectual leadership dimensions of competence (IQ) are represented by critical thinking, Vision and strategic perspective;

- the managerial leadership dimensions of competence (MQ) are represented by managing resources, engaging communication, empowering, developing and achieving;
- the emotional leadership dimensions of competence (EQ) are represented by self-awareness, emotional resilience, intuitiveness, sensitivity, influence, motivation and conscientiousness.

Muller and Turner identified that all but one of the 15 leadership competencies (that of intuitiveness) are significantly stronger in the managers of successful projects than in the managers of less successful projects. Across all high-performing projects, the EQ leadership dimensions of conscientiousness and sensitivity, and the MQ dimension of engaging communication, correlate positively with project success. The better the project manager is in these elements of leadership, the higher the level of project success.

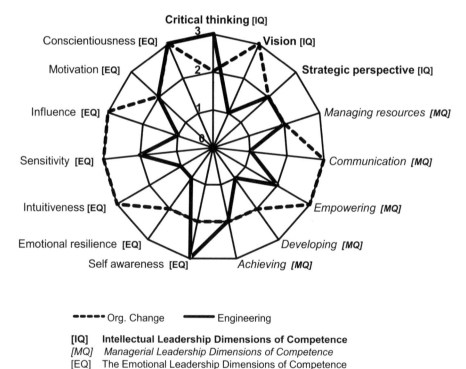

Figure 3.4   Personality profile of successful project managers in different industries

Source: Adapted from Muller and Turner (2010)

How can the organization match a project leader to a project to increase the chances of success? We described the continuum of concrete, occasional and open project types earlier so we know that particular types of project lend themselves to particular project leadership skills. Where an organization recognizes the lack of particular project leadership skills they have the choice as to whether they buy in those skills, whether they develop those skills in-house or indeed whether they plough on with the project regardless. Alternatively, where an organization is in the enviable position of having access to a number of project leaders, it might become a question of further professional development for a particular project leader. These issues will be discussed in further detail in Part 4.

The relationship between project leader and the project, and the way each impacts the other, ultimately impacts the performance and success of the undertaking.

We have already discussed the diverse range of projects undertaken by organizations. This diversity is not just about project size, industry sector and expected benefit but also clarity of purpose, the level of experience of the organization itself in successfully delivering projects. Are some project leaders much better suited to particular types of projects than others? Or, can an organization equip their project leaders with a single comprehensive skill set to help them successfully deliver against any type of project the organization may choose to undertake? This continues to be debated with no consensus. Table 3.6 looks at the advantages and disadvantages.

We suggest that the ideal situation is when the project leader does have the expert knowledge of the type of project or industry, but also that this is complemented by their understanding of the disadvantages that this may cause so that they can plan how to discharge their role effectively.

The project leader is not always simply there to lead or manage but often has, either by design or default, multiple other roles. These secondary roles such as signing off technical specifications or appointment of specialized support will require in-depth knowledge of the project technologies or equivalent and may even be required to act as a technical authority.

Clarity is therefore required of the role of the project leader as these secondary responsibilities may be just as important as their role as the leader.

Table 3.6   Implications of no or expert knowledge of the type of project or industry

	No knowledge or understanding of the type of project or industry	Expert knowledge on the type of project or industry
Example	Limited or no experience in the industry or sector or with the particular technologies and specialisms that are key to project success	Experience of the industry or sector and with an understanding of the technologies and specialisms that are key to project success
Advantages	• Brings fresh thinking and approaches (but may not be applicable or appropriate which may not be immediately evident) • Challenges existing ways of working (which may have been honed over a long period of time and therefore resentment if challenged)	• Technical understanding of what is being done and why to inform decision making (so possibly confusing responsibilities if making decisions of a technical nature) • Respected by specialist teams • Can 'hit the ground running' (but may therefore not reflect on the context)
Disadvantages	• May not immediately gain the respect of specialist leaders and teams; however, primary focus is to augment existing expertise not to replicate • Cannot challenge (although you could argue that is not the project leader's role)	• Can be too close and therefore not question underlying assumptions or structures as overly familiar • May take on a role which is more technical in nature rather than a leadership role

3.5   Methodology and its Implications on Leadership Style

There is a further, and often overlooked, factor that impacts the project leader, and that is the nature of the methodology or approach adopted for the project. This ultimately defines the tools you have at your disposal to monitor, coordinate, report and the many other functions that are needed to ensure success. Organizations have increasingly adopted proprietary approaches or developed their own, or more likely have developed hybrids, which take the best of both worlds. The impact on the project leader to do their job easily and efficiently can be considerable.

Methodologies, the term we will use to describe the structures and processes with which organizations use to deliver their projects, come in varied levels of comprehensiveness, intentionality and complexity. They should be designed to meet the needs of the organization and potentially tweaked to the type of project. This is unfortunately not the case in many organizations resulting in methodologies that are not suited to their culture. We will consider two extremes, shown in Table 3.7:

Table 3.7   Characteristics of flexible and fixed types of methodology

Formality or flexibility of the methodology	
Flexible	• Could be either a proprietary approach which was, or has been, subsequently simplified or an emergent methodology which has evolved and grown from within the organization
	• More informal and flexible approaches are often favoured by more people-centric organizational cultures to allow freedom and expression
	• May cause issues when governing or assuring portfolios of projects where there is inconsistency in terms of approach and outputs
	• More likely to be adapted to suit the individual project needs but requires an experienced leader who understands the implications of impacting the methodology
	• Collaboration with other areas of the organization may be easier to initiate but working together may be challenging as there is no commonly understood approach
Fixed	• Typically proprietary which has been modified and adapted. Exceptions are often corporates where they have the resources to develop their own methodology
	• Can be become limiting if it does not allow a certain level of adaptability with respect to the type of project and culture within which it must be delivered
	• Excellent basis for governing or assuring a portfolio of projects if the methodology is applied consistently (just because you have one it does not necessarily mean everyone will use it!)
	• Ideally it should allow for different types of project and describe the adaptations to the approach. For example, for a less complex project there may be a lower level of assurance and mandatory number of processes which must be applied such as earned value. The project leader should discuss with the team how the methodology supports effective working practices. For example, the need for reporting and assurance

Should project leaders adapt the methodology to meet their style or adjust their style? Is there a style of project leader best suited to a particular methodology? The project leader may be in a position where they are able to influence the methodology used. The implications are identified below in Figure 3.5 of each scenario against the two extremes of methodology discussed above.

At a more practical level, each person perceives and uses a methodology differently. When working with individuals and teams who wish to improve their performance, it is worth considering how different styles impact the performance of the methodology and what adaptations the project leader

		Low — Project leader influence on the methodology — High	
Fixed ↑ *Formality / flexibility of the methodology* ↓ **Flexible**		**Ham strung** • Potentially a far from ideal situation for the project leader if the methodology does not fit with the desired style of project leadership or type of project • The project leader should invest time up front to work with the team to understand how they will use the methodology and changes that they should campaign for	**I want this all the time** • Consideration as to the value of any potential changes before making them as the methodology is likely well embedded, understood and accepted • Focus should be on changes that are clearly beneficial to the project; for example, change in stage gate approval process or the level of planning at different stages through the project • Consideration as to the impact on organisational governance and assurance of any changes
		Constrained • Opportunity exists to make selective changes only so the team and project needs should be identified and considered. For example, change in reporting cycle or the way risks are handled	**Ideal case** • Opportunity to adapt to suit the type of project is high and the approach being taken towards delivery • Project leader must consider the value that will be achieved from a wholesale change as this may impact performance in the short term

Figure 3.5 **Impact on project leader and form of leadership of the type of methodology**

can make to the methodology to suit the collective style of the team or behavioural changes with key individuals or with the team. It can be helpful to get the team to consider the following questions in relation to a particular process used in managing a project, in this case as described below for Planning.

- Why (Value): Why do it? What value does it add? What is its purpose?
- Who and where (Engagement): Who should be involved? Should they be involved as a one-off or continuously? Where should it take place?
- How (Process): How should it be carried out? Should formalized techniques and processes be used?
- When (Time): When is it best to plan – early or a little later? Should it be continuous or one off?
- What (Output): What level of detail is appropriate? How should it be presented?

By considering such questions for the whole methodology, or key processes, the project leader can gain insights that may help to explain issues such as the quality of planning, monitoring, control or management of risk. Ultimately a methodology is a static description that will work for some and not others.

Conclusion

Each project demands varying capabilities from the project leader. An individual's preferred way of working may be better suited to one type of project than another. To help inform you, consider looking for distinctions between projects, as identified in the models above, and then consider how you will adapt your leadership approach. Another key consideration is the methodology and, dependent on the influence you have over its use and modification, how you may have to change how you adapt your leadership to suit. Whatever changes you may consider, it is key that you take the time to reflect and consider, demonstrating to the team and sponsor that you are informed, flexible and adaptable.

Key Questions

- Is there a single 'best' style of management and leadership for projects?
- Does a 'best' style of project leadership really depend on the nature and circumstances of the project?
- How should the project leader impact the project in relation to how it is delivered and what is delivered?
- How could the style of project leadership impact the success of the project and what safeguards are required?
- What actions should the project leader take, including the design of the team, to offset any perceived 'weaknesses'?
- What type of projects does your organization run and how does it take into account an individual project leader's preferred way of working?
- Are you clear about the methodology that will be used to deliver the project and how you may have to adapt your own leadership style and the way the team works?
- Consider your own project against each of the NTCP model axes. How does this impact your role and how you deliver the project?

References

Briner, W., Hastings, C. and and Geddes, M (1990) *Project Leadership, First Edition* Gower Publishing Limited, Farnham, UK.

Muller, R. and Turner, R.J. (2010) *Project-Oriented Leadership* Gower Publishing Limited, Farnham, UK.

Obeng, E. (1997) *New Rules for the New World: Cautionary Tales for the New World Manager* Capstone Publishing Ltd, Mankato, MN.

Obeng, E. (1996) *All Change!: The Project Leader's Secret Handbook* (Financial Times Series) Prentice Hall, Harlow, UK.

Shenhar, A.J. and Dvir, D. (2007) *Reinventing Project Management: The Diamond Approach to Successful Growth and Innovation* Harvard Business School Press, Boston, MA.

PART 2
LEADING THE PROJECT

The instrument of leadership is the self, and mastery of the art of leadership comes from mastery of the self.

Kouzes and Posner

In Part 1 we looked at leadership, project leadership and the breadth of competencies and skills required for a project leader to undertake the project leadership role to drive the project to its successful conclusion. In Part 2 we look at the project itself: how the lifecycle of the project is divided into logical phases and the activities required of these phases to ensure it is shaped, scoped, started, delivered and closed effectively and efficiently. Different organizations and project management methodologies have their own preferences about how projects are constructed, governed and run. However, for ease of discussion, we look at a generic version of the project lifecycle in order to explore four key phases: shaping and scoping, start-up, delivery and close.

Our particular focus here is the aspects of the role of the project leader during these key phases, not the mechanics and technical detail of these phases. We will explore how the focus of the project leader changes with various stages of the project's lifecycle. In the early phases, the project leader needs to:

- understand constraints, assumptions and the various ideas of 'success';
- identify and develop strong durable links with key stakeholders;
- assemble the project team and develop a set of very diverse individuals into a high-performing team;
- create the project culture that will deliver the project performance needed and to align effort.

As the project progresses, the focus shifts to maintaining momentum and keeping on track, to measuring performance and responding to uncertainty and change. At closure of the project the focus again shifts to closing down in a controlled manner, ensuring business readiness and handing over to the client, identifying lessons learnt and ensuring they are fed back into the organization, in providing feedback and even references for project team members, ensuring that longer-term benefits measurement is planned for even as the project team is dismantled, and finally to considering your own future.

> **Completing the Eight Lookings Diagnostic will provide you with an indication of how much your focus is on:**
>
> **Looking backwards – at the Past**
>
> **and**
>
> **Looking forwards – to the Future.**

We recognize that this part of the book is the richest in terms of explanations and detail, so we have provided a summary of the activities across the four generic phases of the project lifecycle (see opposite).

In Part 2:

- Chapter 4 describes the first phase of the generic project lifecycle, that of shaping and scoping.
- Chapter 5 looks at the activities involved in starting-up the project including formulating the approach to the project, gathering the team and getting it to work effectively together, and detailed planning.
- Chapter 6 covers the delivery phase, keeping your finger on the pulse of the project and reviewing, checking and anticipating.
- Chapter 7 looks at giving the project a definite close regardless of whether this is a forced or natural close. This involves:
  - ensuring the client is ready to receive the outcomes and output;
  - final reviews or audits are completed and knowledge gained disseminated into the organization for development and improvement;
  - the project team's involvement is brought to a structured finish;
  - you have considered your own future.

Shaping and Scoping	Start-up	Delivery	Close
Not all PLs have the opportunity to get engaged at this early stage. Where they do, typically they need to:	Here the project leader needs to:	As the project progresses the focus shifts to keeping your finger on the pulse of the project and reviewing, checking and anticipating:	At closure of the project the focus again shifts:
• Understand how the project is being shaped, given the hopes and ambitions of those who want to benefit from it	• Identify and develop strong durable links with key stakeholders to gain support and commitment: the sponsor, the client, the project team	• Remain aware of insidious and unanticipated ways in which slippage can occur	• Close down the project in a controlled manner regardless of a natural or forced closure
• Understand the organization's Big Picture and how the project fits with the organizational strategy	• Assemble the project team: visible and invisible	• Use appropriate monitoring tools and processes to provide rapid feedback on progress	• Understand this new version of the relationship with the client
• Support the development and presentation of the business case, ensuring the investment decision is sound so that it will deliver the proposed benefits	• Accelerate team development and cohesion through forming, storming and norming to develop a high-performing team.	• Provide regular opportunities for the team not only to review progress, but even more important, to anticipate problems	• Identify lessons learnt and ensure they are fed back into the organization
• Support the development of relevant success criteria for the project for performance monitoring during delivery and handover to the client at closure	• Define the way you and the project team will work cross-functionally, multi-located, cross-culturally	• Control, monitor and report	• Handover to the client
• Support the development of a project vision to provide focus, clarity and alignment	• Develop the project plans: 'what' needs to be done (understanding the activities and tasks) and 'how' it needs to be done (ownership and responsibility, quality, project culture)	• Maintain momentum	• Provide feedback, appraisals, references for project team members
• Ensure a definition and scope is put around the project	• Develop appropriate communication plans and feedback mechanisms	• Keep delivery on track and in line with the plans derived from the start-up phase	• Ensure the client organization is linked into the project so that they can use outputs and deliverables confidently
• Understand the constraints, assumptions and the various ideas of 'success'	• Assess project risks in detail	• Measure performance	• Review the project lifecycle and processes
• Begin to estimate what kinds of capabilities the project requires for successful completion	• Formulate the approach to the project	• Review health of the project	• Adjourn the project team
• Start to assess the risks of, and the quality required for, the project	• Create the project culture that will deliver the project performance needed and to align effort	• Respond to uncertainty and change	• Celebrate and enjoying the success of the project
• Develop a change control process: managing change to scope is an inevitable part of every project	• Anticipate change to scope, market context, project success criteria and personnel	• Continue to communicate and invite feedback	• Ensure the project Vision and success criteria have been met, or handed over for further benefits tracking
• Stakeholder mapping techniques and dialogue are especially useful to the project leader at this early stage.	• Launch the project formally	• Actively market the project to build support and commitment	• Consider your own future
		• Take the time simply to think, plan and reflect	
		• Hold project reviews, to include performance, progress, risk, quality, communication and so on	
		• Celebrate success along the way	
		• Respond to change	
		• Challenge underperformance	

CHAPTER 4

Phase A – Shaping and Scoping

Begin with the end in mind.

Stephen Covey (1989)

Introduction

In Chapter 4 we look at the first phase of the generic project lifecycle, that of shaping and scoping. We describe how:

- the project is initially shaped within the organization, given the many hopes and ambitions of those who want to benefit from it and given the organizational strategy;
- the organization ensures the investment decision is sound so that it will deliver the proposed benefits;
- success criteria for the project are developed and agreed for performance monitoring during delivery and for handover to the client at closure;
- a definition and scope is put around the project.

This is part of the process to ensure that we help the 'right' projects get the necessary agreement, support and resources. By 'right' we mean ensuring that any projects taken forward are aligned with the strategic aims of the organization and will deliver value, so protecting the organization's investment.

Not all project leaders have the opportunity to get engaged with the project at this early stage. Where they do, they become a point of continuity throughout the project as well as providing support for the development and presentation of the business case, ensuring the investment decision is sound so that it will deliver the proposed benefits, and support for the development of relevant success criteria for the project.

4.1   Shaping the Project

Organizations choose to undertake projects for many different reasons. A project may be a particular piece of work contracted for with a client, it may be the result of research and development or it may be a pet scheme. Even before the project is explored in terms of scope, boundaries, terms of reference, expected outcomes or business case there is a huge amount of work which takes place to move the initial whisper of an idea through the muddle of ambiguity and choices, and convert it into a cohesive and accepted 'sense' that is a project. These, then, are the front-end conceptualization activities which crystallize an idea into a defined concept.

The idea of 'project shaping' is fairly new and essentially represents the ideas, concepts and activities that lead up to a more detailed scoping. Smith and Winter (2009) looked at the 'complex and messy social processes' that lead to a particular project being proposed, understanding that projects are created and shaped by a diverse range of individuals and interests within the organization. Why is this so important for the project management community? Simply because we recognize that for projects to have a good chance of success they must be soundly based; it is difficult to recover downstream from a project that has been poorly conceived.

The 'project shaper' is the person or group of persons who determine the form a particular project will take. They have to negotiate through the various power bases and interest groups within the organization using influence, negotiation, persuasion and facilitation to make sense of the requirements, benefits and outcomes wanted. They have to decide which are important, pertinent and priority and to draw together these diverse strands into a coherent form. Shaping the project serves to address and resolve conflicts upfront, and to help all the various groups gain clarity about what they really want to achieve rather than what they *think* they want to achieve.

The project leader will have a role to play in this shaping if they are fortunate enough to be engaged this early, along with other individuals who have specific vested interests and agendas. It would certainly be in the project leader's own interest to get involved in this stage of the project lifecycle since they will have the opportunity to engage with groups who have a keen interest in the outcomes and so are likely to become key stakeholders, to understand their concepts of value, and to get involved with shaping the project into a form which has a good prospect of success.

Figure 4.1 illustrates the six significant influences that Smith and Winter identified in shaping the project. These six significant influences are detailed in Table 4.1, p. 84.

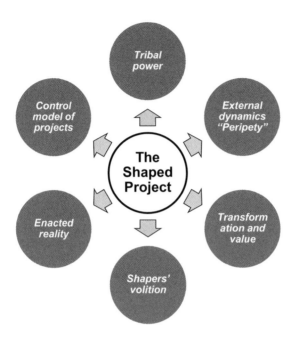

Figure 4.1   The six significant influences of project shaping
Source: Smith and Winter, 2009

Project shaping is not a single conversation at a single point in time. It is typically a series of discussions over a period of time, visiting and revisiting points and previous conversations before a arriving at a plausible shape to take forward into scoping.

4.2   Understanding Scoping

Once the project has a shape, direction and an understanding of what it needs to achieve, more detailed scoping can take place. Scoping is another early stage process through which clarity, agreement and commitment are obtained for the project throughout the organization. It helps identify the terms of reference for the project, the vision for the project and how this aligns with the organizational strategy, what constitutes success for the project, and the constraints and assumptions under which the project will be working. In doing so, it helps to kick-start project planning which will determine and document a list of specific project goals, deliverables, tasks and deadlines. That is its overt purpose.

Table 4.1   The six significant influences of project shaping

Influence	Description
1: The control model of projects	Work in organizations has often been loosely defined, tracked and distributed between multiple different parties. Such work is increasingly undergoing 'projectification'; that is, being brought into the structure and framework of a controlled project with defined outputs and outcomes, defined processes and activities, specific roles and accountability.
2: Tribal power	Projects emerge from the input and manoeuvring of various groups each with their own agenda, and with their own ideas of success and value. It takes time, negotiation and persuasion to consolidate these wants and needs into a plausible concept that can then be moulded further into an acceptable and defined scope. The project shaper recognizes these diverse 'tribes' can impact the success of the project, and works to facilitate and create 'projects with drumbeat'.
3: Transformation and value	The alignment of projects with a need for organizational transformation and the drive for 'value' that goes beyond the obvious and immediate product or service delivery. This value may be as diverse as an improvement in communications between organizations, new product development or divesting part of the organization.
4: Enacted reality	This encompasses two main areas. Firstly, the production of tangibles such as project mandates and documentation that explain and codify the project essentials; these help to provide stability of purpose for the project. Secondly, actively making sense of and trying to align the requirements and agendas of the various groups.
5: External dynamics – 'peripety'	This relates to how responsive the shape of the project becomes to the dynamics of the wider environment. Sometimes, something appears which leads to a reframing of the understanding of things that have already happened or been discussed. This might include movements in the external environment such as legislative changes or market forces. It is not only the outcomes that are changed as a result, but the question that originally framed the thinking and planning. This may require a significant and sudden shift in organizational strategy and hence to the projects which have been defined as a result of that strategy.
6: Shapers' volition	The identity that shapers individually and as a group bring to the process so that, for each project, the scope is formed through the action of individuals who choose to shape it in a particular way.

Source: Adapted from Smith and Winter (2009)

However, scoping also has the covert purpose of helping the key players in the organization to rehearse mentally what the implications of the project might be across the organization, how these might affect the project definition, and how they might be anticipated and prepared for. These implications may include:

- funding and budgets;
- resources (skill sets as well as capital equipment);
- project team building;
- risk identification and management, including health and safety;
- dependencies on other individuals, teams or projects for their deliverables;
- planning, control, monitoring and reporting;
- governance;
- stakeholder communication and dialogue;
- benefits realization;
- project branding and marketing;
- product testing or service and project success criteria;
- quality assurance and the use of quality management systems;
- the use of an appropriate project management methodology or approach, whether industry standard or in-house.

This covert purpose has many similarities to ideas of 'mental rehearsal', which are now widely used in the field of sports psychology. The act of imagining the whole cycle of a project, anticipating what can be expected and what might be unexpected, helps to iron out problems before they occur in the way that a pilot may learn to deal with many different situations in a flight simulator.

Together, the overt and covert purposes of scoping help the organization to identify its own appetite for the project as well as its capability and capacity to deliver it. Gathering contributions from different stakeholders and collectively anticipating problems is the crucial element in building a team of people committed to the project. A further positive function is to enable the project leader and the project team to gain sufficient understanding of the complexities involved in the project to increase their chances of success. This depth of understanding of the project's implications is also an important prerequisite if a credible and persuasive bid for the funding and resources required is to be made.

Even at this very early stage, stakeholders' expectations fall across a continuum. They may be unclear about benefits for themselves or their teams or they may have extremely unrealistic (and sometimes quite fantastical) views on the benefits the project may bring to themselves or their teams. As project leader, your job is to engage in a dialogue with them to help them to think through their expectations, and to begin to point out where different expectations may conflict with each other. At this stage it is also important that you challenge one-track thinking about solutions. It is vital to explore alternatives if the real problem is to be solved.

At the same time, throughout the scoping process the project leader is trying to build people's confidence in him or her and his or her credibility to handle problems. At this early stage, key players are already making judgments about the project's chances of success and about you as a project leader. The scoping process also represents a quality gate where the idea can be agreed, killed or delayed for further investigation. The idea may be killed off at this stage because it doesn't fit with the strategic direction of the organization; perhaps it duplicates other organizational projects; perhaps it falls outside the risk profile of the organization or perhaps it is doubtful it will fulfill the success criteria required.

4.3   Five Critical Questions

Figure 4.2 provides a structured approach to the scoping process by posing five critical questions that need to be answered as you start to prepare the ground. Each question is expanded in Table 4.2.

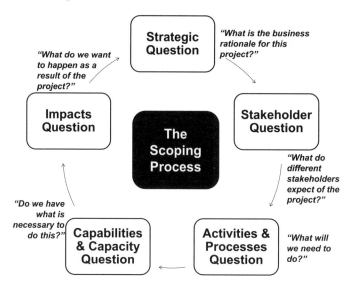

Figure 4.2   Five critical questions in scoping a project

Table 4.2   Five critical questions in scoping a project examined

Question	Discussion
Strategic question: What is the business rationale for the project?	Working with a wide range of organizations across industry sectors, we have found a major problem that lurks in those in-house projects which are the whim of some individual or department and which, on detailed examination, are not related to the strategy or Big Picture of the organization. The Major Projects Authority talks about the 'right projects, done right', so aligning projects with the strategic aims of the organization. Project leaders need to be positive but challenging in asking questions regarding relevance, rationale and value to the organization. On the positive side, we also find that increasingly organizations are expecting a project feasibility study or business case to be completed which documents the business rationale, identifies the range of anticipated benefits and spells out when these are expected to cut in.
	In developing the business case, organizations want to be able to determine whether the project merits investment. Since financial and other resources are finite, there is often a hurdle that projects need to cross before being deemed acceptable to the organization. This hurdle will typically be higher for riskier projects than for safer projects. The business case may also explain what type of financing is required for the project and how this will be achieved, how the client (whether internal or external) will be contracted with, what other resources will be required. Business cases won't just cover activities and budgets allocation for project delivery; they will also cover activities for the whole of the project lifecycle including handover into business-as-usual operations. Organizations often specify financial hurdle rates or internal rates of return for proposed projects, which include the whole life costs involved in products or services.
	Calculating the business value of a project is not an exact science. Assumptions are made and refined based on commercial perceptions at a single point in time by individuals who have particular agendas, bias or requirements on them by others. Flyvbjerg, Bruselius and Rothengatter (2003) asks the question, 'Is delusion necessary to get projects started?' in the context of multi-billion dollar mega-infrastructure projects and experience tells us that there are three factors which contribute to the expected business value from project investments not being achieved as shown in Figure 4.3 (p. 89).
Stakeholder question: What do different stakeholders expect of the project?	Even where the business rationale has been well established, there will still be many different views within the organization regarding what the project must deliver. An important element in the scoping process is to establish who the various stakeholders are and subsequently to understand their particular interests in and expectations of the project. Much of this work may have already been completed during the project shaping. As a first step, brainstorm with your sponsor and perhaps with one or two other interested parties to identify who the key and secondary stakeholders in the project might be. This 'stakeholder mapping' (see section 4.7) is one of the cornerstones of the project that will enable you to build relationships, influence and support. Not only can stakeholder mapping help you actively cultivate relationships with those people who can help you move the project forward, it can also help you to understand which individuals or groups you shouldn't upset or exclude.
	The project sponsor is one of the key stakeholders for the project. Where one is appointed, and not all organizations do this, do use your project sponsor to make introductions where necessary in order to meet and talk to other stakeholders using those interviewing and probing skills which will enable you to draw out of them their interests in the project and their expectations about what they, their team or department will gain from the project. This will also be the first step in defining success criteria for the project (see Chapter 10).

Table 4.2   Five critical questions in scoping a project examined (*concluded*)

Question	Discussion
Activities and processes question: What will we need to do?	Your sponsor and stakeholders will often be anxious about any new project at this early stage, particularly where it is a project characterized by uncertainty. What they are really looking for as a result of the scoping process is an informed idea of what kinds of activities might be necessary in order to successfully complete the project, and how they might need to support the project in terms of manpower, budget or knowledge. In short, they need to understand what the organization is letting itself in for. Whilst there is no way that you can produce detailed plans at this stage (you're simply not advanced enough in your thinking), what you *can* do is to begin to sketch out some of the broad activity areas in conjunction with other people who may have a contribution to the project, and identify areas where there may be overlap or hand-offs between functions, departments or teams. Some of these activities will emerge from your deliberations quite clearly. Other areas will be very vague: for example, where there is little previous experience within the organization. This question also helps different people to think widely about the implications of what is being proposed.
Capabilities and capacity question: Do we have what's necessary to do it?	Your initial consideration of stakeholder expectations and activity areas will help you begin to understand the kinds of resources and the volume of resources the project might require. By this we mean a range of resources from the obvious tangible resources of capital equipment or the use of a project management office (PMO) through to money, time and materials. We also mean those intangible resources of technical skills, risk management, quality management, performance monitoring and communications skills, and the vital intangible of commitment and support from particular people within the organization and outside it. What you are really doing is assessing where the organization may have capacity or capability gaps, and where the areas of difficulty in delivering aspects of the project may lie. There may be a requirement to subcontract specific operations and delivery due to particular skill or capacity restraints in-house.
Impacts question: What do we want to happen as a result of the project?	Traditional project management thinking focuses on inputs and outputs. Our own experience has shown us that this is too narrow a focus and that wider questions about deliverables and outcomes should be asked to provide a full view of all benefits. See Chapter 8 for further discussions on 'success'.

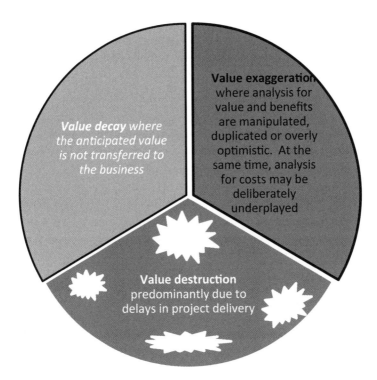

Figure 4.3   How value from projects is manipulated or lost

One project leader described to us an urban regeneration project he had been working on, explaining that the various benefits, including a better living environment, increased local employment and an enhanced local economy, would cut in over a 25-year period. Such a long timeline for benefit realization is not typical for commercial organizations, which prefer to see business benefits during a shorter timeframe. Companies sponsoring the London Olympics 2012 paid large sums of money to sponsor particular events, the Olympic Park and other features of the games each representing significant investment for the sponsoring organizations and necessitating the design and delivery of large projects. In some instances, sponsorship deals involved over £100 million. What benefits did these organizations hope to achieve as a result? In the main, the results were tracked as brand recognition, market share and revenue increase over the period of the games and over the following years. In May 2014 the British media reported that London Olympic 2012's economic legacy reached £13 billion, that expertise gained by British companies from the Olympic Games helped to secure further contracts at home and abroad, and that the Japanese prime minister signed a memorandum of cooperation paving the way for close collaboration between Japan and the UK for the planning of the 2020 Games in Toyo and the 2019 Rugby World Cup.

Part of the project leader's job then is to understand the business context of the project, to identify the sort of impact the deliverables of the project should have and to find answers to the question: 'How does this project contribute to customer service and our competitive position in the market?'

We know of a project set up to develop a training programme for project leaders. The project group set to with great enthusiasm, interviewing individual project managers about their needs, and then began to define deliverables such as training materials, reflective journals, coaching and training programmes in line with the responses.

Nobody thought to ask the questions: 'Why do we want to train these project managers?' 'What is the impact we want to have on the organization as a result of their training?' In reality, the desired impact was to change the organization's whole approach to managing multiple projects. Once this was realized it became clear that training was required not only for project managers but also for senior managers in their roles as project sponsors and as part of project governance groups. Further, the requirement for the development and implementation of new information systems to keep track of simultaneous projects was identified, as was the requirement for a PMO to support the control, monitoring and progress reporting of multiple projects. The result was a significant change project to develop and embed project management capability within the organization with all the associated communications and engagement exercises across the organization.

This consideration of impact, rather than simply tangible deliverables, helped the team to redefine the scope of their project substantially and to satisfy the multiple stakeholders considerably more. You should therefore *start* by considering your project's desired impact on the organization and then work backwards to consider what kinds of deliverables would achieve that. You can now see clearly that starting with the understanding of impact brings you back full circle to the strategic question of the business rationale for the project.

Regardless of whether the project is a sporting event, software development or major construction, a set of agreed and well-documented criteria of performance established up front defining what 'success' looks like will save a lot of time and negotiation later when the project is handing over to business-as-usual and requires a sign-off from the client.

4.4   Iterative Scoping

Particularly with open projects, you may find that you need to go round the cycle of the five questions a number of times. Each cycle will gradually refine and clarify everybody's concept of what the project will involve, until it is sufficiently defined that you can sensibly begin to make plans about how to implement it. This is 'iterative scoping' and it is a fundamental approach even for apparently clear, concrete projects. The reality is that even clear terms of reference are interpreted and manipulated differently by different stakeholders. For this reason, it is often useful to make explicit what will not be in scope, recording those ideas that have already been visited and rejected, as well as what is in scope.

Iterative scoping is the process that not only builds clarity and a common picture but, crucially, also builds the commitment of the key players to the success of the project. Although many will say it's taking too long, time taken at this stage will pay handsome dividends later in shortening the implementation process.

4.5   Making the Case

Once you have this overview of your project you are in a strong position to make the case for it to be properly resourced and supported.

4.5.1   MAKE A GOOD CASE

'If I understand their reasoning and have the impression that they have thought the issues through, then I am likely to believe their budgets' was the advice of one sponsor who had to decide how to allocate limited resources between several projects. There are two parts to making a good case:

- Show that the basis of the estimates is reasonable. This means that if you have used firm historical data you must say so, and illustrate the risks that you have experienced in the past due to arbitrary cuts. Alternatively, if your project is at the open end of the continuum, you must indicate that this is a best guess, which will be reviewed after certain events have clarified the resource demands. It helps to demonstrate that you have consulted others thought to be sound when you were putting your case together.
- Structure your information well for the sponsor to understand. Excessive detail is difficult to take in and if it looks unstructured it will not give the sponsor confidence that the project is in good hands. Instead, use simple visuals and graphical summaries where possible.

4.5.2   BE CREDIBLE TO THE STAKEHOLDERS

Knowing the Big Picture and being organizationally intelligent, that is familiar with the power bases and political network of the organization, will help you to present your case. Highlight aspects that you believe will be seen as important in the wider company context. You can afford to push hard on these, whilst soft-pedalling on demands likely to be perceived by others as less important.

Showing that you understand the trade-offs that have to be made between the range of projects will earn you respect in your sponsor's eyes.

4.5.3   KNOW WHEN TO BE FLEXIBLE

Even the most genial people can become obstinate and difficult when it comes to budgets. The adversarial approach rarely gains the best outcome, but that doesn't mean you have to fall over in the face of opposition. You must choose your battle. As a project leader objectivity is key, so if your project is threatened with resource reduction take a step back to understand not just what impact this will have on your project, but also why this is being contemplated by the organization at all. Show that you are aware of the commercial considerations which management will be taking into account. Then you are in a good position to consider what your next step will be.

4.5.4   INTANGIBLE RESOURCES

Other projects and departments will be fighting equally hard to obtain resources. To be sure of securing those you require, you therefore need to draw on your own intangible resources: the confidence, trust, ideas and active support of individuals outside your visible team, whether they are sponsors or invisible team members in other departments, such as finance, marketing or personnel. Your own network and credibility within it will help you to gain support when you most need it. You will have to be prepared to help others out in return, so understand the reciprocity involved. Intangible resources work on an informal basis of mutual give and take. Your own informal network of contacts will provide that mutuality and reciprocity to help you find different approaches to getting things done. Especially with open projects, intangible resources will be your main resource bank. Build and nurture them. They have a high yield.

4.6   Mistaken Beliefs about Scoping

Regardless of your type of project there are a number of mistakes that project leaders and their senior management sponsors often make at the early stages. This is true whether your project is concrete (where there is strong definition of output, considerable previous experience within the organization to draw from and there are clear systems and procedures) or open (where possible outputs are unclear, there is little previous experience and procedure in the organization to draw from). These mistakes typically stem from a number of erroneous beliefs:

- the belief that senior managers give a lot of thought to what they want from a project before they give it to the project leader;
- the belief that the senior manager's definition of the problem or solution should be accepted because he/she has thought about it or has more experience;
- the belief by senior managers that what is obvious to them must be obvious to the project leader or project team;
- the belief that clients commissioning the project ought to have a clear idea of what they want;
- the belief that if the terms of reference of the project are documented, they will be understood and accepted;
- the belief that the project must accommodate all the desires and ambitions of all the stakeholders.

Again, to have a good chance of success projects must be well shaped and scoped since it is difficult to recover from a project that has been poorly conceived. Poorly shaped or scoped projects often result in disappointed sponsors and clients, and in disillusionment among project leaders and teams. This in turn results in recriminations, witch hunts and extensive rework to recover the situation or the scrapping of the project altogether. They can also be career limiting.

In its review of the FiReControl project to replace the 46 Fire and Rescue Services' local control rooms across England with nine purpose-built regional control centres linked by a new IT system, The National Audit Office (2011) described it as ' … flawed from the outset because it did not have the support of those essential to its success – local Fire and Rescue Services … these local bodies prize their distinctiveness and the freedom they have to choose their own equipment'. In particular, the NAO noted that the rationale and benefits of a regional approach were unclear and badly communicated to locally accountable fire and rescue services. The Department rushed the start of the project, failing to follow proper procedures. Ineffective checks and balances during initiation and early stages meant the Department committed itself to the project on the basis of broad-brush and inaccurate estimates of costs and benefits and an unrealistic delivery timetable, and agreed an inadequate contract with its IT supplier.

Source: National Audit Office

4.7   Tools for Scoping

There is no standard methodology for scoping, but we present below two techniques and skills that can be useful, which we now describe briefly. These are:

- stakeholder mapping
- dialogue.

4.7.1   STAKEHOLDER MAPPING

Stakeholders are those individuals or groups who have an interest in, a role in or are impacted by what you are doing, or what you propose to do. All those who have a significant contribution to make to the success of the project must be seen by the project leader as part of the team, because they are the stakeholders on whom lasting success depends. You perhaps need to think of 'contribution' in a wider sense than usual. People contribute not only through their special skills and expertise, but also through being supportive and by expressing their expectations clearly. The project leader's task is to establish the different types of contribution needed and the impact of each one, and to devise ways of mobilizing all the contributions towards the same end.

It is helpful to have a simple map identifying and linking the stakeholders. Every such map will show a unique pattern, but some features have been found to appear frequently and Figure 4.4 illustrates a familiar sort of pattern.

Here, the three broad groups are:

1. *Internal stakeholders*
   These are typically:
   - The project leader – who wants the project to be successful, aims to be effective and competent, and will want to maintain a good reputation within the organization.
   - The core members – who are the regular contributors, who may be full or part time, each of whom has a particular skill. They are seen by themselves and others to be formally associated with the project. They are usually the visible team. They want sufficient scope and resources to do a good job and make the project a success, and thus gain personal satisfaction as well as enhanced reputation.

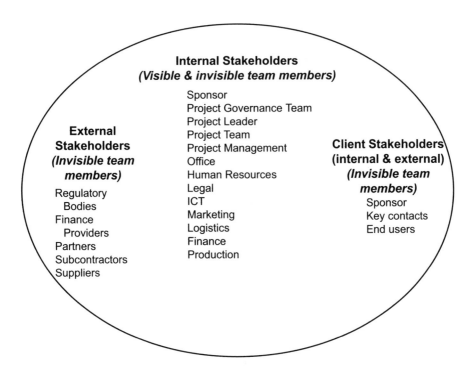

Figure 4.4   Internal, client and external stakeholders in a project

- The project sponsor – is the person who has the most to gain from the success of the project and is typically seen as the key link between the business and the project. In many cases, the sponsor is responsible for ensuring the business case and the ongoing business benefits, but is not directly involved in operational details. As project leader you have delegated responsibility for the success of the project, but ultimately the buck stops with the project sponsor. As such, they should also be appropriately positioned within the business to influence and open blockages at senior level, open up his/her network of top-level contacts, call in favours and use his/her extensive knowledge of the organization and industry sector to smooth the path of the project on behalf of the project leader and to actively promote the project. This is a key relationship for the project leader who should ensure there is strong agreement about respective roles, responsibilities, progress reporting and clear communication channels with the project sponsor. The sponsor is primarily concerned, if the project is an internal one, to maintain credibility and currency within the organization, but he or she may also have personal ideas or interests that need to be taken into account. If the project is for an external client, the sponsor has the organization's interests uppermost and is concerned with costs and reputation.

- The other members – who are typically described as the suppliers of services that are part of the project. They are frequently specialists who give functional advice or administrative support, usually in departments such as Finance, HR, Legal, ICT, Operations or Production, Marketing and Logistics. They won't be permanent or full-time members of the project team, but they will be brought into and exited from the project for specific reasons as required. However, they will want to know when and to what extent their services will be required, and will want to understand enough about the project to be able to deliver to the best of their abilities.

2. *Client stakeholders (external or internal)*

   Every project has an ultimate client or customer. The expectations of the client may be clear or confused, but it is the client who accepts or rejects the project team's output. Identifying and clarifying their ideas of 'success' for the project and the success or performance criteria for sign-off at this early phase of the project will help you when you come to handover the deliverables.

   Many projects are delivered for internal clients: for other departments or companies under the umbrella of the same organization. A common example is the ICT department, which develops bespoke software for the marketing, finance or distribution department of the same organization. Internal clients deserve the same care and attention as external clients. Assumptions based on historical prejudice are often made about other departments and these have to be challenged. End users will have different perspectives and interests that need to be understood and taken into account. It is easier to show this understanding if the client stakeholders are at the very least perceived as team members, and better still become actual members of the team helping to shape project design, delivery and testing.

3. *External stakeholders*

   There are many different kinds of external stakeholders. Some of the most common are suppliers of raw materials and products, specialist advisers or consultants, subcontractors and third parties who do part of the work, governmental bodies who execute statutory requirements as inspectors, interest groups including trade unions, lobbyists, voluntary group opinion leaders and the media.

There exists an 'adversarial' view in which all those inside an organization are seen to have common interests which are not shared by those outside it and are likely to be opposed by them. The idea of 'organizational networking' (Hastings, 1993) fundamentally challenges the adversarial view. It does not deny that there are conflicts of interest, but it approaches them as problems to be worked through, by building robust links with outsiders on the basis that there are benefits to be gained by all involved. Instances where suppliers or subcontractors have been brought in to work closely with the project team show that the speed and quality of communication, and therefore appropriate action, increases dramatically. The message is to bring in from the cold the main outside players, work continuously with them and not against them, and ensure that they work with you.

4.7.2   DIALOGUE

Dialogue covers a great many techniques from one-to-one interviewing, facilitating workshops and discussion forums, through to brainstorming and clustering to capture and consider the vision, success criteria, appropriate project phasing and activities with a variety of stakeholders. Additional techniques such as the Six Thinking Hats® (de Bono, 2000) help to focus discussion and to weed out inappropriate or irrelevant ideas to help develop a cohesive and coherent project scope. One of the particular and important things about dialogue is that it is a two-way interactive process, not just a broadcast of information.

Interviewing and questioning

Interviewing will take place across the project lifecycle for all kinds of reasons. It is a strong technique to tease out the business rationale in the early stages of a project when people themselves may not be very clear. How do you find out what stakeholders want from the project when they haven't had much time to give it thought? The answer lies in being very skilful when you approach them to talk through their thoughts. During this interviewing process, the first step is to know how to develop rapport with the people you are interviewing.

This will help them feel at ease. Be open and explain to them broadly what the interview is about and why you are doing it. The second step lies in the quality of the questions that you ask. At this early stage it is very important to ask open questions (those that elicit an elaborating response from your interviewee) rather than closed questions (those that just elicit a yes or no answer). You also need to become skilful at listening for small clues, sometimes disguised, which if probed and investigated further might lead to useful information. This has often been described as peeling off the layers of an onion: each question delivers a response which is then unpeeled to reveal more so gradually working your way through irrelevant information to get at that which is really important to the individual. This requires interviewing skills such as summarizing, paraphrasing, probing and asking for concrete examples as a way of helping people to articulate more clearly what they are after.

Brain storming and clustering

Group brain storming is a very good way of rapidly sketching out some of the central activities and processes that might need to be undertaken in the project. It also helps to start the conversations about risk, resourcing, communication and other aspects of the project. Keeping the group energized and enthusiastic helps provide momentum. Multicoloured sticky notes are a basic tool. Give the group a briefing of what you know about the project so far and any thoughts that you have on it. Ask them individually, as you talk, to write down on the sticky notes any actions, tasks, activities or processes that they believe might need to be carried out to realize the project. These can then be stuck up on a wall or flipchart for everybody to see. Quantity not quality of ideas is the most important consideration at this point. People should not feel they have to be 'sensible'.

You can then work with the group to cluster groups of notes into related activities and apply judgment to prioritize or schedule the phasing of these activities. This quite rapidly gives you both a high-level plan and some elements of lower-level plans that are good enough at this stage, and which can be carried forward to further detailed planning.

4.8   Capability Audits

Having seen some of the suggested activities, you are then in a better position to begin to estimate what kinds of capabilities you might require to complete the project. You can do this by yourself, but again, using a group of people makes the process more efficient and more complete, particularly if you can pull together people who have either some interest in or contribution to the project. This can be done quite rapidly.

A key question is 'What will we need to be good at in order to achieve this project successfully?' You can use a number of triggers for your thinking. Obviously, the outline activity plan drawn up from the brainstorm is one. Another might be to ask yourself what skills and resources you will require, under the following headings:

- technical skills;
- commercial skills;
- political skills;
- financial skills;
- communication skills;
- marketing skills;
- managerial skills;
- gaining commitment;
- planning skills;
- monitoring and reporting skills;
- developing contacts and networks;
- securing resources.

Such an audit would rapidly enable you to see which capabilities lie within the organization, together with their likely availability, and which capabilities you will either have to develop internally or buy-in from elsewhere. A good example of this might be a project management office (PMO) function. These are your capability gaps, and filling them is frequently a time-consuming business much underestimated in planning by project managers. This is a common source of delay and slippage.

4.9 Dealing with Uncertainty and Change

The process of scoping helps provide transparency about the project, its outcomes and deliverables. At this stage, ideas are already being formulated about how the project can be chunked down into smaller work packages to help with the subsequent detailed planning process; looking at particular resources for skills and availability during the project lifecycle; considering benefits realization and success criteria for handover.

It is also not unusual for the scope to vary and change through iterative scoping to a lesser or greater degree. One project leader described the process for her as being particularly painful as each of the stakeholders tried to insist on benefits from the project quite unrelated to the drafted scope; another described trying to align the various stakeholder requirements as 'nailing jelly to the wall'.

Once the scope and terms of reference are agreed and the project starts, do ensure that a change control process is put in place for capturing and assessing potential changes to scope. Managing change to scope is an inevitable part of every project. Understanding the impact of these changes on the scope, budget and resources is imperative and often leads to regular review and re-estimating. It is usual to regularly review progress in order to reassess, especially for open projects, which by their nature are uncertain and ambiguous in their outcomes and path.

Further, ensure that the project team understands the importance of capturing and assessing each of these no matter how seemingly insignificant, no matter how they are described and regardless of whether they are a result of chance meetings, conversations over coffee or a friendly email. Trying to downplay the significance and impact of a change by describing it as an 'issue-ette', 'de minimus' or 'something that was mistakenly left off the original specification, but which *obviously* has to happen' by the client or a stakeholder is not uncommon.

Often these 'minor' project changes can cause significant friction later on between client and contractor if not properly dealt with. We've known instances where the situation has accelerated rapidly into contractual and financial arguments because changes have been pushed through or accepted 'under the radar'. A lesson well learnt is that requested changes must be captured through a robust change control process, then assessed and, if accepted, reflected in the project plan which is in turn made transparent in the project schedule, budget, resource plan and risk register as appropriate.

4.10   Understanding Project Risk and Appetite

At the same time we also need to recognize the degree of uncertainty about the scope of the project and its outcomes at this early stage, especially for those occasional and open projects. As a result, the concept of risk is often also introduced at this early stage to help understand the organization's appetite for risk, and to make plans and forecasts about risk as robust as possible. Each of the key stakeholders should be considering this, as should the organization. Often the questions are around risk capacity, risk appetite and risk tolerance. Pullan and Murray-Webster (2011) define risk as 'uncertainty that matters' and look at three groups of influences on the perception of risk as shown in Figure 4.5.

Figure 4.5   Three groups of influences on the perception of risk
Source: Pullan and Murray-Webster (2011)

One way which is often used to help start the conversations around risk even before the project has started is to establish a meeting bringing together those key players (stakeholders and project team members) who are likely to have significant involvement or interest in the project, along with members of previous project teams and stakeholders who have knowledge and experience of these areas to share. These forums are also known as 'Peer Assists'. Here, the new project team lays out its draft plans, concerns, ideas and any specific questions for the visiting project team who shares what insights it can bring to the new project team. The new project team then uses these insights to revise its plans and also as input for the risk analysis of the new project.

As a result of these discussions, create and start to populate a risk register. Typically this will detail identified risks, their possible impact and probability, and mitigating actions. This is not a one-off exercise; as part of the normal governance process, risk identification and mitigation actions, review and reporting will need to be revised and updated as the project progresses. Some organizations have a preference for a RAID register which identifies and tracks Risks, Assumptions, Issues and Dependencies. Figure 4.6 illustrates a typical risk management process.

Figure 4.6   A typical risk management process

4.11   Quality

In the past, quality management was viewed as relevant only for manufacturing processes relying on consistent standard of production. It was later taken mainstream into other industry sectors and used as a competitive advantage. Led by the work of Deming, Juran, Feigenbaum, Taguchi and others, the attitude to quality has changed and it has become a 'hygiene' factor. In other words, organizations need to pay attention to quality in all aspects of their operations as an integral part of what they do. This holds just as true for projects as for any other operation, and it must be planned and managed and be part of the way the project leader chooses to run the project.

Harrison and Lock (2004) write that, 'Every project has an anticipated level of quality for the project deliverables. Project quality management is the process to ensure that the project fulfills its obligations to satisfy the project needs.' It is now commonly understood that in practice this is not just about ensuring project deliverables are tested and signed off as being acceptable to the client; this is also about the way in which the project will be run and delivered. So as one of many project documents the Project Quality Plan outlines how the project will be governed, led and managed during its lifecycle, how risk and change will be assessed and responded to, any quality gates involved, which project methodology or approach will be taken, how outcomes will be performance tested, how periodic reviews will be undertaken and the knowledge gained fed back into the project and organization. The BSI Group (www.bsigroup.co.uk) and ISO (www.iso.org) both provide principles and guidelines for the management of projects. They aim to help individuals and organizations deliver projects efficiently and effectively, as well as to contribute to the learning within projects and so continually improve their organization's project management capability. The principles provided are as relevant to small organizations and for small projects as they are to major organizations with multimillion pound projects spanning several years.

4.12   Visibility

By the end of scoping, you should have a good understanding of the visibility of the project. High-visibility projects are usually expected to make a more important strategic contribution. The dimension of visibility influences the number and scale of project risks. The amount of political attention tends to be greatest for high-visibility projects. The risks and political activity mean that the project leader will have to put effort into managing the stakeholders and the organizational dynamics. Figure 4.7 illustrates this idea.

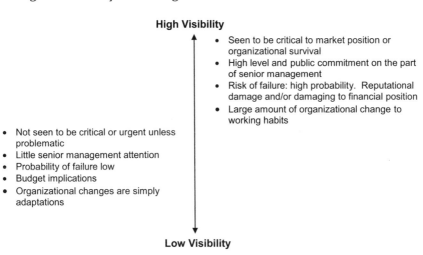

Figure 4.7   Spectrum of project visibility

Conclusion

Projects are shaped and scoped within the context of an organization and should contribute to its strategic purpose. These early stage activities help the organization reflect on its risk appetite, and on its capacity and capability to undertake the project. Scoping has both overt and covert purposes and the scoping process should be both highly supportive and highly challenging; it is the basis for a project's success and at the same time represents the source of many project problems if undertaken poorly. Supporting the organization to respond to the five critical questions will help ensure there is alignment with the organizational strategy, as well as understanding the value of the project to the organization and the resources that will be necessary to make it a success.

Stakeholder mapping and effective dialogue help to support project scoping, and to begin the process of understanding and developing success criteria for the project: those critical indices against which the project and project team's success will be judged. Initial conversations around project risk and organizational tolerance around risk will later help detailed risk assessment, plans and forecasts. Finally, recognizing the organizational culture within which the project is to be delivered helps us to appreciate the possible dynamics between the project leader and the organization.

Key Questions

Shaping and scoping

- How do projects get shaped in your organization? How can you get access to these discussions and to the decision makers in order to contribute at this early stage?
- Are you under early pressure to 'just get on with the project' without due consideration to shaping and scoping the project first? This should alert you to possible scoping problems.
- Can you answer the five critical questions for the project you are involved in? If not, why not?
- How effectively are you able to make the case for your project to be properly resourced and supported? Can the visibility of the project help you in this?
- Which tools and techniques do you typically use for scoping the project? Can you use any others to greater benefit?

- How do you and your stakeholders view uncertainty and change?
- How would you describe your organization's appetite for risk:
  - Generally?
  - Specifically for your project?
- How do you weave quality throughout the lifecycle of your projects?

References

BSI Group (www.bsigroup.co.uk).

Covey, S.R. (1989) *The Seven Habits of Highly Effective People* Simon & Schuster Ltd, London.

De Bono, E. (2000) *Six Thinking Hats* Penguin, London.

Flyvbjerg, B., Bruselius, N. and Rothengatter, W. (2003) *Megaprojects and Risk* Cambridge University Press, Cambridge, UK.

Harrison, F. and Lock, D. (2004) *Advanced Project Management: A Structured Approach (4th edition)* Gower Publishing Ltd, Aldershot, UK.

Hastings, C. (1993) *The New Organization: Growing the Culture of Organizational Networking* The IBM McGraw-Hill Series, New York.

International Organization for Standardization (ISO) (www.iso.org).

National Audit Office (2011) 'The Failure of the FiReControl Project'. Report by the Comptroller and Auditor General. HC 1272 Session 2010–2012, 1 July 2011.

Pullan, P. and Murray-Webster, R. *A Short Guide to Facilitating Risk Management* Gower Publishing Ltd, Farnham, UK.

Smith, C. and Winter, M. (2009) 'The craft of project shaping', *International Journal of Managing Projects in Business* 3 (1), 46–60.

CHAPTER 5
Phase B – Start-up

Planning is an unnatural process; it is much more fun to do something. The nicest thing about not planning is that failure comes as a complete surprise, rather than being preceded by a period of worry and depression.

Sir John Harvey Jones

Introduction

You've completed the shaping and scoping process and provided clarity about what you are trying to achieve and the organizational commitment to it. Now you move into the start-up phase, another of the early phases. By 'start-up' we mean assembling the project team, defining the way you and the project team will work and together develop the project plans. Here we are not discussing the mechanics or technicalities of start-up; instead, the emphasis is on the project leadership aspect of this phase, and what the project leader needs to be doing. So during the start-up phase, the focus for the project leader is on three aspects in particular:

- formulating the approach to the project;
- gathering the team together, getting it working effectively and doing this fast;
- detailed planning.

Taking time for reflection at the start of a project is not easy. As project personnel we typically like to get into the 'doing' and are very task-oriented. Time is money so clients and our organization like to see things happening and the project up and running as soon as possible. Thinking and reflecting does not give the impression of urgency or of getting on with the project. Again and again, in training simulations, in work-based projects which form part of a development activity and in real-life projects, we discover the tendency to plunge into the project or task without taking adequate time to clarify:

- *Why* are we doing this project?
- *What* are our assumptions and expectations about the project and about our roles, responsibilities and accountability?
- *What* is our approach to this project?
- *How* are we going to operate as a team?
- *What* plans do we need to put in place for the project?
- *Who* do we need to get involved to help make this a success?

So, let us begin to look in more detail at what the important issues are in this phase.

5.1   The 'Who': The Project Team

The project team are certainly among the key players and stakeholders for the project. The success of the project is their success; equally the failure of the project also reflects on them. Below we look at how the team is brought together as a functioning whole. Team start-up is one of the most critical parts of the project; this is more than just assigning roles, responsibilities and accountability. Certainly, all projects suffer if teams cannot be assembled quickly enough. However, the project leader is also responsible for ensuring that this diverse set of individuals come together quickly and effectively, and for developing them into a high-performing team.

5.1.1   ASSEMBLING THE TEAM

We all want a 'Dream Team' for our projects. We want our projects to succeed and we want the recognition that goes with this success. Throughout our careers, we've worked with multidisciplinary teams, with virtual teams, with multicultural and multi-located teams. From this, we are able to say that we want to work with particular individuals because we understand their strengths, their commitment and what they can bring to the project. But we can't always get these people. We don't always have the luxury of being able to pick and choose our own team. Sometimes it is simply about who is available at the time or who is deliberately assigned to the project.

5.1.2   FITTING THE TEAM TO THE PROJECT

There are two theories about the relationship between task, people and roles. The 'classical' theory starts with analysing the task and activities to be undertaken, and from that defines the roles that are needed. You then look for people who can best fit those roles.

The alternative theory starts with the task but focuses on success criteria. It then looks for the people who would be committed and able to contribute towards fulfilling those criteria. Their roles are then evolved in line with what they can contribute. This latter approach is more flexible and suits the needs of more open projects since temporary and open project teams are often unclear about the roles and structures they will need. Forcing them into a traditional structure restricts individual contributions.

5.1.3   THE POLITICS OF TEAM SELECTION

Many large organizations work with the notion of a 'bench' where project personnel who are not currently involved with any project are allocated. Individuals with particular experience and/or expertise are then allocated from the bench to projects as and when they are required. In smaller organizations, individuals with special talents or with the eagerness to be involved are usually in greater demand, so they go to the highest bidder. Other organizations allocate individuals to project teams who happen to be available at the time, or who require such an experience as part of their Personal Development Plan, or who simply have to manage their work with the project alongside their usual workload.

A different view of team selection revolves around how visible the project is within the organization, to the client and to the wider community. The project leader is more able to negotiate for experts and the best available with a high-visibility project. Most difficulties are encountered with projects that are more open and have low visibility; here, the most relevant negotiating tactic is to appeal to and foster an individual's personal interest.

In short, in some circumstances the project leader is able to influence the selection process. In others, instead of being able to fit the team to the project, the project leader may be given a set of individuals for the project and have to work within these parameters. These individuals will differ not only in their skill sets and levels of experience, but also in their attitudes and their motivations. They may not have the appropriate levels of authority or delegated responsibility. Yet other organizations leave project leaders to identify, persuade and cajole appropriate in-house personnel or even select and recruit external personnel to work on their project. Particularly where you are leading a multi-located team and/or multicultural team, you may be depending on the in-country management to provide you the best fit possible.

Figure 5.1 illustrates the relationship between the capability of the team and the project leader's ability to influence project team membership.

High	**Thankful!** • A good place to be for the project leader; the focus is on successful delivery without the need or ability to change the team • If changes to team membership are allowed they must be well considered as few will be possible	**I want this all the time** • An ideal place for the project leader • Project leader aims to identify only selective key interventions as the team is capable, wants to progress the project without hindrance and will not readily welcome team membership change • Focus is on performance improvement rather than on the day to day challenges of delivery • Project leader needs to understand the dynamics and impact of any team membership changes and sell robustly as many would ask 'Why?'
Capability of the project team	**Not where I want to be** • A most difficult and potentialy high risk situation requiring the project leader to exhibit all their leadership skills • Team will require extensive guidance and support (Part 4 provides some ideas as to what these interventions could be) • Robust and pragmatic planning is required to identify and mitigate the implications of the lack of capability • Project leader should campaign for the resources to improve the capability, basing the case on the implications of no or ineffective action	**Could be worse** • Project leader will rarely be able to replace all areas where they believe there are capability issues because of contractual, political or social factors • Project leader must balance the benefits (from the improved capability) and the "costs" of any change • Changes should be made purposefully with appropriate communication focused on the benefits to the project and customer
Low		
	Low Project leader influence on team structure **High**	

Figure 5.1   The relationship between the capability of the team and the project leader's ability to influence team membership

5.1.4   ENSURING THE RIGHT MIX

Whatever the realities of the organizational politics, the project leader will want to ensure that, no matter why they were selected, team members have the time and ability to contribute to the project. Where a degree of choice is possible, project leaders should consider the following criteria for selecting team members. Where no choice is possible, they can be used to assess the skills mix:

- Who is interested in this project?
- Who is keen to contribute and believes the project is important and desirable?
- Who has specific technical skills/expertise/experience that is needed?
- Who can represent important interest groups (clients, end users, other key stakeholders)?
- Who will 'fit' with the way we want to work?
- Who has organizational clout/credibility/connections to help the project?
- Who represents/understands opposition or reticence to the project?
- Who would benefit through self-development or corporate exposure from being associated with this project?
- Who has external networks that might be useful to the project?
- Who has special non-technical skills (for example, communication skills, good networking skills, political access and so on)?

5.2   Accelerating Team Development and Cohesion

However the project team is assembled, it is the responsibility of the project leader to take this disparate set of individuals and turn them into a high-performing team. How do good project leaders work with such a situation?

We know of project teams that launch their projects by gathering the visible and invisible teams together to outline the Vision of the project and how it fits with the Big Picture, that is, the organizational strategy. Perhaps more important is the opportunity for members of the team to put names to faces and to start building the identity of the team. One large contractor working in the Far East found that a banquet, which should have been held to celebrate completion of the work, had been organized to take place before the job had started. The mistake turned out to be the single most useful event in the early stage of the project. Communicating with people in the team was much easier after the banquet. Organize something together, preferably informal and not too project-orientated, so that people can get to know each other in a relaxed way.

5.2.1   THE RATIONALE

Getting together is a good start but it won't be enough by itself because high-quality teamwork does not come naturally. Individuals coming together need to understand in more detail what impact they should be making. They come with their own agendas, pressures and limitations. Becoming a 'team' is not an instant process: it takes time and needs skill to facilitate. The team has to go through shared experiences: dreaming, exploring, creating, stepping on each others' toes, stepping over potential offences, victories and setbacks.

Few members of the team will understand the skills a high-performing team needs; individuals will bring elements, but not the whole. And even skilled teamworkers, when they come together, have to go through the normal team development stages of 'forming', 'storming' and 'norming' before they can really start 'performing' (Tuckman, 1965). Your job is to accelerate their progress through these stages, to do this by finding out the most appropriate ways to work together using the full resources that the team members bring and to make this happen rapidly. And this, paradoxically, takes time but it is an investment that will repay you handsomely in terms of much-reduced wasted time, effort and slippage at later stages. And because it takes time, it does need to be planned for.

5.2.2   WHOM DO I INVOLVE?

Obviously, your core team members will be the main project drivers and are the ones who need to be involved in project start-up activities, workshops or conferences. There is no simple rule. Just ask yourself: 'Who will benefit by being involved?' We have run start-up workshops for project teams involving between six and 60 people! The team may not only be people within their own organization, but also within partners', contractors' and other groups' organizations. This provides a rich diversity of skills and experience, which prove useful for identifying and analysing risk, planning, problem solving and decision taking. Rarely do project leaders have such a full understanding of their project that they know exactly what needs to be done when (although work breakdowns and scheduling do like to give us that illusion!), the challenges that will be encountered during delivery or the many relationship issues that will inevitably arise.

The invisible team link

Like temporary or open project team members, all invisible team members have other demands on their time. The task of the project leader and core team members is to make it as easy as possible for invisible team members to come into the team at the appropriate time and contribute of their best. Negotiate the nature and extent of the contribution each invisible team member is to make so that your expectations of them and they of you are compatible.

Near the time of their actual involvement, invite them to meetings and brief them extensively on the Vision of the project and how it fits into the Big Picture, how the team works and its operating ground rules. It is just as important as for visible team members that they understand how their role fits with everyone else's and that they see some of the benefits for themselves. Give them as much notice as possible so that they can plan their commitment to the project team around their other responsibilities.

It is common to devise a 'buddy system' where every invisible team member has a contact person in the visible team to whom they can relate and who is responsible for keeping them in touch with everything that is happening. We have seen this system used to great effect in a complex shipbuilding project involving very many different contractors. The strategy here is one of involvement, not exclusion. The high-performing project team works hard to break down any barriers between themselves and external stakeholders. This is the essence of collaborative working.

You can extend this to bringing members of your client's organization into your project team. We know of several project teams working on large projects where the client has representatives sitting in the same offices as the project team members. In one oil exploration project, the contractors have moved most of their people into the client's offices. In this way, the team and its relationships are dramatically redefined.

5.2.3   A TEAM DEVELOPMENT AGENDA

In the early stages of start-up, you should set yourself seven objectives:

- To get to know each of your team members not just to know their names but also their history, skills and interests and to use this insight to quickly build a relationship with them.
- To create some sense of team identity.

- To begin to discuss and share perceptions of the overall team purpose and success criteria.
- To begin to answer for each team member the question 'What's in it for me?'
- To draw out the underlying concerns that individuals have about the project or the team or any other issues that might make them hold back their commitment.
- To help each team member understand their own role, responsibilities and accountability along with those of the other team members. This will help to understand how the team members complement each others' roles and identify any gaps.
- To help the team identify how they want to work together. This is especially important for cross-functional and/or multi-located and/ or multicultural teams. It also provides them with the mandate to challenge each other over inappropriate behaviour where necessary.

We've provided below some specific ideas and tools for achieving these objectives. Involving the core team members in the planning process is not only a recipe for more effective and realistic planning, it is also the major mechanism that you have at your disposal for welding the team together rapidly into an effective unit.

Just as we suggested some psychometric profiling tools in Chapter 2 to enable the project leader to understand more about their personal style, project team members can also benefit from these. Especially in relation to team roles, these tools can help team members understand the type of role each member is likely to take in the team and their impact on other team members, how other members of the team work and so what the relationship dynamics are likely to be.

5.2.4   THE TEAM MANAGING UPWARDS

Just as you, the project leader, will be managing upwards to the project sponsor and to the project governance body (in whatever form that might take), the project team members will also be managing upwards to you. They need to understand how they can be good team members and followers, just as you need to understand how you can be a good leader.

How will you describe your own leadership style to them, how you work best and how you would like to be managed up to? How will you explain your own role, responsibilities and accountability? How will you help them to understand what you want from them, when and how? How do you like to be kept informed? You've had those discussions in order to contract with your own sponsor, and you will need to do the same with your team members. One project leader told us, 'I had just negotiated my way through a particularly difficult decision for the project and felt rather pleased with myself. Then I received a note from my number two, who I rate very highly. His message was short and to the point: "Good call, but you forgot to take your project team with you." It was my wake-up call and I appreciated that he felt he was able to tell me.'

5.3   Virtual, Multi-located and Multicultural Teams

Projects are increasingly being run with cross-functional, multicultural and multi-located virtual teams in the client–contractor relationship or even in-house. Additionally, almost all (94 per cent) UK organizations now offer their personnel some form of flexible working and flexible working is now standard practice in half (50 per cent) of the companies surveyed by the Institute of Leadership & Management (2013). It is well recognized that technology has been a key driver in changing where we work, who we work with and the way we work. Managing these different dimensions can lead you as the project leader to question your own innate assumptions and working preferences.

5.3.1   VIRTUALLY WORKING OR WORKING VIRTUALLY?

Virtual working, whether from home or from another remote location, whether on-site in client offices or at a contractor site, is becoming the norm for a growing number of personnel. In the past few years several technological trends have emerged that significantly reduce our dependence on physical offices. Research (Hertel, Kondradt and Voss, 2006; Lin, Standing and Lui, 2008) into successful virtual teams have identified:

- strongly clarified, focused and communicated objectives;
- the use of appropriate technology to facilitate two-way communication;
- a joint responsibility for outcomes and deliverables.

Whether you are working with virtual or multi-located teams at a number of different sites, keeping engaged with project team members helps to ensure that things are happening as they should and to strengthen working relationships. In other words, the key to being a 'remote' project leader is in not being remote. When the danger is that the only communication you will have with the more remote members of your team is electronic, formal and written, how can you ensure you remain connected to your team whether they reside over the other side of the city or of the world?

Projects are about creating value together. We are a very social species. Interaction with others is important to us, especially where we rely on others to play their part. Certainly from a technical point of view, we have the tools we need to do our jobs most anywhere we choose and the tools to share information across continents. Cloud computing has made information sharing and remote access easy. Mobile phones, tablets and laptops have better functionality and are more robust than ever. Organizations are increasingly adopting information-sharing tools as well as social-collaboration tools as enablers for remote working. These have significantly changed the way we interact with each other while working so that we can communicate rapidly and feel that sense of team, whether we sit in the same building or on opposite sides of the globe. And the technology is not just helping us to share information. It is also helping us to get face-to-face time using tools such as video conferencing and Skype. Being able to see someone's body language in communication is just as important as hearing or reading the words.

> One project leader led a collaboration between a UK and a US business which were working together to develop a particular software product to bring to market. The same language but different nuances; a similar approach to the project but different time zones; the understanding and support for team building but different continents. The project leader understood the success of the project depended on collaboration and the freedom of sharing know-how, and managed to negotiate additional budget from the partnership to allow the UK team to travel to the US, and for the US team to travel to the UK at different points during the project. In the interim, discussions and progress reviews were done via conference calls and video conferencing.

Don't just visit the remote sites when there is a problem. Watch out for the little things that can leave people feeling isolated. Too often those team members who are out of sight at other locations can too easily be out of mind as well. This has the effect of marginalizing team members, which doesn't support collaborative teamworking and can often build resentment. The initial start-up meeting as a face-to-face meeting helps to build relationships, networking and collaboration within the team even if this means digging deep for the budget to allow this to happen. Periodic face-to-face meetings help to solidify and continue relationships, networking and collaboration.

5.3.2   WORKING CROSS-CULTURALLY

Cross-cultural project teamworking has accelerated rapidly over the years with the rise of organizations expanding their global reach, outsourcing and ease of access to foreign suppliers and markets. Increasingly, we find project working between teams that seldom, if ever, actually meet face to face. Even within a single multinational organization there can be a diversity of cultural 'norms'. In Sweden, for example, it is quite usual to question your boss, whereas in Japan it demonstrates a lack of respect. In working with different cultures you don't need to ignore or negate your own core beliefs, but you do need to be flexible to practices different from your own. These might be around ways of looking at the world as well as the more usual working hours and working days of the week, national and religious holidays, and time zones. Establishing open lines of communication from the outset and speaking openly with your team helps everyone understand different behaviours and values.

We all recognize the danger of making sweeping statements about a particular culture, race or gender. We all recognize that everyone is individual; however, there is such a thing as a cultural norm so that 'the inhabitants of any country possess certain core beliefs and assumptions of reality that will manifest themselves in their behaviour' (Lewis, 2006). Although we have both worked extensively with multinationals in the UK and abroad during our careers, we recognize that we are writing *Project Leadership, Third Edition* from a predominantly Western (more specifically British) viewpoint. From our own experiences and those of project leaders we have talked to, understanding and respect goes a long way to help build these multicultural teams and relationships. Cultural competence or intelligence is about being understanding of and sensitive to cultural norms. Understanding the way other cultures work and think will help you as a project leader frame information and effective communication; it will also help you in decision making, dealing with conflict and gaining approvals at senior levels for the project, quite apart from adding to your own experiences.

One project leader worked on the new Hong Kong air cargo terminal on Chek Lap Kok which opened in 2013. He explained his approach to helping his largely Chinese team to succeed. He recognized it was important to treat local people with genuine respect and to listen well. This is important, not only because of the different intonation and pronunciation in spoken English, but also because of making a genuine effort to understand the sentiment being expressed beyond the words: in general, 'Westerners' are more explicit and outspoken in saying what they think (which can in itself cause problems) than local people, who understate their strength of feeling and may not say what is the issue or point of view explicitly, apparently agreeing in order to save the face of the Westerner. He found that because of the complex and many influences on Hong Kong culture, with its origins in China, influence from British rule and later American culture, as well as Confucian and Taoist values and beliefs, more reverence was paid to hierarchy and age with particular importance given to avoiding 'loss of face'. This can make it difficult for managers to admit what they don't know or that tasks are behind target. In solving complex problems or addressing slippage, this presents some difficult challenges to maintaining respectful relations but still keeping the work on track. To overcome this potential obstacle, he found that issues needed to be discussed one to one, in private and behind closed doors, so that in group meetings the focus was on what needed to be done for the future and not on what should have been done in the past. This project leader also noted that some Westerners did find it difficult working with the local Hong Kong people; some tried too hard to fit in and others found it too difficult and became impatient or withdrawn rather than trying to engage.

Another British project leader worked for a private telecoms network in Oman with a multicultural team comprised of nationalities from 11 countries including Omanis, Indians, Chinese, English, Australians and Phillipinos. He described his biggest lesson as humility, understanding that the diversity of experience and viewpoint in his team was one of their greatest strengths.

Most project leaders we talk with agree it is important to present a sincere and professional face without pretence, which of course, will undermine credibility. You must feel respectful and genuinely curious to understand other people without pre-conceptions about the superiority of whichever culture you come from. This is much harder than it sounds and trying to understand different beliefs is only possible with a genuinely open mind. In authentic leadership, however, it is essential.

5.4   The 'What': Planning

When we talk about 'planning' we typically mean planning the 'What'. When we are faced with large, complex problems we chunk them down until we find them manageable. This is about breaking down the project to define the more tangible activities and tasks, to develop the work breakdown structure, content and timing, resourcing and budgeting, milestones and contingencies, interfaces and dependencies, to understand risk, to identify when benefits are expected and the critical path through the project. Planning ahead helps prevent identified problems from happening, and identifies the contingency needed for dealing with them when they do occur. This is a team sport and is best done together. It is based on the original high-level scoping output from previous discussions and conversations during the early activities of shaping and scoping. That way you can ensure all aspects of the project plan are covered and integrated end to end, and that it reflects what has been agreed and contracted for.

> The project leader working for a private telecoms network in Oman described how he was required to develop a project to replace most of the network with new technology. The breadth of the scope was enormous covering a country-wide network of 40 microwave stations, three main camps in the Omani Desert, and numerous drilling camps and exploration sites with mobile/portable voice and data communications. A significant result of a series of brainstorming meetings focusing on how to go about this massive challenge was the realization that it did not have to be one big bang implementation. Instead, they could renew equipment as and when it aged. In this way, the job could be broken down into a number of smaller projects whose technical risks could be easily managed. This amounted to a programme of 20 separate projects implemented over six years, and the approach cost little more than the cost of maintaining the system over that six-year period, significantly reducing the original cost estimates. He was present for the start of the programme and then had to leave for another posting, so led the work on detailed plans to ensure things would progress properly. He was fortunate enough to go back to Oman seven years later and had a meeting with the telecoms manager who told him that they were just completing the final project, still using the original plan. The final project was only six months overdue on the predictions seven years earlier. He felt a very proud man.

5.4.1 SUCCESS CRITERIA

We talked in Chapter 4 about success criteria for the project, those critical indices against which the team's success will be judged. The team will need to understand both the stated purpose of the project as seen by key stakeholders (for example the sponsor, client, yourself as project leader), and also the unstated purpose. Purposes may be unstated because they are politically unacceptable, because they are not really thought through, or because they are not readily quantifiable. Success criteria are used as the basis for metrics for monitoring performance and for handover to the client.

5.4.2   WHO DOES WHAT, WHEN?

The high-level plans prepared during the scoping phase are a good place to start. The next step is to get more detail and agreement. This is best done in facilitated workshops with team members together using flipcharts, coloured pens and sticky notes. Use the brainstorming and clustering techniques described in Chapter 4 to develop plans in preparation for the next phase of delivery. These plans should detail all aspects from delivery, testing, organizational readiness, implementation, handover and closure to progress and risk reviews and communication.

   Prior to this team development event ask each of your core team members to work up draft plans, at an agreed level of detail. These can then be presented to the whole group. Subgroups can then split out to look for possible clashes, confirm dependencies and handovers between parts of the project team, possible interface problems and ways of cutting out wasted time, and also suggesting intermediate milestones: those highly visible points at which progress and achievement can be marked out along the way. In this way, many good ideas come up and the team as a whole comes to feel that it owns and understands the plan, and how it all fits together. Through this collaborative planning process they all have the necessary overview and commitment to be able to act more responsibly as the plan unfolds. Ignorance, on the other hand, breeds indifference.

5.4.3   SELECTING THE RIGHT PLANNING TOOLS

Project management has grown up over the last decades around the development of sophisticated computer-based estimating and planning tools. These have been invaluable in large-scale projects, but can be too complex and specialist for many organizational projects.

   Given our strong belief that planning should involve all core team members, what simple tools and techniques seem to work?

- **Plan backwards not forwards.** This may sound perverse but it produces good results. Get the team to focus on the *end results* that you are trying to achieve. This should be clear if you have done your scoping well. Then get the team to work backwards, thinking of everything that has to be done in order to achieve that goal.

- **Brainstorming.** In trying to imagine all the possible tasks and activities you will need to carry out, start off with no particular structure, inviting members to shout out their ideas. These should be recorded either on flipcharts, or even better on large Post-it notes, which can then easily be categorized and sorted into an outline schedule.

- **Work breakdown structure.** You can also sort the Post-it notes into different levels of detail. High-level activities or clusters (for example, 'internal communications') can be broken down into lower-level categories (such as 'workshops', 'newsletter', 'informal briefings') and so on into further detail.

- **Bar charts.** Sometimes known as Gantt Charts these are a very simple way of showing the essential high-level activities in a project visually, so that the whole team can quickly understand how the different parts are related. In a more complex project, you can send a subsection of your team away to work up more detailed plans on one of the 'bars' (as in our example above about 'internal communications'). They can then come back and summarize their work with another (lower-level) bar chart.

- **Dependencies.** Many tasks can be undertaken in parallel, and you should strive for this for speed's sake where possible. But some tasks cannot start until others have been completed. You and team members should be very clear about these linkages and the necessary handovers between parts of the project team. Failure to spot them will cause you many problems later.

5.4.4   ENSURING PLANS ARE REALISTIC

Whichever tools you use, it is your job as project leader to take steps to ensure that the plans that emerge are realistic. One of the major sources of slippage in projects is that the initial plans were based on poor analysis of what needed to be done and/or naive estimates of how long different activities would take. Many project-based companies working in software development find it difficult to estimate the time it will take to develop and test a defined piece of software. They underestimate. So they need to build up data about how long a project actually takes, using that as a standard for estimating and identifying where the blockages or deviations occur. As the experience of projects builds up, guesses and hypotheses are turned into reliable data.

Project leaders also frequently feel under pressure to deliver. In the worst cases their sponsors or clients have already committed themselves to completion dates without consultation. It takes a tough project leader to challenge this *fait accompli*. It is often tempting to go along with it and just pray that it works out! But where the stakes are high, no self-respecting project leader should allow themselves to be set up for failure in this way. Good scoping should have already confronted this issue. But equally, good-quality, credible plans and estimates are powerful data with which to argue for more realistic timescales or more resources, or for a compromise in the scope or success criteria.

So what can you do to check that your plans are realistic?

- Ensure that the people who will actually carry out the work draw up the estimates. You need to have discussed the ground rules for estimating beforehand so that team members don't play games with overestimating to give themselves contingency time, which can result in repeated overestimating and substantial project delays.
- Consult others with previous experience in some aspects of your project. For example, we discussed the use of Peer Assists in Chapter 4. Some organizations also create their own catalogue of activity estimates, especially where particular activities are commonplace, refining these as further information is available.
- Ensure that team members build up their time estimates from the detailed list of tasks in the work breakdown structure that the team has developed. This makes the estimating process more structured and precise. Do not accept the back-of-envelope or finger-in-the-air approach from your team members.
- Be aware of the types of tasks that are somehow never considered in the planning process, and are simply left out. Some of these are vital tasks which are time-consuming but intangible, many of them to do with managing the 'How' (see below) of the project rather than the 'What'.

The most common invisible time-stealers and activities that are frequently ignored in plans are:

- **Communication processes.** The process of informing people, helping them to understand, updating them and getting feedback, and reviewing.

- **Key decision milestones outside your control**. For example, gaining approval for a primary project element at a Board meeting or a particular committee. If you miss a specific meeting, there is often not another one for months, and you may have to devote a great deal of time to seeking approval individually from committee members.
- **Building a high-performing team.** Individuals do not come together, instantly gel and become high performing. This takes time and needs to be planned.
- **Team members representing other functions or external agencies**. Unless they have delegated authority, they may have to constantly refer back for decisions.
- **Organizing meetings.** The difficulty of coordinating diaries for meetings which need to involve several busy people.
- **Warming up end users.** The need for end users to be brought up to date, test the outputs and be trained ready for implementation and handover.
- **Selling ideas.** Warming up key decision makers in advance requires meetings and conversations so that they have all the information necessary to understand what you are asking of them.
- **Commissioning services from external providers**. Often there are particular organizational commissioning and procurement processes to be adhered to, so any lead time here will need to be taken into account. For significant work, this may take a formal route over several months. Even seemingly insignificant details like installing a special telephone or a PC for a new team member can have overly long delays.

Traditional project plans, particularly those developed by less-experienced project leaders, simply fail to reflect the time and resources required to resolve some of these issues. Allocating contingency is simply no substitute for being realistic about some of these less visible activities that lie behind the success of a project. They need to be made visible and estimated realistically, and creative ways need to be found to eliminate problems at source.

Finally, when the plan is almost finalized, bring the core team together for a session where you encourage everyone to think of ways in which you could do things more efficiently. Is there duplication, for instance? Could particular activities be done earlier or in parallel to save time? Are there short cuts that could be taken that would not compromise quality? These types of questions should not only be asked now, but continuously throughout the project and especially at review points.

5.4.5   PLANNING SOFTWARE

When project-planning software originally came to market, project leaders would have seen the use of sophisticated software as the prerequisite for success in implementing a project. Today, however, there is a plethora of project-planning software available. Many of the software systems available have functionality for timesheets, resource and budget control to help monitor and report on usage, as well as being able to integrate into other software systems. Even the most basic of these packages help to illustrate not just phases, activities and tasks but resource requirements and dependencies. A word of warning though: there are a number of caveats to its purchase and use. The project drives the software, not the other way around. Such systems:

- must *not* be seen to *control* the project, but to *provide information* to *enable* the project team to manage the project effectively;
- must be *simple* to operate and understand, and must *not* be an end in themselves;
- must be used with the *full support* of the project team, who must have confidence in the validity of the information being generated and in the way particular targets are set and monitored; they must *not* feel threatened by the system.

The mantra of many project leaders is to keep everything as simple as possible. The simplest of monitoring and planning techniques is the Gantt Chart which is also flexible and visual. There is a time and place for sophisticated software on complex, concrete projects with many tasks. There is also a time and place for using the software as a disciplined aid to thinking through how the different tasks and activities are related to each other, and to model different scenarios for the project. One particular advantage of project planning software is that it can provide many views of the project very easily, from resource usage to critical paths. It can also summarize the whole project on a single sheet of paper, which we've found to be so vital when explaining project progress it to sponsors, stakeholders, team members and others who just aren't interested in the detail.

5.4.6   ANTICIPATING CHANGE

Change happens. Change in project scope, market context, project success criteria and team personnel. In this section, we will address changes to the project team. Personnel come into the project and exit the project during the lifecycle simply because their particular skill set is needed at a particular point. You, as the project leader, may be one of a small core set of personnel who represents continuity across the whole of the project lifecycle.

How do you welcome personnel into the project part way through and get them up to speed? How do you let them depart once their role is completed and their skills are no longer needed? We tend to think of project teams dismantling or adjourning at the end of a project. In reality, team members come and go as needed. Helping to articulate the story so far and providing a buddy system with another longer-serving project team member are ways to induct new team members into an already high-performing team, get them rapidly up to speed and get them to gel with the team. In reality, you may not need to do all this depending on the time they will spend on the project, how integral their role is to the project and where they are physically located. Equally, as project team members leave the project when their role is completed, it will be necessary to make sure that they have completed their role as required, that a structured handover to the project team or to a new team member is completed and that any particular thoughts and ideas they have on the project are followed through.

Another form of change to the project is change to scope and requirements. This is about the client or stakeholders raising formal, or more likely informal, requests for change. It is important to be able to capture and analyse these, simply because they can impact the project in relation to time, budget, scope and outcomes. Chapter 6 discusses in more detail how to manage this type of change in the project.

5.5   The 'How': Planning

Planning the 'How' is about developing and agreeing the ground rules and processes that describe the functioning of the team and how the project is going to be run. It is about how the project will be run in terms of quality and health and safety, and how interfaces work with the project governance team, the client, partners and contractors. It is also about developing the project culture for the project team to understand 'how things are done around here' (variously attributed).

5.5.1   CREATING THE PROJECT CULTURE

Creating the project culture is about defining and creating the environment that will deliver the project sucessfully and in which your team can thrive by defining how you will work together. By 'environment' we mean the physical (for example, office space, access to pcs and hardware, and so on) and the psychological (for example, clarity over the performance expected from individuals, the support to achieve this, understanding level of delegated authority, receiving communication and the ability to feedback, and so on). This is typically the point at which values are defined with the project team. This:

- articulates how the project team works best together and with stakeholders;
- encourages team member empowerment;
- allows challenge to inappropriate behaviours and working practices.

Your objective under this heading is to begin to discuss 'the way we will behave and do the project' in order to be successful. You'll be starting discussion about the norms and ground rules, as well as the quality management processes that are vital. Discussions of these 'soft' issues are not always easy and do not come naturally, especially to technical specialists. But we know that the 'How' factor is *the* difference between failure and success. Planning the 'What' is more comfortable; it is necessary but, unfortunately, not sufficient in itself. So you have to be patient and allow your team members to learn this new language slowly and focus their attention.

The project leaders we talk to understand that by creating the project culture it allows them to create the environment and set the tone for the project; further, that they have considerable influence over the culture within the project they lead and that they are responsible for exemplifying the behaviour they expect from their team. They tend to establish a project culture that prizes behaviours that emphasize trust, personal responsibility and doing the right thing so setting the team up for success. They also recognize this has to be a conscious decision, else the culture may develop outside their control. Those project leaders who have the responsibility of leading multicultural and multi-located teams tell us the concepts and values within the project culture are easily transferable across these teams; that in some instances there was a 'central' project culture with local variations to accommodate local sensibilities. One example was where the UK branch of a multinational led a particular project and promoted the use of first names across team members; however, the Middle Eastern branch of the same multinational was particularly uncomfortable with this.

Questions for the dialogue around creating the project culture should include:

- **How will we manage the outside?** How will we position and market the project in our organization? Who actively supports us, is neutral, or might block or act against us? What help and resources do we need from outside the team? What help and resources do we need that we don't have in the core team?
- **How will we manage our external relationships?** How will we build relationships and interface with subcontractors, our client, the media? What information can we/should we share? Is there a single point of contact through whom any information should go externally?
- **Leadership and followership.** What do we expect of the project leader: for example, providing the Big Picture, keeping the team on track, marketing the project, being positive and driving confidence? What do we expect of team members: for example, taking responsibility, being accountable, fulfilling commitments, keeping others informed? Who will provide drive and energy? Who will be keeping us on track? Does the project leader have to provide all the leadership? What are the different ways team members can contribute to the leadership role? Are we aware of all our collective skills and experience? Which are delegated responsibilities and which ones should be shared collectively?
- **The team apart.** How will we stay in touch between meetings? How will we deal with competing priorities: the project and our other commitments? Do we follow through and do what we say we will between meetings? How will we keep information flowing? What systems and technologies can help?
- **The team together.** As a diverse group how will we manage our meetings productively, and ensure they re-energize us, not drain us? What style and format will suit our personal preferences and the project needs? How can we use these most productively to generate and test ideas? Do we have the luxury of a 'war room' where we can meet, where project documentation is physically stored and where charts hang on the walls? How often will we meet? How will we manage conflicting views/priorities/style?

- **How will we manage conflict?** How will we manage and resolve conflict whether in views, priorities or ways of working within the team? Pinto (1996) categorizes possible conflict resolution methods into three fundamental philosophies: avoidance, defusion and confrontation. Each has its own benefits and drawbacks, and each can be an appropriate response under certain circumstances.

5.5.2   INHERITING A PROJECT CULTURE

What happens when a project leader is placed to lead an existing team who have been working together for a while? In this instance, the team members have already worked with each other in other projects, understanding differences and complementary skills, and working their way through the phases of forming, storming, norming and performing. In this scenario it is the project leader who is new and unknown, and who will walk into the project where team dynamics have already been set and a culture has already been established. Figure 5.2 illustrates the relationship between the established team and how familiar the project leader is with the team.

5.6   Assessing Project Risks

At what point do you properly understand the risks in your project? Can you confidently identify these during the shaping process, by the completion of scoping, perhaps during start-up? What would you have done differently if you had spotted some of the surprises that crept up on you during the project? Assessing project risks is perhaps the most crucial step in preparing the ground because if you know the sort of project you are leading then you, your sponsor and core team members can identify at least 80 per cent of the anticipated risks, and plan contingency actions.

Thinking the project through in the early phase has a number of benefits:

- You and your sponsor gain a better understanding of what the project involves, so you start your relationship on a sound footing.
- If you think the project is not viable, you can make a decision regarding the conditions you need to have in place in order to continue, or withdraw from the project, making your reasons clear.

	Short ← Team history → Long
New (Project Leader familiarity)	**Unknown quantity** • Project leader has no history with the team who are also new to each other: start of a process of discovery • Team dynamics will not be immediately clear • Project leader needs to allow a period of investigation and planning before finalising structures and approach; accepts this may be uncomfortable for some • Progress may have to be made in the short term so the project leader may wish to have a temporary structure while developing plans for the long term	**New kid on the block** • Potentially the most challenging position for the project leader. They may be replacing a previous project leader who will have had their own way of working or an existing team has been re-tasked on a new project • Project leader has a very short period of time to understand the project and culture including where the power lies, how decisions are made, etc and then to make any necessary modifications • Novelty can be helpful as it allows norms to be challenged and a fresh approach introduced if appropriate; however, don't change things just because you can!
Existing (Project Leader familiarity)	**All in the same place** • Some project leaders would say this is the ideal position to be in as they can shape the project and team from the start • The team will look to the project leader to provide clear direction. Typically the project leader has only a few months to build the trust of the team by demonstrating they know where they are going and how the team will get there • Project leadership style will likely be directive in the early stages • Relationship building is critical even although planning will be important; aim to do both by involving the team in the process and demonstrating their importance	**One of us** • The team is familiar to the project leader • Relationships will have been formed previously but these may not always be positive or supportive • Project leadership style is less directive as the team understand how they function together and how to get things done so only the direction needs to be set

Figure 5.2   The relationship between the established team and how familiar the project leader is with the team

• You can put into place an appropriate planning and decision-making infrastructure that will help to deal with issues as they arise. For example, you might walkthrough the project in a Peer Review with personnel who have knowledge and experience of similar types of projects, to help educate

yourself and the team. You might plan a series of workshops with users to define needs and build prototypes with more stakeholder involvement.
- You can assess the overall probability of the project failing as a result of traditional risks, such as new technology, natural disasters, the financial instability of a partner, legislative changes or the loss of vital experts.

Where there are high risks, you can start to minimize them at an early stage and devise alternative plans of action, highlighting critical points during the project's life where you might start to see problems occurring. This proactive risk management should run throughout the project lifecycle.

5.6.1   MAPPING PROJECT RISKS

At an early meeting during project start-up, the project leader, sponsor and some key clients, contributors or suppliers need to map the risks by going through a structured process. This might include:

- brainstorming possible risks;
- considering what has gone wrong in similar projects previously;
- clustering into related topics;
- weighting risks for impact and probability;
- focusing on the very serious and highly probable;
- defining the project type, and reviewing typical risks;
- planning how to run the project with the risks in mind;
- highlighting where in the project the risks will be most critical;
- deciding how to reduce the risks so that the chances and consequences of failure are minimized.

5.6.2   CHECKLIST OF POTENTIAL PROJECT RISKS

You will need to develop your own checklist for projects in your organization, focusing particularly on the areas where projects typically go wrong in your environment. The checklist in Table 5.1 is a starting point rather than a definitive list, but it will help you think of some areas you might otherwise overlook. High-visibility projects, particularly open ones, benefit from this mapping exercise. Project leaders need to understand what they have really taken on at an early stage where they can do something before the focus on the consequences of failure makes it very hard to discuss the options.

Table 5.1   Checklist of project risks

Business impact and benefits	Strategic impact? Widely supported? Quantum leap or incremental step? Confidence level? Expected return on investment? Success criteria, deliverables, outcomes and so on defined?
Organizational impact	Who is affected and how? Level of cultural change? Legacy of change? Resistance levels? Who will be 'winners' and 'losers'? Business readiness? Communication and feedback plans? Reputation risk?
Project	Budget? Timescales and resources allocated? Geographic location(s)? Level of experience of team members? Success criteria, deliverables, outcomes and so on defined? Scoped and defined? Project sponsor assigned? Decision-making process defined? Project governance process and structure defined? Appropriate process and methods for defining deliverables? Organizational success criteria, client success criteria, project success criteria? Stakeholder mapping and engagement? Planning, tracking and performance monitoring? Communication and feedback plans?
Technical risks and complexity	Level of experience with technology? Suitability for purpose, reliability, performance standards? Knock-on effects? Reliability of suppliers: technical, commercial, and so on? Nature of relationships with key/secondary internal/external stakeholders? Interdependencies: volume of, criticality, impact?

5.7   Project Launch

The formal launch of the project can happen at a number of points during the early phases of the lifecycle: at completion of scoping, once the project has been ratified and signed off, at project start-up or just before project delivery commences. It may also depend on the project management methodology you have adopted, which can be quite definite about when the project launch must take place. There can also be a 'soft' launch (where the project is given the go-ahead by the business to commence planning work or even delivery) and a 'hard' launch (where any necessary contracts have been signed or the business is sufficiently confident that they will be and so is happy to make a formal announcement to the market). At whatever point you choose to launch, make sure the project has a definite start, just as you will ensure it has a definite end.

The project launch is not just a formality. It signifies the beginning of something new and ambitious for the organization. It helps to:

- build enthusiasm for the project among the project team who will be doing the work and the project stakeholders who will be participating in many ways in the project;
- communicate information about your carefully developed plan;
- identify the major deliverables and outcomes of the project and how these benefit the organization;
- signify the end of the early stages of the project (shaping, scoping and planning) and the beginning of project executing and monitoring;
- ensure that the team members understand how the activities and tasks they will work on fit into the project.

Conclusion

The start-up phase is one of the most intense. It focuses on getting the right mix of skill sets and volume of personnel to fit the project type and objectives, on facilitating the rapid development and cohesion into a high-performing team, on ensuring the team understands what it is trying to achieve and how it will need to operate regardless of where team members are located. Teamworking is also a development experience. The team that you start with is not the one you finish with (even if it comprises the same members!) and typically team members will move in and out of the project team as required during the project lifecycle.

It also focuses on detailed planning of the 'What' and the 'How'. Both are team sports and best done with team members and, if possible, with other personnel who have had experience of a similar type of project, to help educate yourself and the team. Planning ahead helps to ensure all activities are covered and integrated, to prevent identified problems from happening, and to identify any contingency needed for dealing with them when they do occur. Planning is also about developing and agreeing the ground rules and processes that describe the internal functioning of the team and how they will interface with outside stakeholders such as subcontractors. It also allows the project leader to consider and create an appropriate project culture to support how the project will be run.

Those initial conversations around project risk and organizational tolerance around risk are developed and detailed further during the start-up phase, so continuing to inform project planning and delivery. Finally the start-up phase is typically when the project is formally launched, signifying the beginning of something of significance for the organization.

Key Questions

- What is your preferred way of assembling your project team and developing these individuals into a high-performing team? How else might you do this for greater benefit?
- What specific actions have you taken to influence how effectively your team members work together, or have you just hoped for the right chemistry?
- How clear are all your team members about why the organization wants your project and precisely what impact it is designed to achieve for both the organization and the client?
- If you are working with a multi-located team how will you reduce the impact of being a 'remote' project leader?
- If you are working with a multicultural team how will you work effectively with different cultures and ensure project team members work together effectively across these cultures?
- How does your project view and work with risk?
- How do you typically mark the project launch? How else could you do this to better effect?
- Do you use project management software? If so, how does your project team view this, and what are the advantages and disadvantages of your particular software for your project?

References and Supporting References

Hertel, G., Kondradt, U. and Voss, K. (2006) 'Competencies for virtual teamwork: Development and validation of a web-based selection tool for members of distributed teams', *European Journal of Work and Organizational Psychology*, 15 (4), 477.

Institute of Leadership & Management (2013) 'Flexible working: Goodbye nine to five'. March 2013 https://www.i-l-m.com/~/media/ILM%20Website/Downloads/Insight/Reports_from_ILM_website/Research_flexibleworking_march2013%20pdf.ashx, accessed 20 September 2014.

Lewis, R. (2006) *When Cultures Collide: Leading Successfully across Cultures (3rd edition)*. Nicholas Brearly Publishing, Boston, MA.

Lin, C., Standing, C. and Lui, Y. (2008) 'A model to develop effective virtual teams', *Decision Support Systems*, 45 (1), 1031.

Pinto, J.K. (1996) *Power & Politics in Project Management* Project Management Institute, Upper Darby, PA.

Tuckman, B.W. (1965) 'Developmental sequence in small groups', *Psychological Bulletin*, 63, 384–399.

CHAPTER 6
Phase C – Delivery

I have always found that plans are useless, but planning is indispensible.

Dwight D. Eisenhower

Introduction

You've prepared the plan and defined the activities and dependencies, your team is up and running, and you've ensured that all your stakeholders are being kept in the picture. You've started 'doing' and are now in the thick of the delivery phase of your project. This isn't about leaving the team to get on with it, now that the plans have been developed and are being executed. As all experienced project leaders know, it doesn't work quite like that. This phase involves keeping your finger on the pulse of the project and reviewing, checking and anticipating.

In practice, of course, we all know that delivery has its own difficulties, and there is a danger that the project leader's role becomes one of firefighting. Whilst the track may be fairly clear for concrete projects it is often indistinct for open ones, but all types of projects need to be kept moving. If your organization has adopted a particular project management methodology, this may proscribe the governance, planning, control and monitoring processes. Regardless, some basic principles can be applied and there are common and straightforward ways of ensuring your project is moving forward and on track.

You need to ensure that you:

- and your team are acutely aware of insidious and unanticipated ways in which slippage can occur;
- use appropriate monitoring tools and processes to provide rapid feedback on progress for the project team, the sponsor and other key stakeholders;
- provide regular opportunities for the team not only to review progress, but even more important, to anticipate problems.

6.1   Keeping on Track

Once your project moves from scoping and planning into delivery, you will probably encounter things you didn't cover off in the planning or risk identification meetings. However, it is your responsibility to understand what is actually happening as opposed to believing what you are told is happening. That way there are no surprises for you, your sponsor, your governance team or your client. So what can happen to mess up your day?

Alarm bells ring in project leaders' heads at the very mention of the word 'slippage' which tends to be defined as an activity taking longer than was estimated. However, research we have carried out into sources of poor project performance in companies highlights that there are a number of other sources of slippage which do not occur directly as a result of overruns against estimates in the project plan. So how does slippage occur and what lessons can we draw?

6.1.1   DUMPING

Project leaders, especially those who also have a 'day job' or who are running multiple projects, complain that their managers and other instigators allocated projects to them but took no account of their existing project and line management workload. This is particularly acute where organizations have de-layered and made redundancies. Effectively, these project leaders felt they were being dumped on.

Few project leaders feel that they can say that they are overworked or can question the validity of the project, for fear that their careers and employment prospects might suffer. One way they handle this issue is simply to make their own decisions about the range of projects they are running, sometimes in ignorance of many wider business or strategic considerations. They might decide to put some projects on the back burner, compromise on quality by taking short cuts or simply let projects quietly die and sink into oblivion.

6.1.2   ORGANIZATIONAL NAIVETY

Functional specialists or young and inexperienced executives placed into project leader roles may have very little idea of how the rest of the organization works, of how and where important decisions are made, and of where power and influence resides. This naivety about some of the realities of organizational life can result in them overlooking some simple organizational considerations in their estimates and plans. For example:

- Underestimating the time it would take to assemble a team of people to carry out their project. In one case, a project leader told us that she had assumed she would be given a group of people and that she would have the team up and running within a week. However, she discovered she had to go out and find, persuade and generally cajole people to come to work on her project. It actually took her three months to call the first meeting.
- No allowance made for what might be involved in obtaining decisions from various departments, divisions or from the Board itself. Don't underestimate the amount of lobbying, information-giving, influencing and general preparing of the ground that will be needed to bring other people to the point of making decisions. Crucial decisions are often made at particular points in the calendar, such as regular monthly Departmental or Board meetings, and papers and other information for these meetings need to be circulated well in advance. Additionally, most important decisions are made in the lead-up to the meetings that ratify them. Many of us assume that a decision is made at the meeting, but organizational reality is different. The project leader who waits to argue his or her case at the meeting itself will typically loose out to the project leader who has been informally conversing with the decision makers, building support and commitment in the lead up to the meeting.
- Taking account of people's diaries and competing priorities. It can take a while to get space in particular people's diaries, especially when their time is in demand. Do you have the ability to reconfigure activities to help decrease the impact?
- Lack of available meeting rooms. Simply delaying meetings until a room is available will cause slippage, so look for alternatives.
- Even having named individuals in the project team won't guarantee a smooth ride. In some cases, these individuals may be reluctant to commit themselves to decisions without referring back to their departments. As the project leader you may need to negotiate team members' authority levels and delegated responsibilities with their respective line managers, as well as negotiating their availability for the project.

Most of the answers to these issues lie in anticipating where the next problem will be and looking several steps ahead. Finding the gatekeeper in these circumstances, whether it is a personal assistant to the chair or the administrative assistant who runs the meeting room bookings, is imperative. Make use of your sponsor and networks to understand how the organization works, how decisions are made and where they are made, how to influence and persuade effectively, and at what point you need to rely on someone more in tune with the organizational politics to work on your behalf.

One of the causes of delay and disruption to projects is the client themselves. This can be due to clients not turning around documentation or decisions within agreed timescales, but expecting the overrun to be absorbed into the plans so that the project still hits its key milestones. In other instances, the client might be trying to micro-manage the project, causing confusion in the project team and so delay. Again, getting buy-in to the plans, agreeing ground rules with the client, especially around roles, responsibilities and accountability, will help to reduce the impact of these challenges.

6.2   Keeping Score

Projects are dynamic and so we need to ensure we are able to control, monitor and report on progress. What works for one type of project may not be suitable for another. For example, a well-defined project with clear, hard success criteria and a highly visible full-time team mean that you are able to use far more clear-cut systems and procedures than will be appropriate to a more open project with only part-time team members.

We need to keep track of events and costs for two main reasons:

- so that we can make modifications and adjustments as the project progresses;
- so that we can identify points of particular progress and completion and can understand the value and benefits derived from the project at that point:
  - as part of contractual payments from clients or to subcontractors;
  - to bring in or release resources as necessary.

Benefit realization, value management and earned value management are specific areas of project management which aim to state the expected value of a project during the early stages, and monitor and measure the value during delivery and beyond. We're going to avoid being purist here since our focus is on project leadership; instead, for ease of discussion, we will deliberately use the generic term 'benefit' to cover the range of benefit, success criteria, value, outputs, outcomes, results, deliverables and so on of a project.

The function of project control systems is to provide the project team with reliable tracking information, as well as guidance on which to base decisions. Every project leader needs to decide which areas or activities are critical and need to be monitored closely if the project is to succeed, and which are not. For example, in a project to develop a new drug it is essential to set and monitor stringent quality control standards. You cannot disregard test results in order to achieve your budget. On the other hand, if you are responsible for an office move it is unlikely that you will ever get everyone to agree on the colour of the tiles in the toilets; you have to take a decision based on a reasonable degree of consultation, and then press ahead.

With an open project, where the objective is less clear, and where strict control of resources is perhaps inappropriate, it is nevertheless important to set some overall targets. For example, if a group of people are meeting informally to see how they might be able to improve customer care in a certain area, it is important to set some specific intermediate goals in order to maintain momentum otherwise commitment levels will gradually fall away.

One drawback of the term 'project control system' is that it implies inflexibility. It creates the idea that, having made a plan, all you have to do is to control the project in accordance with it, and success will be inevitable. Of course, this is not so. A changing market or economic context can mean that the client or the organization varies the project specification in accordance with these changes; moreover, the more high-performing a team is, the more it wishes to deviate from the original plan and improve the specification as it goes along. Under these circumstances a good project team and an effective leader check the changes with the necessary stakeholders, identify any problems, re-plan where necessary, and renegotiate resources and support if required. These activities can only be carried out if you are aware of the project's progress. This means that projects need something more than planning control systems; they need planning review systems to enable the project to move forward. Our 'plan–do–review–check' system is based on Deming's Plan, Do, Check, Act (PDCA) cycle. This cycle, or similar, is often used in professional services firms to ensure the quality of output in legal cases, audits and so on. At its simplest it provides a lifecycle for the work that they do which project leaders would class as projects although they may call them matters, cases or assignments. The underlying premise is about learning and ongoing improvement: learning what works and what does not in a systematic way (see Figure 6.1) and making any necessary adjustments in the light of this.

Figure 6.1   The 'plan–do–review–check' cycle

These review cycles are extremely important in maintaining the commitment of stakeholders and the interest of the team. Being in control of the process in a way that enables the project's performance specification to be improved will provide encouragement. In effect, the implementation phase is a series of continuous plan–do–review–check cycles, with the centre of gravity gradually moving forward with time and effort, as shown in Figure 6.2.

As each activity is tested and receives the support of the sponsor and the other stakeholders, the team develops cohesion in the way it works and becomes more confident in pressing forward with the project. As the project leader you can encourage everyone to think of ways in which things could be done more efficiently. Is there duplication, for instance? Could more be done earlier, or in parallel, to save time? Are there short cuts that could be taken that would not compromise quality or requirements? Are there new ways of doing things and innovations you can adopt? This all helps the team to face the uncertainties that arise in any project with a much greater degree of purpose.

Whilst the concept of continuous plan–do–review–check cycles provides a useful framework within which to work, you need to identify the points in the project which delineate each cycle. These are typically particular milestones reached after a sequence of activities. Not every element of a project is equally crucial to its success, and you need to identify at the outset which ones are. It is particularly important to identify those tasks that must be completed before

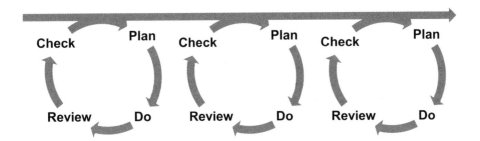

Figure 6.2   Series of continuous plan–do–review–check cycles

another can begin. Once this has been done, you can set up the appropriate monitoring processes. We discuss below four categories that affect success and need to be monitored:

6.2.1   CRITICAL EVENT-TIMES OR BOTTLENECKS

Critical event-times and bottlenecks occur in all aspects of the project. Some will be within your own direct control or be capable of being directly monitored by you. Others will occur in the work of subcontractors, or outside your direct knowledge. Different systems and procedures will be needed for different situations.

For example, the successful execution of a building project depends on component parts being ordered at the right time. A temporary project, such as the development of a strategic plan, may require you to meet the timetable of a series of meetings, each of which may deal with elements of strategy if you are to arrive at the boardroom with a comprehensive plan.

6.2.2   COSTS INCURRED AND RESOURCES USED

Costs and resources are elements that also need to be monitored continually. Normally, these are identified in the project plan. Sometimes cost limits are very clearly set out and relatively easy to monitor. On other occasions cost limits are not well specified, and extra costs may be permissible if certain results are achieved. This can all be spelt out in a project cost plan agreed at the outset. Projects at the open end of the continuum generally have very loose cost estimates and these are often capped, requiring the project leader to go back for additional funding where needed.

Direct costs are fairly easy to identify and monitor, usually using a monetary measure. Other types of resources are not so easy to identify and track. Take specialist skills or materials needed at certain points in the project: have these been identified at the outset? Have you decided how to check on their availability and their usage? Appropriate monitoring procedures need to be established for any items of this nature, and to understand earned value in the project so far.

6.2.3   QUALITY ASSURANCE OR PERFORMANCE SPECIFICATION

Concrete projects have quality assurance and performance specifications set in the original project definition. The success of open projects often depends as much on *how* you do things as on *what* you do.

It is important to be very clear as to who is the most important party to satisfy on a particular quality target or performance specification. Who has set the standard to be achieved: is it the client or the end user, or even a third party such as a regulatory body? Alternatively, you and the project team may have set your own performance specifications. This will determine how you monitor a particular quality target and the degree to which you could vary the specification if necessary. For example, there may be hard specifications set down by a regulatory body from which you cannot deviate, while end users may be flexible in some aspects of their final requirements.

6.2.4   EXPECTATIONS OF STAKEHOLDERS

Individual stakeholders establish their own success criteria, which are well-defined in some types of project, less so in others. For example, the development of a corporate strategy plan is a very ill-defined project, with the individuals concerned possibly having differing personal objectives. You will know these from scoping, and they will help you identify the particular elements that need to be monitored in addition to the fundamental time, cost and resource usage elements.

6.3   The Project Management Office

How do you monitor the progress and performance of the project? Using project management software is one way, but during delivery the project management office (PMO) function comes into its own. Organizations typically have a PMO for any or all of the following reasons:

- to make more efficient use of project resources by using a 'shared service' across projects to monitor performance and provide progress reporting;
- to make more effective use of scarce skills and resources across projects;
- to develop and disseminate good practice, standards and education to the project management community within the organization;

thereby increasing the success of projects in delivering the business value expected.

Some project leaders have described their relationship with their PMO to us as 'crucial', so as a project leader what support can you expect from your PMO? This certainly depends on the type of PMO within the organization. Different organizations use different PMO configurations so in Figure 6.3 we illustrate a spectrum of these configurations in use:

Centre of Excellence which supports and develops the capability of the organization by implementing good practices and standards across the project management community

Enterprise-Wide PMO which provides processes and routines for the control, monitoring and reporting of projects

Individual PMO which provides a range of project support services as a temporary entity established to support a specific project

Ad-hoc provision of monitoring processes (for example, spreadsheets).

Figure 6.3   Spectrum of project management office (PMO) configurations within organizations

Typical services provided by the PMO include supporting data management, coordination of governance and reporting, and administrative activities to support the project team. Well-established and experienced PMOs can take a lot of the routine control, monitoring and reporting burden off the project leader's shoulders. The requirement for, availability and use of, a PMO or equivalent should be agreed during scoping.

6.4   Reviews

Reviews provide health and sanity checks for the project. They are opportunities for the project as a whole to reflect on its impact and effectiveness. Typically they are held at key points during the project in order to identify lessons learnt and knowledge gained so that these can be disseminated into the project management community and be integrated into the project for future and continuous improvement, but can in fact be done at any time. Project management methodologies build in what are typically known as gate, after action, quality or end-stage reviews. These are ways for everyone in the project team to learn quickly from their experiences to date. The project team has an opportunity to talk about what happened so that critical lessons and knowledge are explored and transferred immediately to get the most benefit. They are also ways to identify underperformance and provide the opportunity to address the situation in a timely manner.

It is typical to hold periodic reviews throughout the project lifecycle as well as at the end of the project as part of handover and closure. This might be after each phase of the project, stage gate or key milestone has been reached. These are natural points through the project lifecycle that can be used to:

- look backwards to understand what went well and why;
- look forwards to anticipate what needs to happen next and adjust plans to maximize progress;
- recognize how working processes may have evolved;
- capture lessons learnt to date to help inform how the project might proceed;
- celebrate the successes along the way to generate and sustain morale;
- reassess and update the risks, assumptions, issues and dependencies;
- review the relative importance of stakeholders to the project, and the way you engage and interface with them;
- reassess and update project communications and marketing.

These intermediate reviews are variously named depending on the project management methodology adopted, but for ease of use we're going to use the term 'After Action Reviews'. First introduced by the military and subsequently adopted by other sectors, the intent is to capture and review lessons learned after any significant event, so that any corrective or supporting action can be implemented immediately. Our own experience is that these are natural breathing spaces for projects which could otherwise be very full on. The ground rules are simple:

- Project team members and key stakeholders are invited, and are expected to attend with open minds.
- An agenda incorporating:
  - a recap of objectives: what actually happened and how this differed from the intent, what can be learnt from this difference, and who to share the lessons learned with;
  - Looking forward to and reviewing the plan for the next set of activities in view of what has happened previously, and finding efficiencies.
- No blame is attached to any individual or teams, so avoiding the fear of witch-hunts and recriminations.
- Lessons learnt are shared with everyone relevant whether inside or outside the team.

6.5   Reflecting

Introspection, self-analysis and quiet reflection do not come naturally to people who like to do and to make things happen, including the project community. Looking and being busy has become something of a status symbol: if we are busy, we are important and we are making money for our business; if we're not busy, we're almost embarrassed to admit it. Busy-ness is validating but taking the time simply to think, plan and reflect has its own rewards. Research into effective learning confirms the importance of the natural process of reflection, and pulling back from day-to-day concerns to gain a holistic and systemic perspective. One project leader commented on flashes of insight when shaving, another whilst walking the dog or jogging.

Researchers at the Royal Dutch Shell Company identified what they called the 'helicopter view'. They found it to be the best single predictor of suitability for senior management and it is now used in industry as an essential leadership competency. It is often referred to by various other names such as 'peripheral vision', 'breadth of vision', 'power of anticipation' or 'clarity of purpose'. The helicopter view refers to the ability to rise above the specifics of a particular situation and to see it within the overall context. It is the ability to see the Big Picture without losing sight of the details and their implications. The same is also true for effective project leaders. They consciously build in time to reflect, to survey the whole picture and, above all, to review their own performance. This can be done with a colleague or team member, or increasingly with a coach or mentor, to provide the necessary mixture of constructive challenge and objectivity. This is just as true for the project team as for the individual project leader, and reviews are also opportunities to do just this.

If things do go wrong, you will need space to help you clarify and understand what has happened and to make decisions about what to do next. You can problem solve using the diverse points of view and experiences that come with the diverse project team, the wider stakeholder community you have already identified and the strong relationships that you have already built. This is the time you need to rely on the resilience you have built up, to stay calm and reasoned and not to start the blame game.

6.6   The Importance of Celebrating Success

Celebrating success shouldn't just come at the end of the project. Effective project teams and leaders help themselves to maintain momentum by celebrating their collective and individual achievements and successes along the way. Celebrating success is also a visible statement to the wider stakeholder community, to the client and to the organization to help convince sceptics, to raise the profile of the project and so build support, and to create a feel good factor. Some project leaders argue for the multiplier effect of small wins and successes.

Interim targets are important markers of success. Project leaders are always looking for ways of recognizing and celebrating achievements and contributions in ways that reflect the scale of the achievement, to support team morale and motivation and to make the team feel appreciated and recognized for their efforts. Ways in which you can do this include:

- Simple and instant rewards. For example, sending a personal handwritten note offering congratulations and thanks; saying 'well done' and 'thank you' spontaneously; inexpensive gifts.
- Spotlighting. For example, talking or writing publicly about individual team members who are outstanding, describing what they have done and why they were so successful; allowing team members to nominate their own heroes.
- Away days. For example, holding an impromptu party or get-together to celebrate success; allowing team members to take a break at the organization's expense.

- Providing free time. For example, days off in lieu or finishing the week early.

One project leader we know of made a point of ensuring not only the team member benefitted from a prize of a weekend away, but that his whole family accompanied him, understanding that the family had supported him during an intensive time of the project and so also deserved the organization's thanks. Team members will respond in different ways. Experience and observation will help you discover the best approach in each case.

When commenting on the results produced by a team member, outstanding project leaders often say: 'It takes a very special sort of person to do this work.' They are modest about their own contribution, making sure it is not more highly valued than that of other team members. Respect for the capabilities and efforts of others in the visible and invisible team is a common characteristic of individuals whose teams produce good results.

6.7   Change

Change happens regardless of the type of project, and it needs to be dealt with appropriately. We talked in Chapter 4 about how it is also not unusual for the project scope to vary and change during the lifecycle, and in Chapter 5 about anticipating personnel changes within the project team.

Understanding the impact of changes raised by the client, stakeholders or by external influences on project progress and outcomes is imperative since they are likely to affect budget, resources, timescales or other success criteria. Any changes which are agreed to be taken forward should be consistent with the Vision and outcomes of the project, else these could take the project significantly off-track. Capturing these changes by means of a defined process, registering and analysing them for any impact on the project, will help you keep the project delivery on track and the stakeholders informed.

One project leader explained her issue around 'minor' project changes. She was employed by a blue chip telecoms company and led a particular outsourcing contract on behalf of the business, which was worth tens of millions of pounds sterling. This involved the movement of over 50 IT infrastructure, development and maintenance personnel under a Transfer of Undertakings Protection of Employment (UK) (TUPE) agreement from the client to the telecoms company. Although on paper the employer had changed for these 50 IT personnel so that they were now relying on pay and promotion from the telecoms company, in reality they were still sited in their original offices, with their original equipment, having lunch and going out socially with their original colleagues. What this meant was that their former colleagues would continue to walk down the corridor to ask them, 'Can you please just … ?' And of course they were happy to be as helpful as they had always been. Unfortunately, it was these 'justs' that had such an impact on the bottom line of the outsourcing contract. Contract performance was not up to anticipated levels before handover to business-as-usual was complete. None of the 50 TUPE'd personnel owned up to what was happening but it was clear timesheets were telling one story and actual productivity another. So the project leader decided to spend a greater portion of her time exclusively on site, sitting in the open office with the TUPE'd personnel, noticing everything that was happening and listening to the conversations around her. It was then that she understood the problem and took the steps to resolve the issue.

One of our colleagues also talks about the 'Friday afternoon calls'. These typically happen when the contractor calls the client to make claims on them for work carried out over and above the contract. The Friday afternoon call ensures the client is about to leave the office for a well-earned weekend. The contractor's claims often come as an unwelcome surprise, if not shock, especially if the client has not introduced a robust change control process. The lesson? Don't be an arrogant client and expect your purchasing power to allow you to get your way. Rely instead on a robust change control process to register, analyse and report on financial, scheduling and other impacts to the project.

6.8   Keeping the Team Members on Track

Deciding what items you need to monitor, and how you're going to monitor them, is only one aspect of keeping your project on track. The information provided by such monitoring systems has to be put to good use by the project team. After all, there is no point in having first-class information if the team continues to operate inefficiently.

Ideally, a project team develops its own momentum and energy, and drives the project forward with commitment and enthusiasm. They trust their colleagues to back them up, and actively promote the Plan–Do–Review–Check philosophy outlined earlier in this chapter. In concrete projects where the team members are very visible and come together often, this level of teamworking is fairly easy to develop; people are accustomed to handling problems and conflicts which surface in meetings. But in temporary or open projects with less visible teams, identification of potential problems or conflict areas is much more difficult. People who disagree with the way the project is going, or who are encountering their own local difficulties, tend just to shelve the issue or give up and hope the problems will go away. It is at this end of the project spectrum that your personal leadership skills and style are really put to the test.

One way of thinking about how you can keep your team's motivation and performance high is to think of the team under two headings:

- The team together. How can you get the best out of them when the team meets? What actions can you take to make the meetings more productive?
- The team apart. How can you maintain momentum when they are not meeting regularly and are in different locations? Do you keep in touch with the team members, and support them when they need you?

6.8.1   THE TEAM TOGETHER

There are always project meetings: regular in the case of concrete projects, occasional with less-defined projects. Effective meetings don't just happen. They have to be worked at. Your first job is to ask the question: 'Is this meeting really necessary?'

Regular meetings are not ends in themselves. They can turn into tedious rituals if they have no real purpose. There are three main reasons to call a meeting:

- to communicate information;
- to solve problems;
- to make decisions.

From your point of view, meetings also serve a number of important underlying purposes. They:

- create identity, cohesion and a sense of 'togetherness' for the project team. Meetings help to make the team visible to each other;
- help to make team members feel involved in discussing and arriving at decisions. This in turn produces a sense of ownership and commitment to those decisions;
- develop synergy, that creative energy that helps the team achieve more collectively than individual members could on their own;
- help to reinforce the team's ground rules. Meetings are times when these rules are seen in action and are reviewed, renewed or enforced;

- provide an opportunity for teams to celebrate their successes together so generating and sustaining good morale, and revitalizing team members after intense periods of work.

Whatever the type of project, you will probably find it necessary to schedule some regular meetings of all team members, which may or may not take the form of the type of review discussed earlier. These help to keep the project on track.

It is crucial that you use these team meetings in two different ways. The first is the traditional feedback route – looking at what has actually happened, comparing it with the plan and working on resultant problems. But probably a more powerful technique, and certainly one that is used infrequently in our experience, is to 'preview': to anticipate what is coming up, to 'feed forward' problems and blockages that team members foresee. In this way you can solve problems before they occur, or at least have the opportunity to minimize their consequences and carry out damage limitation exercises in advance. Remember, everyone involved with projects tends to hate nasty surprises that come out of the blue. Forewarned is forearmed. However, day-to-day issues may have to be resolved by other meetings, often impromptu or at short notice. These may not involve all the team, but just those who need to talk about something together.

Finally, meetings may also not always involve you or be led by you. Effective delegation is part of good team leadership!

6.8.2   PROJECT MEETINGS – THE 11 'GOLDEN RULES'

To help you in your task, we have prepared what we regard as the 11 (not content with 10!) essential rules for running meetings successfully, shown in Table 6.1.

One last idea is to build in enough 'silly time'. When members of a team have been apart for a long time they often need to get to know each other again and reform the team. You should allow some informal time for this bonding process to take place. We call it 'silly time' because it is often spent catching up on gossip and exchanging light-hearted banter. But it is important. Meetings represent valuable time, and are held to help keep the project on track and moving towards completion.

Table 6.1   The 11 'golden rules' for meetings

1.	**Preparation**	Circulate an agenda and relevant papers sufficiently in advance to allow team members to read and prepare. Take into account any preparation or recommendations of subgroups created in past meetings. Nominate a minute-taker
2.	**Purpose**	Think carefully, if appropriate with other team members, about what you want out of the meeting. Make sure everyone is quite clear why they are there so add a set of objectives to the agenda
3.	**Agenda item leads**	Not all meetings or all agenda items need to be led or should be led by you. The team and the project will benefit by having a team member lead on their own area of expertise
4.	**Time scheduling**	Structure the available time to ensure an appropriate airing for each issue. Encourage brevity to help achieve everything on the agenda
5.	**Create understanding**	Try to ensure good communication between team members by *listening* actively to others and responding to what they say; by *asking for clarification* to clear up confusion, and by *summarizing* to keep the group on the right track and check for understanding. Encourage other team members to do the same. You only learn when you listen, not when you talk
6.	**Staying on track**	Ensure the meeting is chaired effectively. Stick to the agenda and stop team members (or yourself!) from wandering off the subject. Do not allow team members to introduce personal hobby horses or red herrings, and park these firmly when they are aired
7.	**Use diverse experience and skills**	Encourage the active participation of *all* team members, especially the quieter ones. Avoid dominating the discussion yourself or giving too much time to contributions from over-assertive team members
8.	**Creative problem solving**	Encourage the team to be positive, whilst learning to love the monitor-evaluators in the team. Reframe the negative in favour of 'what if', 'how' and 'what do we want this to look like?'. Use the full diversity of the team as a source of ideas
9.	**Check for agreement**	Don't assume that silence means consent. Check everyone for agreement, especially the quieter members of the team. This is particularly important in decisions to which widespread commitment is important
10.	**Review the working of the team**	Encourage brief but honest feedback about performance at the end of each meeting. Ensure that basic ground rules are still appropriate and working well
11.	**Action**	Ensure that all actions agreed at the meeting are summarized and understood. Identify clearly the individuals responsible and ensure that realistic deadlines are specified. Circulate this summary in writing to all concerned within 24 hours to act as a reminder

6.8.3   THE TEAM APART: SOME MORE 'GOLDEN RULES'

As we said earlier, the real work of teams takes place outside meetings. In some types of project the number of formal meetings is actually very small, although there may be a number of ad hoc meetings. There is no point in agreeing a series of actions at meetings if all that occurs at the next meeting is a series of carefully thought-out explanations of why individual team members have failed to carry them out. A large part of the responsibility for ensuring that they are carried out falls on your shoulders. So once the meeting has finished, here are some guidelines (Table 6.2) for ensuring actions are completed and the project moves forward once team members have dispersed back to their usual place of work.

6.8.4   CHALLENGING UNDERPERFORMANCE

Being clear about the performance expected for the project and how this defines the performance expected from each team member is part of providing the Vision and Big Picture, and part of defining and establishing the project culture and the way the project team is expected to work. In the many organizations we have worked in or with, we have noticed two types of leaders: those who make things happen and who work to the benefit and interest of their organization; and those who look to their own interests and 'play it safe'. A common complaint from project team members is that where there is underperformance within the team it is often not quickly and effectively dealt with. Particular team members may be taking too long to undertake their tasks or activities, they may be hiding behind others, they may not be as qualified or capable to undertake the role to which they have been appointed. If you choose to shy away from the issue and it becomes the 'elephant in the room' that everyone is aware of and no one is willing to address, and this can easily become a cause of demotivation, frustration and disengagement so impacting the project.

The project leaders we have talked to about this have two typical responses. Firstly, project leaders who are slow in challenging underperformance, or who are not willing to have those difficult conversations, face loss of confidence and frustration from other members of the team. These are things that need to be addressed at the time at which they occur. Wait until the next review or appraisal and the relevancy and urgency of the issue will have been lost. Secondly, by building that positive and constructive project culture, project

Table 6.2   The rules for dispersed teams

Rule	Description
Who does what and when	Before the team leaves the meeting, make sure that everyone has a clear idea of what they have been mandated to do, in terms of actions and results within a specified period of time. Encourage each member to see themselves as a team ambassador, entrusted with the responsibility of managing those outside the team with whom they come into contact.
Holding on and letting go	Encourage each team member to hold on to the lines of support you have created but at the same time to let go of your apron strings and work responsibly alone. At the same time, make sure that you let go of team members. Trust individuals to meet deadlines, trust their commitment and let go of the tasks you have delegated to them. Interference through distrust or anxiety will produce a negative reaction.
Protect members from distractions	Even with full-time team members, events sometimes occur outside the team's work that require a response from an individual team member. If possible, try to act as a shield for them by handling some of the pressure. Encourage them to approach you if they need support. At the other extreme, where the project is a part-time activity, team members need encouragement from you to avoid your project being seen as just a distraction.
Maintain momentum and commitment	It is far easier to create excitement at the start of a project than to keep generating it when the team is working apart. You can help to sustain momentum by providing team members with constant reminders of their priorities. This is particularly true of part-time members who have conflicting responsibilities. Without interfering with the work of team members, you must try to keep them motivated. Keep in touch with each member, be available when needed and provide support. If the pressure is too great, you may need to renegotiate success criteria with the sponsor or client or make some kind of deal with those who control other aspects of the team member's responsibilities. Even if the team is unhindered by outside commitments, you still need to maintain momentum by finding ways to show each of the members how valuable their contribution is and by reminding them of how their part fits into the Big Picture. Open projects, with less structured reporting, require you to make special efforts to maintain momentum.
Create active communications	Your role when the team is apart is rather like a spider weaving a web. You are at the centre, but you are constantly making the links between one point and another by staying in touch with individuals and passing information between different members and between them and the centre.
Create 'early warning' systems	A major cause of project failure is where problems are not foreseen, or worse, where a problem is foreseen by one team member but hidden from the others because of worry over being blamed. Encourage the adoption of a ground rule that any problem encountered by any team member, particularly if it might affect others, is to be signalled to you early. 'No surprises' may be one of the ground-rules you set with your team from the outset. Create a blame-free atmosphere where it is acceptable to share problems, to ask for help and to admit to being stuck. Encourage the frequent, fast and frank exchange of information and the idea that it is a cardinal sin to let another team member down.

leaders enable team members themselves to challenge inappropriate behaviour or underperformance in the project team objectively and without fear or intimidation.

6.9   Keeping the Stakeholders in the Picture

Even if the sponsor, client and end user are unable to attend your project meetings frequently, they must be kept fully informed and able to communicate with the team.

In a concrete project, the main stakeholders often attend all project meetings and have instant access to all necessary information. In other types of project, you may have to make special efforts to keep in touch, employing the most appropriate methods. Do they like informal chats over a cup of coffee? Do they need regular presentations with slides or graphs? What is the best method of getting them involved in the project? Perhaps a site visit or involvement in a prototype demonstration?

All contacts with stakeholders enable you to pick up signals, both explicit and implicit, on how they see the project developing and whether their expectations are changing. For example, if end users are excited by seeing the possibilities of a new software system, encourage them to talk to their boss (the client) about any enhancements they would like to see. Get them on your side, make them part of your team and keep them committed to your project.

Conclusion

The delivery phase of a project is the busiest and most intense in terms of 'doing'. It is also arguably the most challenging and exhilarating. Keeping a project on track involves agreeing a plan, issuing instructions and checking to see that everything is being carried out accordingly and this means reviewing and anticipating for change, risk and slippage. It's also a matter of the project leader being acutely aware of the subtle but significant shifts of opinion, desires or expectations of the people who make up the project team and stakeholders. You are responsible for progress, for keeping the monitoring and reporting systems finely tuned, and for ensuring the team continues to work in the most effective way possible regardless of location and culture. This might mean confronting and dealing with underperformance. In the daily rush to move things forward, do take the time to recognize and celebrate the small successes that are important as motivators for the project team as well as for the champions and stakeholders of the project.

Moreover, this is a time for reflecting not just on the performance of the project and the project team, but also on your own performance. Having the personal time to think, plan and reflect helps to keep focused and to build your resilience. There's a tremendous sense of achievement when you come to close and hand over the project.

Key Questions

- What are the root causes of slippage for your projects?
- How clear are you about what basic information you and the team need to keep control of progress?
- Are your project review meetings constructive and problem solving, or blaming and scapegoating sessions? How can you make them motivating rather than de-motivating for team members?
- How do you handle success?
- When do you build in time-out for reflection?

CHAPTER 7

Phase D – Closure

Starting strong is good. Finishing strong is epic.

Robin Sharma

Introduction

A project is 'determinate'. From the outset it is known by all participants that it will be terminated at some point in the future, whether a natural or forced close. All projects need a formal close and a process to close down, hand over and wind up. This is about closing down the project in a structured way, learning from what has happened and feeding back into the organization, handing over and winding up, and asking, 'Where next for the project team and project leader?'

Even when a project appears to be completed, there is often much work still to do. Business cases for projects won't just cover activities and budgets allocation for the delivery of a project. They will also involve handover into business-as-usual operations and often cover whole-life costs. Certainly, the final verdict on the 'success' of the project will depend on the success criteria chosen, and the view of some of these success criteria can only be finally decided months or years after project completion.

Maintaining high performance right up to the last minute, keeping the momentum of the project and the motivation of the project team going towards the completion can be a problem. Project team members may already have one eye on the door ready to move onto the next exciting challenge or may be fearful of what the future holds for them. It is particularly this final phase of the project that demonstrates how successful the project leader has been. Three areas to consider in particular are:

- ensuring that the client organization is linked into the project so that they can use outputs and deliverables confidently. Few projects start this process soon enough or put enough effort into it;

- making sure the client is ready to receive the project outcomes, and that it lands well;
- reviewing the project lifecycle and processes, building on strengths and attacking the weaknesses identified. This means taking on and embedding individual and organizational learning from such reviews. Experience without review and feeding back into the organization means that mistakes are liable to be repeated;
- adjourning the project team and moving on, celebrating and enjoying the success of the project so that you and your team feel rewarded and recognized for your achievements.

Sometimes letting go is not as easy as it sounds. You may well have built up a sense of ownership of the project over the months or years it has taken to bring it to completion. You may be reluctant to see it taken over until you are sure it is really fulfilling its purpose. This can often cause difficulties with the client who is, after all, the real owner and beneficiary. You need to recognize that you are done, the project is completed and that particular journey is over.

But project closure is not just about wrapping up and heading off. It is also about learning from everything that has happened during the project so you can carry forward the lessons that you have personally learned for your own development, helping your project team to reflect and carry forward the lessons they have learned, and also helping the organization improve the way it shapes and scopes, starts, delivers and closes projects.

The following guidelines for this final stage aim to help you become a project leader with a high reputation for seeing the job through to lasting performance.

7.1   Give it a Definite Close

Give your project a close with a definitive set of closure activities relating to personnel, handover to the client, reporting and communication (see Figure 7.1). At the most fundamental level, project closure is a notice to:

- identify and release available resources, although this might have also been happening through the natural course of the project;
- inform the operational team of the upcoming handover to allow them to get mobilized;
- prepare any necessary performance evaluations in preparation for handover to a previously agreed standard of performance;

Figure 7.1   Give the project a definite close
Source: © Oliver Widder. Reproduced with kind permission

- inform specific parts of the organization, for example the Finance department and HR department;
- conduct internal review processes;
- prepare the client for signing off the project.

'Natural' project closure occurs when the project scope has been met. However, not all projects can or should reach a natural conclusion. 'Unnatural' or 'forced' project closure occurs for a variety of reasons and often involves having those difficult conversations with the organization, the project team and the client. The most frequent causes of unnatural closure include:

- insufficient time or inadequate project funding;
- culling projects which duplicate results;
- sufficiently poor project performance that the organization or client calls time on it and accepts sunk costs;
- the client or requirements have changed;
- original assumptions that the project was originally based on are subsequently proven to be false so that the rationale for the project is no longer valid;
- context for the project has changed as a result of pressures or factors external to the organization;
- pet projects with no supporting or valid business case.

When completed, natural project closure verifies that all the agreed and defined phases, activities and tasks are completed, that the client has accepted the results and that the project is no longer active. It is at this point the client must honour their responsibilities to sign-off and accept the product or service once they have confirmed it is fit for purpose. Unfortunately, it is not uncommon for clients to drag their feet at this point and to become reticent about putting their signature to paper, particularly because they understand that the handover suddenly makes them responsible for taking on the outcomes. Part of your role as the project leader is to make this go smoothly, and to do this effectively there must be a set of well-documented criteria of performance in place from the beginning of the project. Essentially, this is what 'success' looks like. Tangible, objective and measurable criteria are of most use since intangible, subjective criteria are risky and open to interpretation. There should be no room for doubt or ambiguity, although this is often difficult to achieve. This is obviously easiest for concrete and occasional projects; for open projects 'success' is often just agreeing that there is a next step!

Typically, the benefits owner is responsible for the continued tracking of the project benefits. For some organizations that person may be the project sponsor or the client, in others it may be another specified individual. It is this tracking which will in part determine the success or otherwise of the project.

7.2   Business Readiness and Handing Over

If project leadership is about driving the project and project delivery is about implementing the project, then business readiness is about receiving the outcomes and outputs, and ensuring these land well. Since it is the client that will be signing off and taking receipt of the project outcomes, it is the client who will be asking the questions, 'What and who needs to be ready?' 'How ready is ready enough?' And 'Whose viewpoint should be used when judging readiness?' (PMI, 2014).

If you've followed our approach of involving all main stakeholders early in the project lifecycle, then you will have already started the conversation about preparing the client and handover at the beginning of the project so that the final handover should contain no surprises. The difficulty can arise from this new version of the relationship with the client. The client is no longer specifying results and setting policy guidelines; the client at this stage becomes the actual user, operator or consumer of your project's results. The client has to live with these results, day in and day out, so they need to know the detail of how the product or service is going to work.

The 'client' is, in fact, likely to appear in the form of numerous users, ones that possibly you and your project team haven't dealt with before. The logistics of this absorb a considerable amount of time and are very important. Users are a long way behind you in their familiarity with the project. Yet now they have to live with the outcomes and deliverables. It helps if you try to understand the newcomers who have to be linked into the project at this late stage:

- remember that it's all clear to you because you've lived with it for weeks, months or years;
- remember what it was like when you were groping around in the early stages to get to grips with the complexity of it all;
- remember that is where *they* are *now*.

Once the real users start to become active they find bugs, snags, gaps or unforeseen problems. This is true whether your project is building an airport terminal or a software package, whether it is a concrete project or an open one. There are always genuine, interesting questions to be addressed at the end. The question is how to reduce the shocks in number and severity.

The handover process for open projects can sometimes be difficult to manage because, by their very nature, the outcome is often uncertain. Sometimes there is nothing to show for the project except the knowledge that further work is viable. On the other hand, an open project that is successful usually becomes either a 'temporary' project, subject to a further tentative stage of development, or a concrete project. Many ideas for new product development start as 'skunk works' described in Chapter 3 which go on to become concrete projects. To achieve this, the project leader has to manage the sponsors and the political environment very actively to gain official status for the project.

So handover success is achieved by involving the end users earlier than you might have supposed. We stress this because handover is the point in the project lifecycle where the uncertain areas between the project team and the client are greatest. Starting early to reduce that uncertainty means that fewer critical issues are left out. Even more important, it builds the sense of ownership and confidence of the client. Some methods that can be used at the handover stage are:

- building in link people;
- identifying ways to enhance the handover.

7.2.1   BUILD IN LINK PEOPLE

Assign one team member the specific job of managing the handover. The client should also have assigned an individual or group whose responsibilities include ensuring business readiness and a smooth and seamless transition from project to business-as-usual. Specifying and filling such a role prevents the handover being left to everybody and nobody, and signals that it is being taken seriously. It injects direct resources and commitment into this critical phase. It also ensures that detailed planning and control extend to the end of the project. Increasingly, clients are also making use of 'change managers' who explicitly look at how the project outcomes and deliverables will be integrated effectively and efficiently into their organization.

Consider bringing support people into the project team. They may be concerned with training, helpline services, maintenance, operating procedures, production of reference materials or troubleshooting. Begin to integrate these people as soon as you have an outline or prototype that can give them an idea of what the end product might be like. If you do not start this learning process early enough and don't invest enough time in preparing people (explaining, training, explaining again) then you may have to inject large quantities of resources to rescue the situation later on.

7.2.2   IDENTIFYING WAYS TO ENHANCE THE HANDOVER

Here are some ideas to enhance the handover:

> *Build up the introduction of the product, service or change to the client and stakeholders*. Build their awareness and interest about what is on the way in terms of what's in it for them, and what processes and structures are being adopted. Establish and clarify expectations, and answer their queries (what, when and why?). You can do this in a variety of ways. Use presentation, exhibitions, lunchtime meetings, demonstrations, webinars, written materials, mock-ups, models or tours months before handover to give the client and stakeholders an idea of what will be involved. Write clear documentation, guides and handbooks that are user-friendly. Answer the questions naive clients and stakeholders always wanted, but never dared, to ask. All the above are just as important for less concrete projects with ideas that are difficult to communicate.

> When Siemens designed and constructed a new site in Lincoln, UK, they spent considerable time and effort in building awareness and developing dialogue with their staff. Officially opened in 2013, the site is an integrated manufacturing unit and office consolidating Siemens service employees from other sites in Lincoln into a single location. The centre includes a new workshop with a high-speed balancer, new modern offices and dedicated customer facility. The new site represents a major investment in the service business of around £15 million and it achieved a BREEAM® 'excellence' rating. Siemens also used the move to the new site as an opportunity to consciously develop new ways of working to drive a change in culture in the new environment. During the years of discussion and construction leading up to the move, they deliberately set up two-way dialogues and engaged with their staff, providing regular updates, discussion forums and site visits to build understanding, support and familiarity with the new complex.

Reassure them. Use discussions with client link personnel and stakeholder representatives to answer questions such as, 'How will our work change?', 'What support will be provided?'

Introduce them to the product/service/change in a structured way. This might be using formal training and practice forums. For formal 'classroom' training, provide several short training sessions rather than a single long one over an appropriate time frame. This not only ensures the client and stakeholders aren't overwhelmed by everything at once, but that they have the opportunity to go away, reflect and try things out for themselves. Some of the most important items covered by the training should include:

- gaining skills in using equipment;
- gaining knowledge of what is happening and how to handle links between activities;
- understanding how this new way of working will integrate into day to day operations;
- practising routines, and highlighting how to use manuals and self-help facilities;
- stressing key points for accuracy and control;
- building troubleshooting processes to cope when things go wrong (what is really serious and must be avoided?).

One way we have done this previously was to create a learning centre where demonstrations were provided and individuals could work through particular questions or routines with guidance. Other project leaders have held informal question/answer sessions to provide a safety valve for complaints or hidden problems, conducted one-to-one or small-group simulations of the work environment with all its pressures, and provided forums where end users could talk through their problems and find solutions.

Using coaching and problem solving designed to provide quick help in the early stages of use, to help users to solve their own problems. These can be achieved through informal contacts but should be friendly and readily available. Support and develop 'lead' users who work with other users but who are more experienced and can build the confidence of new users. They can talk the users' language and see the problems from their perspective. Build up a resource of specialist back-up that can be called in to deal with more technical questions or unexpected results. This is vital in concrete projects with high risks depending on equipment functioning reliably. Providing helpline support, so that somebody is readily available to sort out immediate problems, is particularly important for people depending on new technology for the execution of their work.

Review. Use all of the above opportunities for discussions with your client, their link personnel, users and supervisors in order to assess the system's strengths and weaknesses and provide additional communication and training.

The project team, and that includes you as project leader, will be widely considered to be the experts since you have all been instrumental in delivering the results. This can mean that you can live the project indefinitely and become the 'go-to' person unless you can deliberately disengage yourself by stepping aside for the business-as-usual team.

7.3   Learning the Lessons

We've talked previously about reviewing the projects after particular milestones during the lifecycle. The final review, often known as the post-implementation review, looks at the project across its lifecycle. This can also be a project audit which is carried out by an internal or independent body, but which is more 'official'. We've known multinationals that routinely audit a random selection of their projects at various points in the lifecycle, regardless of how they are progressing, in order to understand successful projects as well as struggling projects.

But why worry when the project is completed? Why not let it rest in peace? You and your organization can learn a lot about what to do better next time. How successful were the methodology, approach and/or processes adopted for the project? New good practices can be discovered, and they need to be communicated to project team members, sponsors and the project management community within the organization. Persistent organizational or procedural problems can be dealt with, in order to secure improvements in performance for future projects.

One project-based company asked itself why its projects were failing or producing disappointing performance. After auditing several projects, it found the common features or patterns of interaction that showed clearly the cause and symptom. The company's failures were connected with:

- too many people working on too many projects;
- frequent priority changes;
- projects technically focused, with insufficient market sensitivity.

Typically, project audits reveal weaknesses in three areas:

- poor project definition;
- weak project sponsorship;
- bad project organization.

7.4   Auditing the Project

Typical topics for a project audit include:

- Cost/benefit analysis: how realistic were the original cost calculations, and what benefit has been realized to date?
- Definition of success criteria: were they adequate? How were they arrived at?
- Steps in the project lifecycle: where was the team effective? Where were the problems?
- Project organization and control tools: did they help or hinder?
- What kinds of problems were encountered and how were they dealt with?

- Constraints that were surprising.
- Links with stakeholders: strengths and weaknesses.
- Organization and communication of the core team and project leader.

Here it is important to identify the information from as many directions as possible and to differentiate between symptoms and causes.

If you run an audit, run it as a participative problem-solving process with as many members of the team as possible, including the project sponsor. You need to hear the diversity of views, so give your team members time to reflect on their experience in the project, and tell them prior to the meeting the sort of questions you have in mind. They can also be encouraged to carry out mini-audits with their parts of the visible or invisible team. Your client should be included in some aspects of the audit. Input from the client will enable you to test some of your suggestions for improvement.

One of the dangers of audits is that people, project leaders especially, perceive audits as witch hunts. But this fear can be overcome by making clear the audit's ground rules:

- Concentrate on the issues and problems, the roles and process, rather than the personalities.
- Do not criticize or disapprove of anything unless you can offer something better in its place. We can all push things over. Rebuilding takes effort and genuine interest.
- Tap into ideas that the organizational team members have. They have first-hand experience of the problems, and may well have worked out the best solutions.

Once you have completed the audit, don't forget to let other project leaders or sponsors know what your experience has taught you. Your proposals on how to improve performance are valuable information for the organization, helping to set them apart from competitors. Sharing good practice, informally and formally, is one of the most effective ways of spreading learning through the organization to improve its capacity for achieving results through projects. At a very basic level you can:

- send a summary of bad/good points with recommendations to senior management and other project leaders;
- hold a briefing workshop to test ideas for improvement;

- ensure that a comprehensive financial report is included, with real expenditure compared with original and revised estimates;
- make sure others know why you have been successful. What did you do that was different? Success is rarely just the result of good luck.

The New Ventures division of an international telecommunications organization was experiencing difficulty in bringing an important new product to the market fast enough and at a competitive price. In discussing the issue, the management team realized that there had been several smaller projects over the previous five years that had not been successful either, apparently because of technical difficulties that were insuperable. One team member suggested that this was not really the reason for failure, but was just a face-saving formula that those involved knew would be acceptable to senior management.

The team, horrified by this suggestion, asked one of the previous project leaders to form a small group to analyse the past failures, so that the whole division could learn from them. The group worked rapidly and their report was circulated throughout the division within 10 days.

The divisional director asked each member of the division to put forward ideas about how the lessons from the report could be applied constructively to their own project. Each project team then discussed these extensively and came up with its own 'performance improvement plan'. Each plan had two sections:

- things we can do ourselves;
- things that the divisional Service management team needs to do.

The latter issues were brought together by the divisional director and discussed by the senior team; plans for their resolution, with clear responsibilities and deadlines, were circulated to all. Over the next six months some large changes were made, as well as a whole range of small ones by many people. Morale and confidence rose rapidly and progress towards meeting the main project objectives was generally recognized to have been substantially accelerated.

We've audited projects which have followed specific project management methodologies to the letter, but which have still not been 'successful'. How well do we learn from these discussions and revelations? The National Audit Office, The Standish Group, Gartner and others tell us that, as a project management community, we continue to make the same mistakes in projects. The way that organizations and individuals deal with failure often indicates their attitude to learning. In order to learn, we have to recognize that something didn't go as well as it could have done or should have done. In the rush to finish a project, handover and take that well deserved rest or move onto the next project, we don't always give ourselves the space to reflect, to learn the lessons we need to and to pass these lessons on to others.

Finally, ensure that you too learn from the process. Each project you undertake or lead provides a significant learning experience, which may well prove invaluable in your future career. Consider what you have learnt from your own experience. Try to be specific about the positive and negative events and how you handled them.

7.5   From Lessons Learnt to Knowledge Management

Project reviews, post-implementation reviews, project audits and identifying the lessons learnt are too often tick-box exercises. They can be missed altogether, perhaps because the project team has been dispersed and reallocated to another project, or because there is no project charge code to book the review to. This is a shame since these are all missed opportunities to provide a reflective learning platform for the project and for the individuals involved, recapping the objectives and what actually happened. Project reviews and audits can be used to examine what went wrong, to look at the root causes and how they were overcome (or how they were fallen foul of!). This can be fed back into the organization to help refine estimates for particular pieces of work, and to develop the project management framework and community. Both processes and content should be looked at, ideally immediately after the project has been completed when everything is still fresh in the team's minds and when team members are most likely to be available; then again in several months' time when everyone has had a chance to reflect further and the product or service is being used on a daily basis so that the client and end users can provide additional experience in the evaluation.

For many organizations and individuals, 'knowledge' is still about information which is readily articulated, captured, structured, organized and stored for personnel to access through web-based portals or shared folders to search, retrieve and use. Examples might be good practice programmes, documentation management systems and lessons learnt databases. This codified, explicit and easily transferable knowledge can be used again and again to help educate, train and develop personnel in a range of functions and skills. However, knowing that your feedback and lessons learnt will be documented for all to see and share for all time tends to make people guarded and reticent about what they commit for capture and how they express it. As a result, it can be dry and also sparse on content.

The more interesting question is how we can tap into the deeper, tacit knowledge: those insights, know-how and experiences that are probably jumbled, chaotic and judgmental so require reflection, dialogue, trust and time. This, then, is the challenge for projects, project team members and organizations. Goodman and Riddell (2014) suggest that if 'information management' is to do with the collection, storage, dissemination, archiving and distribution of information, then 'knowledge management' is to do with the use that people put that to, how they apply their expertise to make decisions, how they tap into what they have learned and the translation of personal experience into collective knowledge. This, then, is about sharing knowledge, not just by documenting it but also by sharing it informally, such as through social contact, conversations, trusted colleagues, peer-to-peer connections, mentoring, shadowing, job rotation, communities of practice and storytelling.

We know of organizations that create forums where employees can create a discussion thread for generating and exchanging ideas among the colleagues and peers. These 'creative forums' or 'knowledge cafés' are typically facilitated meetings where the facilitator can encourage the participants to develop and articulate their ideas, ensuring that a few speakers do not dominate the discussion, and that the environment is conducive to trust and discretion. These forums are recognized as places that personnel can be more candid about their stories, descriptions and feelings. They are also recognized as hothouses for innovation and change.

Especially if the organization has hired an external project leader or other project team members, a commitment to knowledge sharing is a feature that would mark someone out as valuable to the organization. No organization likes to think that the experience and knowledge gained by a contracted project professional by virtue of one of *their* projects will simply walk out the door once the contract has expired.

So sharing knowledge develops the organization's capability for deeper learning as well as developing good practice within their project community. Both enhance competitive advantage.

7.6   The Project Team Adjourning

Projects typically start with a great sense of anticipation and enthusiasm. A significant part of the project leader's role is in keeping the momentum of the project team going until the end, even when interest and enthusiasm are threatening to decline. Personnel come into the project and exit the project during the lifecycle because their particular skill set is needed at a particular point, because they choose to leave for their own reasons or because they are managed out when their performance is not sufficiently strong. As the project leader, you will have the responsibility of managing people in and out of the project team along the life of the project. You will probably be one of a small core set of personnel who is a point of continuity across the whole of the project lifecycle, who knows the project history and background, and who can connect current activities back to the original scoping discussions with stakeholders.

As the project approaches its conclusion, a good team will gain momentum. However, individual members often look further ahead and become concerned about their career development and position within the organization once the team is dismantled.

Because of this, the elation of achievement can be speedily followed by depression. You need to help people understand this process and a celebration held at the end of a project is a chance to recognize the work, not only of the team's leaders, but of all its members, both visible and invisible. The end of a project is an emotional event, and a celebration – however small – of its success helps people to come to terms with the change occurring in their life.

The future for team members may well depend on their personal performance and the credibility of the project. If you have been successful, other project leaders may be trying to snap up your people before you are really ready to let them go. You will have some tough decisions to make. Letting somebody who is important to you take up a new post at this stage could be your last visible sign of commitment and support to that team member. It is important to start openly discussing with members what they would prefer to do, what their strengths are, how they might develop or improve, and what you think the realistic alternatives are for them in the organization. One-to-one discussions with yourself or the organization's HR personnel can provide reassurance and moral support.

To prevent unnecessary apprehension, make sure that the sponsor and any other relevant senior executive has planned the future role of project team members well before the end of the project. This must be done and the conclusions communicated to team members in sufficient time to avoid loss of motivation. You need to have established who in the organization is responsible for making decisions on the future use of your team members; contact them, promote their achievements and keep the pressure on to make sure that they are properly rewarded. If you leave redeployment to the last minute, the organization may make hasty decisions that are disadvantageous to itself and to the individuals concerned.

Do write thank yous, provide feedback for appraisals for the project team, and offer to write references for your team. How you exit people from the team and how you bring the project to a close also reflects on you and impacts your image and reputation.

7.7   What Next for You?

So what is next for you? Will you capitalize on your success by moving on to a new and bigger challenge in the organization, or choose to bail out and quit while you are ahead? Being able to plan your own exit from the project is as integral to its closure as any of the other activities. At what point will you have completed the handover and made that clean break? If you've been seconded to another part of the business or have been posted overseas for the duration of the project, it is certainly time to reflect on what comes next and to get your informal network working for you. Are you excited to be going back and do they have a role waiting for you, are your supporters still there or have they reorganized in the meantime and forgotten about you because you've been too busy to keep your profile up and your network going?

What have you learnt from this project that tells you where you want to go next, or the sort of project you are seeking next? Look at the project as a way to recognize your strengths and weaknesses and a way to help you identify where you excelled and where you could have done better. It's not about beating yourself up because you didn't achieve everything you thought you were going to achieve. It is about learning from the project so you can acknowledge your personal and professional growth and development, and carry forward the lessons that you have learned.

> We know of one project leader who worked for a global insurance company. Having successfully led a significant change project for her employer, she was rewarded with a promotion into the leadership team. After a couple of years, she was invited to take the project leader role again for another major change project because of her previous success. She refused the invitation. She explained to us, 'I have a corner office at headquarters, less stress, more regular hours, a high-performing permanent team which I have built and developed over the last three years and increased work–life balance for my family. I worked hard to achieve this. Why would I choose to swap all this for another project leadership role?'

Some months before your project comes to an end you may need to start reminding sponsors and decision makers that you will be available. This is another point at which you can make all that networking, communication, engagement and building support that you have done for the project work for you. Update your CV to reflect what you have contributed and achieved, and how you have developed. Organizations that work with a project management structure are usually well aware of beginnings and ends of projects. So the issue in this case will be to put together your negotiating position on the basis of what you would prefer to do and the type of challenge you are ready to take on. If you are seen to have been successful, you can often afford to be forceful in ensuring that your next project will be set up with conditions that you know will help it to succeed. If you are not a shining star in the organization, review your own strengths and see where you need to build your expertise and organizational visibility.

Temporary projects are very different in that you are likely to have retained your normal job throughout, and have worked only part time on the project. Therefore, you have no expectation of a totally new job. Temporary projects often give both leaders and team members a wider view of the organization and its operating environment, as well as access to a wider network of contacts and influencers. So, when a project ends, it is sometimes rather unexciting to resume business as usual. Reflecting on your own and/or talking to senior managers, coach or mentors about what you have learnt can help you to capitalize on your experience. Understanding how certain ideas can be applied constructively to other situations is one way of moving from a functional to a more general management outlook. You may have discovered other aspects of your organization that you would be interested to explore further. Let your own line manager or sponsor know of your preferences at performance appraisal time or through informal discussions.

So how 'successful' were you personally? We've talked about how to judge the success of the project itself, and now we need to talk about you. There are two elements to this particular question:

- How successful was the project leadership role within the project?
- As project leader, how successful were you in carrying out that role?

These questions give many project leaders we have talked with pause for thought. These questions are about self-reflection and being able to recognize when, where and how you acted well and where there is room for improvement. In Part 4 we will look at ways to develop your own skills and career in project leadership as well as looking at how the organization can support your development and career choices.

Conclusion

Closing down the project, handing over and winding up complete the project lifecycle. Not all projects come to a natural conclusion; some are closed as a result of reasons related to funding, duplication, performance or context.

To complete the natural close of a project, the project leader must ensure a robust handover to the client and look after the interests of the team members as the project finishes. During this phase, the most important activities are:

- The effective handover to, and the formal sign-off from, the client. Develop a plan and framework to involve end users and any operational support staff as early as possible in the project to ensure business readiness and no surprises.
- Learning the lessons and managing the knowledge gained from the project. Project post-implementation reviews or audits are invaluable in helping identify the good and the not-so-good elements of a project. Sharing this knowledge within the organization supports the development of the project management community and builds on experience to continually improve the way projects are shaped, scoped, started-up, delivered and closed.
- The withdrawal of the project team and the phasing-in of the long-term business-as-usual team.
- Closing down your own involvement in the project and considering your own future.

Key Questions

- How did you communicate your last project to the end users and operational support team? Was it reasonably structured, or on a fairly ad hoc basis?
- Consider conducting an audit of your present project. How will you structure it, and to whom will you circulate the results?
- How will you choose to mark the completion of your project?
- Finally, a test of how effective you have been as a project leader: would you like to lead another project? Will you be asked to do so? Will you be able to gain the support of your former team members for your new project?

References

Goodman, E. and Riddell J. (2014) *Knowledge Management in the Pharmaceutical Industry* Gower Publishing Ltd, Farnham, UK.

Project Management Institute Inc. (2014) 'Change readiness: Focusing change management where it counts', PMI White Paper, July.

PART 3
THE CORE

*This may sound simple, but the first characteristic that separates
the really successful PMs is their leadership. They set the tone, they
should be decisive, and have a vision.*

Grauel, Malone and Wygal

In Part 1 we looked at leadership, project leadership and the breadth
of competencies and skills required for a project leader to undertake the
project leadership role successfully. In Part 2 we looked at the project itself:
how the lifecycle of the project is divided into logical phases, their primary
activities and particular aspects of the role of the project leader during these
key phases.

Part 3 covers in detail three core competencies, those things the effective
and successful project leader needs to do and be aware of at all times.
These, then, are the things over and above technical abilities that make the
difference, and they rely strongly on business acumen, interpersonal skills and
organizational intelligence.

The three competencies are:

- Vision and the Big Picture: understanding how the project fits with
  the strategic direction of the organization, developing the Vision
  for the project and aligning key players and other stakeholders to
  the Vision.
- Building key relationships: identifying and building relationships
  with key players including stakeholders and, in particular, the project
  sponsor, client and project team.
- Communication and engagement: looking at the different facets of
  communication, including branding and marketing, which help to build
  engagement with and commitment to the project during its lifecycle.

These three core elements are woven throughout the project lifecycle
discussed in Part 2.

In Part 3:

- Chapter 8 looks at the strategic perspective, that of Vision and the Big Picture. This is part of the early-stage activities of the project during shaping and scoping, and needs to be recommunicated throughout the project. The Vision provides clarity and understanding about the project aims and outcomes, and should reflect the Big Picture of where the organization is heading so that any project is itself a reflection of commercial realities, the market and the strategic context in which the organization finds itself. We also look at project success criteria and ask the fundamental question, 'What is "success"?'
- Chapter 9 looks at how to identify the range of stakeholders for the project, how to identify the various attributes that make particular stakeholders important to the project, and how to develop and maintain strong relationships with them. We look at specific individuals or groups, the 'key players', who are critical to the project because of the role they play and the support they can provide throughout the life of the project. These are the sponsor, the client and the project team and they all have one thing in common: their ability to make your project a success or failure. You need to bring them on board and harness their power. This chapter also shows you how to navigate your way through the power bases and politics within the organization and how to develop your 'organizational intelligence'.
- Chapter 10 looks at communication and engagement. Why is this important and how can a project leader ensure this is done effectively at the strategic and tactical level for the project when cross-functional, multi-located and multicultural project teams and a diverse range of stakeholders represent an increasing challenge? This chapter also looks at project branding and marketing, and the importance of the project leader considering their own image and profile.

CHAPTER 8
Vision and the Big Picture

It all comes down to the ability to go up and down the ladder of abstraction, and being able to see the big picture and the operational implications, which are signs of outstanding leaders and strategists.

Loizos Heracleous

Introduction

Chapter 8 looks at the strategic perspective, that of Vision and the Big Picture, which provide purpose and direction for the project. This is part of the early-stage activities of the project during shaping and scoping, and needs to be recommunicated throughout the project. The Vision provides clarity and understanding about the project aims and outcomes, and should reflect the organization's own Vision and strategy. The Big Picture provides the context of market and economy. As a result, any project is itself a reflection of commercial realities, the market and the strategic context in which the organization finds itself. We also look at project success criteria and ask the fundamental question, 'What is "success"?'

8.1   Providing Purpose and Direction

Project teams, just like organizations, are a collection of individuals and groups aligned and working towards a common purpose. In common with organizations, every project needs a well-defined and well-communicated Vision which describes what the project aims to do and what it is trying to achieve, painting a picture for the future and so providing the purpose and direction for the project. The 'Vision' is not the same as a SMART (Specific, Measureable, Achievable, Realistic, Timely) target. We have worked with a client who set their project Vision as 'reaching £20m revenue by 2020'. Although a great sound bite, it didn't motivate the project team. The Big

Picture provides the explanation of the context for the project and how it works with the organizational strategy. From this the conversation can then move onto aligning the Vision and Big Picture with the objectives, outcomes and deliverables so that the project team, stakeholders and business will be clear about:

- what the project is and why it is important;
- the performance expected of the project team;
- what high performance for the project looks like.

If your team doesn't know or understand the purpose behind a project, it has no meaning for them and although they might go through the necessary actions they will not understand the consequences, so they are less committed to its success. If you want to build a highly motivated and high-performing project team, you need a clearly expressed and articulated rationale and purpose.

Heathrow Terminal 5 is the newest of Heathrow's terminals in London, UK. The design of the new terminal began in 1989, government planning permission was granted in November 2001 and the terminal was officially opened in 2008 at a cost of £4 billion. It was a substantial and complex build, with five floors large enough to hold 50 football pitches, and provides a huge range of facilities including restaurants, shops, hotels, car hire services, business services, parking and bureaux de change facilities. The terminal is used exclusively by British Airways and Iberia.

The Vision for Teminal 5 was to deliver the world's most successful airport development:

- good for passengers;
- easy to operate;
- new standards of HSSE;
- respect for neighbours;
- no disruption to Heathrow Airport Limited.

And the specific project goals included:

- throughput of 30–35 million passengers per year;
- world-class experience;
- zero fatalities during construction.

An initial role of the project leader is to help set the scene for the project (see Figure 8.1). This includes understanding and communicating the rationale for the project within the context of the organization and the client. The project Vision is focused on the project itself, but is informed by the Vision of the organization and from the client's own Vision, both of which

Figure 8.1 Part of the project leader's role is to provide clarity of Vision and purpose for the project

are, in turn, informed by the impact of external pressures (see Figure 8.2). It provides clarity around the aims and objectives of the project, as well as what 'success' looks like. It helps to engage and align others across the project team, organization and client organization. It also helps drive decision making across the project team and the organization, as well as supporting the definition of goals and targets.

> *Completing the Eight Lookings Diagnostic will provide you with an indication of how much your focus is on:*
>
> - *Looking internally – the Organization's Vision.*
> - *Looking externally – the Client's Vision.*

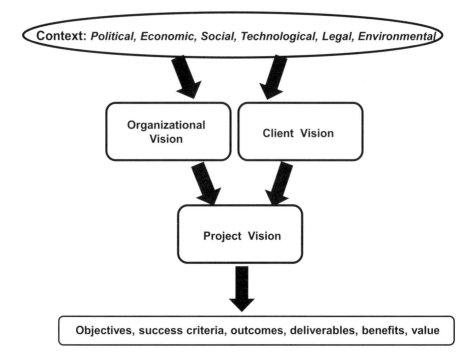

Figure 8.2 Relationship between external pressures impacting organizational and client Vision, providing the context for the project and the project Vision

Further, well-defined projects not only state the benefits expected (in terms of tangible and intangible value, outcomes, deliverables and results) but also state the environment and way it is to be delivered in terms of quality, appropriate technology and project culture (see Chapter 5).

This all helps to keep the focus on the end-game and, more importantly, it helps to inform the project team and other stakeholders and to encourage their buy-in and to align them with project. This becomes even more important at the times when the project doesn't seem to be moving forward as rapidly at it should, when clients want to change the terms of reference once the project has launched or when those key resources you counted on are about to be reassigned to other projects.

The project Vision can be built up by exploring questions with stakeholders and project team members, such as:

- How will this project make a difference to the organization?

- How will we know this project has been successful?
- What do we want this project to achieve?

Translating the answers to such questions into a Vision statement for the project creates a very powerful communications tool, not only for project team members, but also as a way of checking with and communicating to stakeholders and other interested parties throughout the course of the project. It also serves at a later stage to help you to keep the project on track.

> Dounreay Site Restoration Ltd has produced not just words documenting a Vision ('to establish Dounreay as the benchmark in Europe for successful nuclear decommissioning'), but a video to support the visualization of what they are trying to achieve. This is a great use of the visual to build understanding and to engage support. The use of language and the focus on particular themes such as community and the environment are also striking:
>
> *Important aspects of this project include stewardship, not only of the site, but of the surrounding area and the local workforce, with a key responsibility being building trust and relationships over the fifteen year decommissioning period. Another vital element is the development and implementation of constructive solutions to mitigate the socio-economic impact on the local community caused by the closure of the site.*
>
> Source: Dounreay Site Restoration Limited

8.2 Pressures on Organizations

What drives a project may not at first be easy to see. It is helpful to stand back from the specific project objectives to see why the project is significant to the organization in which you work, and also to your client's organization. Keeping any organization viable and competitive is vital to its continued success. New competitors enter markets all the time at home and abroad. Reducing costs, improving productivity, new production methods to improve quality, increased speed and flexibility are constant pressures on organizations. As product lifecycles shorten, the speed of new product innovation has to increase to compensate. Standing still or, alternatively, gradually upgrading existing products and marginally reducing costs is not an option. Radical alternatives have to be introduced and then, almost immediately, challenged again as competitors catch up.

This means that organizations have to recognize trends and movement in the market, competitors, technology and other factors and decide how to act. All organizations, whether public services or private sector and no matter the industry sector, are affected by these types of external pressures which help to clarify and focus their strategic position. The range of these external pressures are often summarized as PESTLE, described in Table 8.1.

Table 8.1   PESTLE – external pressures on organizations

Political	Examples: government policies; government term and change; funding, grants and regional development initiatives; home market lobbying/pressure groups.
Economic	Examples: home/overseas economy and trends; disposable income; inflation; tax issues/relief; market and trade cycles; market routes and distribution trends; interest and foreign exchange rates; international trade tariffs.
Social	Examples: lifestyle trends; consumer tastes, attitudes and opinions; demographic trends and characteristics; media views; target markets; buying access and trends; ethical issues; fads.
Technological	Examples: competing technology development; research funding; replacement technology/solutions; maturity of technology; information and communications; innovation potential; technology access; licensing, patents and intellectual property issues; global communications.
Legal	Examples: current/future legislation for home market and foreign target market; regulatory bodies and processes; employment law; consumer protection; industry-specific regulations; competitive regulations.
Environmental	Examples: ecological/environmental/sustainability issues in home market and foreign target market; customer values; market values; shareholder and stakeholder values.

An example of PESTLE in practice is the 2004 Clementi Report, an independent review of the regulation of legal services in England and Wales which provided recommendations that continue to impact the sector, not least the threat and arrival of new entrants. This was followed between 2009 and 2012 by a 'perfect storm' of recession biting at the lucrative corporate market, more competition as a result of Alternative Business Structures (Legal Services Act 2007), a proliferation of in-house teams as well as increased use of competitive tenders and of panel suppliers.

Why is this important? Law firms continue to see increased price competition and a shift in the balance of power towards the client, and some law firms have gone under. Sector research suggests that law firms may respond to this change by following the route of other professional services which have developed project management techniques in the delivery of their services in order to help refine their offering to the market. Here, the development of project management capability focuses on delivering whole services, not just one technical aspect of it, so managing the implementation of the change within the client organization and providing additional value. This might be, for example, post-merger integration, share scheme implementation, property acquisition and sale. 'Legal Project Management' (LPM) (also known as 'matter management') is still a relatively new concept and is being increasingly used to apply project management techniques to deliver legal services.

Projects initiated and allocated to project leaders may be a direct result of the organization's strategic position, of internal organizational strategic reviews or in response to an external client request for research, product or service. Projects may involve improved product development, manufacturing, administration or selling; they may be aimed at improving efficiency and saving costs through new ways of working; they may be culture change projects aimed at shifting the ingrained traditional, hierarchical and bureaucratic culture to one of flexibility, collaboration, resilience and fast response. Regardless, projects have a context and it should be easily demonstrable how they fit with the strategy, aims and ambitions of the organization.

8.3   Establishing and Reconciling 'Success'

Traditionally, projects and the leadership and management of projects have been judged by the triple constraints of time, cost and scope. Two other factors of risk and quality are also often included. This view of success is very much focused on technical delivery; as such, given this definition, the Sydney Opera House, the British Library, the Copenhagen Metro and indeed Heathrow Terminal 5 would be deemed failures. These traditional factors remain important but they are no longer the final word on project success. In trying to understand upfront what will make a project a 'success' we will be able to understand, at the close of the project and/or throughout the life of the outcomes and deliverables, whether the project has done what was originally envisaged and whether it was money well spent.

An emerging trend is the tangible and non-tangible value that the project delivers to the client. Does value involve managing a particularly disparate set of stakeholders who all have their own particular view of 'success'? Perhaps it is bringing a new product to market fast to beat competitors, or the construction of an architectural showpiece to demonstrate innovation and collaboration. This, then, is 'success' as determined by the client whether they sit within the project organization or externally. Increasingly, project value is determined by the 'recipient' (or client), not the 'provider'. In short, 'success' is no longer purely a technical delivery or financial consideration. It can be measured in a variety of different ways by looking at benefits realization and earned value, and at outcomes as well as outputs.

Success is judged at a point in time based on what is reasonably known at that point. This means that the notion of 'success' can change as the project matures and more is known about its impact and take-up; similarly, during

The UK Forestry Commission use the concept of 'the triple bottom line' to help articulate the benefits and success factors of woodland planning and particular forestry projects, and to help provide a decision support model. The triple bottom line is a concept that takes into account benefits to society, the environment and the economy. Specifically, it recognizes that commercial objectives and the more traditional time, cost, quality considerations of projects should not be to the detriment of these other goals. So, for example, a woodland creation project would generate direct economic benefits (commercial forestry) and environmental benefits (flood mitigation for communities, water quality management, bio-diversity, carbon sink) as well as social benefits (access to woodland, health and wellbeing). In this the Forestry Commission is pioneering work to account for costs and benefits, not just in financial terms, but in terms of their impact on 'natural capital'. Another example, that of building a new public lavatory block for visitors to Forestry Commission land which costs around £500K, might struggle to provide a recognizable return on investment!

One of the characteristics of forestry projects in general is the extended time horizon: it can take up to 40 years for a newly planted forest to reach commercial maturity. Similarly, urban regeneration projects look at an extended time horizon for environmental and local economic improvement. In both cases, benefits and outcomes are tracked long after the completion of the project delivery.

its use and impact in-life and afterwards when decommissioning. This also means that the notion of 'success' can be affected by changes in the business environment. Wembley Stadium was late and over budget, but its 'success' is in the long-term benefit as the national football arena and major gig and event venue.

Flyvbjerg, Bruzelius and Rothengatter (2003) talk about the paradox of the multibillion-dollar mega-infrastructure projects, their complexity and their record of strikingly poor performance records in terms of environmental impact and public support. Yet these mega-projects in transport, telecommunications and energy are often seen as enabling people, goods, energy, money and information to move about easily so making geography and distance less important.

So there is a challenge in reconciling different ideas of 'success' and the various competing needs of different stakeholder groups. We know project leaders who use negotiation techniques under these circumstances, focusing on interests rather than positions because positional bargaining limits the ability to arrive at a wise agreement (Fisher, Ury and Patten, 2012).

8.4   Defining Success Criteria

Success criteria are used by stakeholders to judge how well you are doing. Understanding the different bases for their judgments will stand you in good stead, for they are rarely as simple as they seem. Examples of different benefits for different stakeholders are shown in Figure 8.3:

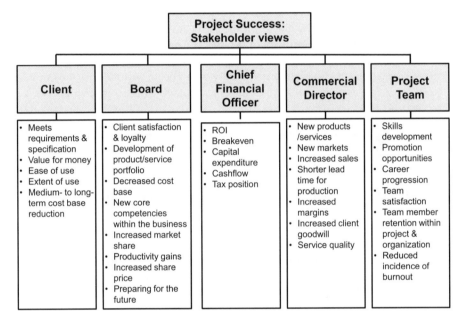

Figure 8.3   Different stakeholder views of project success criteria

Project type can also have an impact. Concrete and open projects, as described in Chapter 3, are discussed in Figure 8.4 overleaf.

Regardless of the type of project, hard commercial and technical criteria are, of course, important. However, they are rarely the final word and should not be used as the exclusive basis for judging success. They may not be the basis of assessment when matters are less straightforward.

Hard success criteria tend to relate to *what* is done. These are the more tangible, quantitative and easily measureable criteria such as:

- deadlines;
- performance specifications;
- service levels;
- specific quality standards;

Concrete projects. Here, the project value and success criteria can be clearly defined. For example, the development of a new aircraft to meet specific operational requirements.

Open projects. Here, the purpose of the project may be to define a desirable output. So, the main success criteria are likely to be the desires/ambitions of the individual stakeholders, which cannot necessarily be measured at the outset. For example, a project team set up to investigate alternative business plans.

Figure 8.4   Project type impacting project success criteria

- cost requirements;
- resource usage.

In comparison, soft success criteria relate more to *how* it is done. These are the more intangible and qualitative criteria. For example, you must demonstrate:

- a cooperative attitude;
- a positive image;
- total quality;
- total project commitment;
- an appreciation of the level of risk involved;
- ethical conduct.

Soft and less easily measured criteria of the project can be more important than the hard and easily measured criteria. You might be installing a computer system for a company; it works very effectively, and is delivered on time and within budget. However, if it is not user-friendly the take-up will not be as planned so the client will not derive maximum value and be satisfied: here, the project will not be a 'success' regardless of the fact it came in on time and to budget. It is part of the job of a project leader to 'tease out' such soft criteria in discussion with the client and end users at the start of the project.

High standards in the less tangible areas associated with both products and services have become crucial to an organization's competitive edge. As a result, soft criteria are not just 'nice to have' extras, but are now seen as essential elements of success. The concept of a 'balanced scorecard' (Kaplan and Norton, 1993) is mainstream to business and industry, and is increasingly being used for projects. It goes beyond traditional measures of financial performance and is used to align the project to the Vision and strategy of the organization, improve communications and monitor perception of the project as well as performance against objectives.

For project leaders, it is extremely important to discover what the success criteria are. Stakeholders will have a set of 'visible' criteria, but you'll still need to check these to make sure they are realistic. They may also have criteria that are 'implicit' but that they have not thought to express and, finally, 'latent' criteria. This last group can be the most challenging because, although the stakeholders aren't consciously aware of them at the start of the project, they will help inform their view of the project once completed.

Interviewing and questioning will enable you to clarify what is in scope and out of scope for the project so that only realistic success criteria relevant to the outputs, outcomes and deliverables of the project are identified and accepted. Table 8.2 expresses this:

Table 8.2   Obvious and less obvious success criteria

	'Hard' success criteria	'Soft' success criteria
Success criteria in the open (Visible) Declared, visible, openly discussed by all parties	Examples: Performance specifications Service level agreements Time Budget Financial return Contractual terms and conditions Delivery terms and quality	Examples: How the project is controlled Review meetings Escalation procedures Communication and feedback
Success criteria under the table (Implicit) Influential but withheld deliberately, undeclared by oversight or not usually discussed	Examples: 'Real' budget constraints that are arising or foreseeable: • delivery dates • resource availability	Examples: Political concerns: • 'don't rock the boat' • 'if anything goes wrong you're on your own' • 'don't reduce my visibility with top managers'
Success criteria which may emerge (Latent) Initially unknown by both parties, but should be dealt with positively when they emerge	Examples: New options arise from practical events and experience The unexpected enforces different constraints Crises as 'Acts of God' Future-proofing the organization	Examples: Risks too large for the client personally Outcomes from joint participants' days of problem solving

Success criteria are also used by you and your team for greater transparency and granularity of the project by providing the basis for performance measurement using benefit realization (Bradley, 2006) and earned value management (APM, 2013) during the delivery phase, handover and beyond.

Finally, once a project has been given the go-ahead, it tends to attract interest from other parties and their requirements simply because it has agreed budget, support and traction. Don't allow stakeholders to hang requirements and expectations onto the project that don't belong.

Conclusions

All projects are set within the context of the organization and the wider context of the market and economy, and are intended to contribute to the strategic purpose of the organization. The project leader needs to understand the trends and external pressures influencing the Big Picture in order to focus the project's intended impact and to be able to develop the project Vision to help articulate what it aims to do and to promote buy-in and support.

Project success and failure is related to the stakeholders' perceptions of the value created, especially the perceptions of the client and the organization. Therefore understanding and defining visible, implicit and latent success criteria for the project is one of the key roles for the project leader. 'Success' is no longer purely about the technical delivery or financial return. The variety of tangible and non-tangible criteria need to be identified during the early stages of the project to be able to judge success at the close and beyond.

Key Questions

We suggest you run through your current project and ask:

- How does your project help support your organizational strategy and the client's strategy?
- What is your project's Vision and how was it developed?
- Looking to the future, when your project has successfully completed, how will the client make use of it?
- What are the visible, implicit and latent success criteria you are dealing with in your current project?

References

Association for Project Management (APM) (2013) *Earned Value Management Handbook* Association for Project Management, Princes Risborough, UK.

Bradley, G. (2006) *Benefit Realisation Management* Gower Publishing, Farnham, UK.

Dounreay Site Restoration Limited video, www.dounreay.com/news-room/dounreay-tv/future-vision, accessed 3 November 2014.

Fisher, R., Ury, W. and Patten, B. (2012) *Getting to YES: Negotiating an Agreement without Giving In* RH Business Books.

Flyvbjerg, B., Bruzelius, N. and Rothengatter, W. (2003) *Megaprojects and Risk: An Anatomy of Ambition* Cambridge University Press, Cambridge, UK.

Johnson, G., Scholes, K. and Wittington R. (2008) *Exploring Corporate Strategy (8th edition)* Pearson Education Limited, Harlow, UK.

Kaplan, R.S. and Norton, D.P. (1993) *The Balanced Scorecard: Translating Strategy into Action* Harvard Business School Press, Boston, MA.

Shenhar, A.J., Dvir, D., Levy O. and Maltz. A.C. (2001) 'Project success: A multidimensional strategic concept', *Long Range Planning* 34, 699–725.

CHAPTER 9
Building Key Relationships

All the world's a stage,
And all the men and women merely players;
They have their exits and their entrances,
And one man in his time plays many parts …
> *William Shakespeare (As You Like It', Act II, Scene VII)*

Introduction

Chapter 9 looks at how to identify the range of stakeholders for the project, how to identify the various attributes that make particular stakeholders important to the project, how to recognize the key players, and develop and maintain strong relationships with them. These key players have one thing in common: their ability to make your project a success or a failure. You need to bring them on board and harness their power.

In Chapter 4 we looked at mapping stakeholders. Here, we look at specific individuals or groups, the 'key players', who are critical to the project because of the role they play and the support they can provide throughout the life of the project. These are the stakeholders whose perspectives you need to understand, and with whom you will need to build strong relationships. The three key players we'll focus on here are the:

- project sponsor;
- client;
- project team.

Relationship-building is one of the key elements of the project leader's role. Research continues to highlight that a key element of project success involves proactive management of stakeholders and their expectations. Just like your own personal relationships, these relationships are not static but dynamic. As such they need active and continued review, reappraisal and renegotiation.

This chapter also shows you how to navigate your way through the power bases and politics within the organization and how to develop your 'organizational intelligence'.

9.1   The Project Leader and Relationships

An extremely useful and often the most undervalued resource you and your team can have is the positive support of your colleagues throughout the organization. This will stand you in good stead later in whatever project bargaining, negotiating, persuading and jockeying for resources and support you need to undertake. Organizations often have a portfolio of projects in progress at any one time and, as a result, it is not unusual to have to argue your case for resources regardless of what has been agreed and signed off upfront. These resources can range from personnel, expertise, budget and technology through to capital equipment and even the resource of time (for example, being given the opportunity to brief senior managers). Raising resources and holding on to them is often a political problem in which the project's credibility rating is important. Both you and your project's reputation for being effective will help you in securing official and unofficial resources, otherwise your bargaining power will be weak.

Positive support is earned through building strong relationships, credibility and trust within the organization. This can all take time, energy and patience. Often you can build this faster by referring to your track record and past successes within the organization, but moving into a new role in a new organization or working as a freelance or interim project leader can mean you are starting with a blank sheet of paper.

We can all identify situations where we were surprised by the support we received, either more or less support than expected. One groundwork's contractor on a large construction project explained to us that during a particular project critical works were identified towards the end of a week that would have brought the project to a halt unless they were completed over the weekend. The project leader had built up a strong and trusted relationship with the contracts manager, primarily through being open on commercial matters (there were often challenges in paying for all additional works) and doing '... on the whole, what I said I would do to help them deliver on their commercial commitments. They took a risk in mobilizing nearly their full workforce to carry out the works when there was no formal and fully costed agreement as to what they would receive for the works. My commitment to them was that I would do everything in my power to ensure they were appropriately rewarded for helping the project progress. They trusted that I could deliver on my word, given they had taken a risk for me'.

So, you and your team members have to build your credits with the organization. One of the best ways of doing this is to understand the perspectives of your senior management, sponsor and other key stakeholders. What will convince them that your project is not only well led but that it is in good health and will be successful? Is it keeping within the traditional budget, time and quality parameters or other identified success criteria?

Having the business acumen, showing that you understand the implications of the project within the context of what is happening within the organization, sector or market, and appreciating the perspectives of key stakeholders help to demonstrate that you are worthy of confidence and support. This can make it easier to push for what you need. At times, however, you may need to push very hard to secure something that's critical to your project and, in doing so, make yourself very unpopular in some quarters. Changes set in motion by projects stimulate political and power dynamics; and dealing with these is part of the project leader's job.

9.2   Introducing Stakeholders

Why are stakeholders so important to the project leader? Stakeholders are those individuals or groups who have an interest in, a role in or are impacted by what you are doing or what you propose to do. Simply put, you need to be able to understand who they are and develop communication and relationships with them to ensure you have their continued support and buy-in.

We looked at stakeholder mapping in Chapter 4, in order to understand who they are. Identifying the project's stakeholders will enable you to prioritize them and develop an appropriate engagement strategy and communications plan: a 'one-size-fits-all' plan of communication and engagement will not suit all stakeholders, and insisting on this may actively alienate them. Prioritizing them ensures their needs and expectations are understood and actively managed throughout the life of the project, which in turn allows you to build credibility and support for the project. How we work with our stakeholders, communicate with them and relate to them is often described as 'stakeholder management'. However, we would argue that instead of simply 'managing' them, the project leader needs to work to actively engage them to build support and commitment.

Identifying and engaging with particular stakeholder groups from the early project activities throughout the lifecycle can also provide you with some insight that you may not have otherwise considered. The more you talk to them, the more you'll find out about what else is going on that could potentially impact your project; for example, helping you identify new risks. Actively engage your stakeholders and manage their expectations, and they are more likely to view your project as a success than those stakeholders who have been ignored. They are also less likely to reject deliverables for not meeting their standards because they will have been involved in the scoping of the project, the setting of success criteria, performance and service levels, and the production, testing and checking of deliverables. Tapping into your stakeholders' skills and interest in the project can also provide additional and extended team members, often for no cost.

It is worth stating that stakeholders are also dynamic in that their relevance, significance, impact and influence on the project can change throughout the lifecycle. As such, stakeholders and relationships need regular review, reappraisal and renegotiation throughout the project. They may change roles and responsibilities, they may need to pay more attention to other projects, or perhaps the project has progressed to a point where their input and support is no longer required. In effect, their relative importance may fluctuate throughout the project lifecycle. Just as risks are identified up front and reviewed throughout the project lifecycle, the same attention will be required for stakeholders. This is about identifying the right stakeholders for the right time of the project lifecycle and developing an appropriate engagement and communications strategy in response. It also relies on the project leader and the team having the personal qualities necessary to build and maintain relationships with the stakeholders identified.

9.3   Ranking Stakeholders

A project's stakeholders are potentially a large and diverse group. How do you rank, rate and define those who will be your champions and advocates, those who will be your detractors and those who you need to spend time with to build credibility and support? A good first step is to brainstorm with your project team members, sponsor and perhaps with one or two other interested parties by looking *upwards*, *downwards, inwards, outwards* and *sideways* to decide who the various stakeholders in the project might be and to share knowledge and experiences about them.

The next step is to identify 'mutuality' (French and Granrose, 1995) in order to understand what each stakeholder wants from the project as well as the significance of the stakeholder to the project. Understanding this helps formulate relationship-building as well as relevant communication plans (see Figure 9.1).

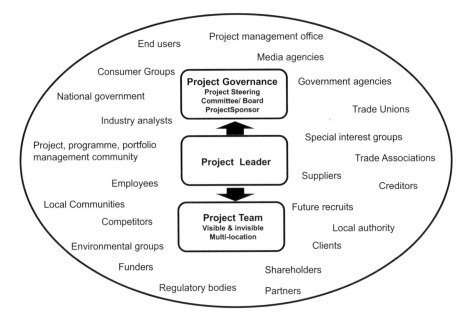

Figure 9.1   Identifying stakeholders

At a basic level stakeholders are divided into:

- 'Primary' stakeholders (key players) are those who have direct impact on the project by virtue of their roles and responsibilities, legal obligation or authority to manage and commit resources. They can reside inside or outside your organization. These are typically the project sponsor, project team, client, functional managers, main suppliers and partners.
- 'Secondary' stakeholders are those who have a strong interest in the project and its outcomes even though they may have no formal or contractual relationship with it. These individuals and groups may be unions, shareholders, other employees, the media, environmentalists, other clients and consumer groups.

Understanding the positions held by the stakeholders you have identified can help you predict their behaviour to understand who will champion and support the project, who will be neutral and who will actively seek to disrupt it for their own reasons. This, in turn, can help you identify who can help you move the project forward. Equally, it can also help you understand which individuals or groups you shouldn't upset or exclude. We typically use the following attributes to highlight stakeholders' relative importance:

- Influence: how much are they able to affect the behaviours and actions of others to impact the project?
- Attitude: are they a supporter, neutral or a detractor of the project?
- Power: is their ability to get what they want done significant or relatively limited?
- Interest: are they paying close attention to the project or is it an unwelcome distraction?
- Proximity: are they closely associated with the project or relatively remote?
- Urgency: are they prepared to go to any length to achieve their outcomes? How critical and time-urgent is the project to these stakeholders?

We can rate stakeholders against these six attributes using a scale of 1 to 10. If any of the attributes are of particular importance to the project, they can be weighted so demonstrating their importance relative to the other attributes. The assessment of each stakeholder based on these ratings then produces a total for each, so providing a priority rating for building stakeholder relationships and an indication of where you need to pay particular attention (see Table 9.1).

Table 9.1   Rating stakeholders

	Influence	Attitude	Power	Interest	Proximity	Urgency
Stakeholder 1	(weighted) rating 1–10					
Stakeholder 2						
Stakeholder 3						
Stakeholder 4						
Stakeholder 5						

An example of how this can be presented is given in Figure 9.2.

You are also in a position to devise your strategies for winning over particular stakeholders or trying to reduce their impact on the project where necessary. So, for example, knowing that a particular stakeholder has a huge influence on, but a negative attitude towards, your project allows you to consider ways of

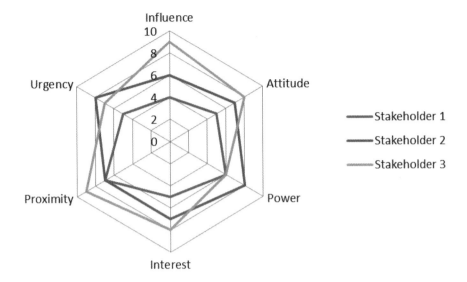

Figure 9.2   Diagrammatic output from rating stakeholders

mitigating this situation that are specifically relevant to that stakeholder: would you consider addressing their concerns directly to get them on side, or perhaps you could work to reduce their influence over the project in some way. Finally, this type of assessment provides a basis on which to plan communications across stakeholders during the project lifecycle.

We ask some fundamental questions in relation to stakeholders:

- Who stands to gain most from this project?
- Who stands to lose most from this project?
- Who are our most important stakeholders?
- Are there any stakeholders who we need to move their positions in terms of influence, interest, attitude, power, proximity or urgency? How will we do this?

From this, we are able to spot potential advocates early and to identify potential conflict, confusion and hostility.

One organization we know of in the property development sector approaches this in a slightly different manner, dividing stakeholders into:

- those in contract, for example the client, partners, subcontractors, project team;
- those in contact, for example the media, local government.

Of the project stakeholders, the key players are typically the project sponsor, the client and the project team by virtue of the fact they each have a particular impact on the project's success.

9.4   The Project Sponsor

The term 'sponsor' is used to identify the individual who is, or individuals who are, the primary beneficiary of the project. The aim, as with all project relationships, is to ensure the sponsor and the project leader work together in partnership for the good of the project towards mutually beneficial objectives.

9.4.1   THE SPONSOR'S ROLE

Projects can certainly succeed without sponsors but it can be a painful, stressful and thankless task if there is no one around to clear the path, navigate the way through organizational politics and champion the project at senior levels. James, Rosenhead and Taylor (2013) describe the sponsor as ' ... the person in the organization who cares most about the project and its success. At least she should be'. As such, the sponsor has executive oversight and responsibility for the project, provides an interface between the project and the organization and may be the primary contact for the client. The sponsor's role is often misunderstood by sponsors and project leaders alike, so it needs to be made explicit. What do you need from your sponsor, what can you expect from them and, in return, what will you provide them?

The sponsor has a difficult position between the project team and the client. It is a balancing act. In their middle position, the sponsor has to look in two or three directions, including outwards to the client. The client may be internal or external, but the sponsor's task is the same: to help define the organizational impact of the project in the context of the Big Picture. Sponsors need to sense changes or shifts of emphasis that will influence the project, especially if it is highly visible. This means heavy involvement in the project in the early stage of scoping. During the start-up and delivery phases it means internal marketing, managing the politics, door-opening, networking and problem solving to make sure that the organizational climate around the project is healthy. The inward-looking facet of the sponsor's role is to ensure that the project leader understands the project's Vision, how it fits with the organizational Vision and strategy, and that he/she anticipates the shifting goal-posts, scoping and re-scoping when necessary.

Organizations sometimes struggle to find a single person to be the 'unblocker': that person, who owns the business case, can be the business conscience and make things happen for the project. Leadership and managing the expectations of the sponsor are two pivotal skills for the project leader and although The Standish Group's 2012 CHAOS report suggests that collaboration between the sponsor and project manager is essential, only 12 per cent of chief information officer respondents considered their project managers to be highly skilled at bonding with the sponsor.

9.4.2   BUILDING THE RELATIONSHIP

Once the sponsor is assigned to your project, how do you manage upwards to encourage your sponsor to do what the project needs? Do you understand their commercial and strategic perspective? How do you have the important conversation with them that confirms your respective roles, responsibilities and accountability so that you can ensure all bases are covered but that there is no duplication of effort? Remember not all project sponsors come from a project management background, so don't assume they will understand project processes or terminology.

> *Completing the Eight Lookings Diagnostic will provide you with an indication of how much of your focus is on:*
>
> - *Looking upwards – the sponsor;*
> - *Looking outwards – the client.*

If this is a sponsor who is new to you, what do you know about them? Talk to others who might have worked with them in the past to find out what the sponsor is like as a person, what experience they have, what their management style is and how they like to be kept informed. Do they prefer a quick chat after close of day, or a formal progress report on a weekly basis? By virtue of the fact that sponsors are senior within the organization, their available time is at a premium. How can you make it easy for them to be updated and to continue to be involved?

It is also worth asking yourself: 'What do I need from my sponsor to enable me to be successful in this project?' Your first meeting should establish the rules of play between the two of you, which continue throughout the whole project. In the meeting, focus the discussion on both your and the sponsor's views of:

- the type of project and the risks expected;
- how the project should be run;
- conflicting priorities with other work;
- 'what if' scenarios to agree how to handle things;
- what you want from each other, such as information, support, meetings, early warning signals;
- which of you should do and be accountable for what in the project.

To do this the project leader needs to use plenty of open and probing questions to make any underlying assumptions transparent. This is a dialogue, a two-way conversation; you are not receiving instructions. Watch how the sponsor reacts: are there non-verbal clues that indicate hesitation, lack of real agreement or discomfort? What lies behind these responses? Finally, summarize verbally, or if necessary in writing, what has been agreed, what is left open for further discussion or what requires additional information. With open projects there may be several phases of clarification and weighing of alternatives before decisions are reached. This ambiguity can cause unease because it appears that no progress is being made, but it is a most important step, as collaboration starts here through clear and common understanding. You are in it together, for better or worse.

One approach that we have used in the past to great benefit is to run through a series of scenarios based around the specifics of the project. The risk register can be a rich source of scenarios. Each scenario can be discussed either informally over a coffee or formally in a workshop between the project leader, sponsor, project team members and other stakeholders and the responses discussed. This may provide you with comfort that support will be available when necessary, or it may raise alarm bells about who will be watching your back when challenges arise. When they do arise and relationships are tested, a positive response will build trust.

> While working with a UK government department we had the opportunity to facilitate a number of these types of discussions. Set up primarily as part of the risk management process and contingency planning, the underlying (and arguably more important) purpose was to build relationships and trust between project and programme leaders and their sponsors. This was done early on in the lifecycle when there was uncertainty regarding

not only what needed to be done but also how it would be achieved. By discussing how each scenario would be perceived and most likely dealt with by each of the parties, insights were gained and approaches developed that would be invaluable later in the project, especially when there was not the time take a reflective approach. Most people found the experience positive although we can remember one discussion that ended up in conflict due to disagreement about the approach to be taken. Fortunately this was resolved after identifying that what were initially perceived as differences were, after in-depth discussions, simply differences in style. Agreement was reached once both parties understood the same outcome would be achieved.

Sponsors tell us two fundamental things about their relationship with a project leader. Firstly, that they need to be able to trust the project leader: trust that what the project leader tells them mirrors what is actually happening. Secondly, that they definitely don't enjoy surprises even if the message is hard to deliver. They want to be told bad news as soon as possible so that they can deal with the politics of the problem before they overtake them. This also allows them to prepare alternative ways forward to replan or renegotiate outcomes in a calmer atmosphere, rather than tense panic. They want to hear news from the source (in other words, from you as the project leader) rather than hear the news in a C-suite meeting where there is scope to be professionally embarrassed.

9.4.3   CONTACT WITH THE SPONSOR

We have noticed that both sponsors and project leaders think that their contact with each other should be minimized. Frequent meetings can imply failure, or that there are many issues that need to be resolved. Unfortunately, infrequent contact is only appropriate for low-visibility projects or where the project leader and sponsor have worked together frequently for a long time. In these cases the project initiation process may be rapid, based on past success and much joint experience. An arm's-length relationship will make any high-visibility project more risky for both the sponsor and project leader. Indeed, it may jeopardize the whole project.

Both parties have to work together and it helps to see the perspectives of the sponsor and project manager as complementary. There will be some areas of specifically separate responsibilities, and other areas where they overlap. In those overlapping areas, they have to decide together what to do and how to do it. In organizations where projects are the way work is routinely delivered, sponsors often take a hands-off position because they assume that the established procedures for project management should cope with everything except a significant disruption. However, the trend towards more open, smaller projects that are more volatile means that there is a need for a much closer working relationship, and closer working relationships help to break down barriers and decrease any negative perceptions such as those shown in Table 9.2.

Table 9.2   Relative negative perceptions of the project sponsor and the project leader

Sponsors' negative perceptions of the project leader	Project leaders' negative perceptions of sponsors
• Promoted technical specialists who don't understand how the organization works or who have no commercial acumen • Talk technical and detail, without seeing the Big Picture and understanding the impact on the organization and its position in the market • Assume the sponsor should know everything by virtue of their seniority and reach within the organization	• Sponsor should know what they want and be able to articulate their requirements • Sponsors don't acknowledge the effort involved in scoping and delivery • Change their minds without understanding the impact to the project • Over-involvement: always there, a 'micro-manager' or 'super project manager' • Under-involvement: absent, invisible, doesn't choose to engage or provide support

9.5   The Client

The client is another key player for the project leader. In some projects, the primary relationship with the client rests with the sponsor but the project leader will still need to build a relationship. This means that you may need to have the same type of discussions with the client around roles, responsibilities, scenarios, contact and communication as you have had with your sponsor.

We talk about 'the client' whether internal to the organization or external, and whether an individual or a steering group comprising a number of individuals. In the latter instance it is usual to nominate an individual to be a single point of contact for, and liaise with, the project leader and the project directly. There is often the assumption that the client will remain the same individual throughout the project lifecycle but, of course, this is not necessarily the case especially for long-term projects. As a further dimension, the client may be located in a different country and different culture. Despite recent moves to align weekends, a Middle Eastern client may require Saturday and Sunday availability to align with their own working week. A Chinese or Russian client may anticipate their contractors working 16–18 hours a day to fulfil their requirements.

A recent trend has been to look at defining what makes an 'intelligent client', understanding that the delivery of successful projects requires particular behaviours from both client and provider. Typically this term is used to describe an organization rather than an individual but the characteristics can be applied to both. It is a call for clients across all industry sectors to be more informed when involved with the procurement and management of work with providers. Maylor and Johnson's work (2009) looking at outsourcing and programme success showed that the idea of the 'intelligent client' is not in contrast to individuals acting 'stupidly'. Instead, it is about the overall effect of corporate policies, systems and attitudes which impact the way in which a client behaves, acts and builds relationships with their providers. This is important to the project leader because it is also about the way in which a client imposes structure or controls on a project: this can range from the use of a particular project management methodology through to particular technology or behaviours. Clients are measured by their own management and it is well understood that measurement drives behaviour. An 'intelligent client' isn't arrogant and doesn't expect their purchasing power to dictate and run roughshod over the project. After all, outsourcing or contracting to other parties is in itself recognition that the client organization doesn't have the skill set and/or capacity to do what is needed.

In our own work with ICT outsourcing, it is quite usual for a client to believe that once a service is outsourced they can relinquish responsibility for it, expect minimal input and a consistently excellent service. Effectively, they believe they are handing off the risk to the provider. This approach is starkly at odds with the £4.5Bn Heathrow Terminal 5 programme being delivered on time and to budget. The phrase 'BAA (the former British Airports Authority – owners of London Heathrow) owns all of the risk, all of the time' was used to describe their approach, which was to take risk away from the supply chain and use pooled benefits to encourage the shared exploitation of opportunities. This was a radical departure from what is still conventional practice and shifted the focus from damage limitation to a search for the best way to get the required benefits delivered.

All this helps us to understand the different possible relationship dynamics between the project leader and the client. Project leaders often describe to us their different experiences of their clients. The word 'trust' often comes up, or more specifically lack of it. One of the most significant causes of delay and disruption to projects is the client themselves; in some instances this is due to clients not turning around documentation, decisions or sign-offs within agreed timescales. In other instances the client tries to micro-manage the project, or the relationship is adversarial which impacts behaviours. However, other project leaders describe very different experiences where their clients make sure there is transparency, reciprocity, sharing of good practice and pooling of opportunities to make efficiencies.

From our conversations with the project community, we've identified various aspects of the client–provider relationship:

- An intelligent client should fully understand and define their requirements from the project. They should also make explicit their role, responsibilities and accountability in relation to the project. They should select the provider competitively and fairly and reward through incentivized contracts, then support the provider and enforce the contract fairly during the project.
- An (emotionally) intelligent client has to understand their own behaviours, how that impacts on others and builds trust.
- The client's own bias and organizational culture can impact a project. For example, a particular risk appetite; the desire for, or avoidance of, new techniques; the drive for innovation through the project processes.

One form of relationship becoming more common is 'partnering' which is increasingly seen as desirable due to the implied equality of the relationship it creates; so far in this book the project leader has taken the role of a 'supplier' rather than a 'partner'. Originally used in the automotive sector, the term 'partnering' is now used extensively across industry sectors to describe a particular form of relationship between buyers/clients and providers. This is more than a simple economic relationship, especially where the project is of strategic importance to the client. Here, a relationship develops which both sides want to be 'satisfying', hence the introduction of the term 'partnering'. The problem is that all too often the relationship is abusive and frequently mutually so. Many providers talk wryly about 'like partnering, but with teeth' to describe the fact that much of their work is still run to contract and that initial action, rather than final action, can be recourse (or threat of recourse) to legal action.

Of course as a project leader, you may also be a client to a provider to your own project. Are you an 'intelligent client' in your own right?

9.6   The Project Team

At the most basic level, the essence of leadership is the ability to create a willing and sustained following: to create in others the desire to want to share the same journey and purpose. This view of leadership is about creating connections, engaging hearts and minds, and building trusted relationships. Contrast this with leadership through delegated authority or organizational hierarchy, which is really about control and compliance.

Part 2 describes in depth the project leader's relationship and work with the visible and invisible project team across the project lifecycle, from the early stages of assembling the project team in the initial stages of the project through to coordinating effort, ensuring the project team is on track with delivery, addressing concerns and monitoring performance of the team, to handover and facilitating the exit of team members at closure of the project. An added dimension is that team members come and go as needed: they come into the project and exit at various points during the lifecycle because their particular skill set is needed at a particular point. Welcoming these new team members and getting them up to speed and getting them to be effective is important, as is letting them go once their role is completed and their skills are no longer needed. As project leader, it is your responsibility to take a changing set of individuals diverse in skills, experience, motivation and location and to develop them into a high-performing team that can effectively and constantly deliver.

Rocky Flats, Denver, USA has been described as 'America's most dangerous nuclear weapons production facility' (Cameron and Lavine, 2006), producing plutonium and enriched uranium triggers for nuclear weapons from 1959 to 1989. The site consisted of around 800 buildings located in 6,000 acres. It became the largest and most complex environmental clean-up project in America's history, and was the first nuclear weapons facility to be decommissioned and closed anywhere in the world. The contract was won in 1995 by Kaiser-Hill and the entire project was completed 60 years early at a cost saving of approximately $30 billion in taxpayer funds.

The project's success was explained by a number of factors: the revolutionary nature of the Vision ('to change the place, we had to create a Vision and mission that the old culture and the old work processes could not achieve'), the removal of old symbols and the creation of new, culture change and embracing new ideas and innovation. Not least, their stakeholder engagement 'intentionally focused on good labor relations' and their other constituencies. One senior manager reinforced the idea that the 'right' people were required to achieve the closure and clean-up objectives: the 'right' people willing to engage, to work consensually and to support one another. The project acknowledged they had personnel who were resistant to change. 'we just mixed them in with the others, and social pressure took care of them.'

Specifically, how did the project succeed with a work force, as part of the wider project team, which had been at the site for many years (some second generation) which were part of a strong community and which were effectively making themselves redundant?

Downsizing was part of the mission so all employees knew that they would eventually lose their jobs. The answer lay in shifting the focus from worker employment to worker employability.

The contractors took on the responsibility of assisting laid-off employees to find employment locally, within the state and with the company elsewhere. They provided training and education, and access to training and education, advertised the skills and capabilities of soon-to-be-available employees, and organized job fairs to bring potential employers to the site. They allowed workers to negotiate the timing of their departure, so helping them retain key benefits and accommodate the transition to new employment. All these measures helped make a difficult transition for these members of the wider project team occur more successfully and led to high commitment among the wider project team who remained at the site.

Source: Cameron and Levine, 2006

9.7   Organizational Intelligence

As a project leader, although you have the accountability and responsibility to produce results you cannot rely exclusively on a formal hierarchical position. Your position is validated by virtue of the project, your project sponsor and the project governance committee. This puts a premium on being able to make sense of the power bases, politics, networks and relationships within your own organization and within other organizations, such as the client's and any key providers'. It is this ability that is paramount to being 'organizationally intelligent'. It is not just about being able to identify and target stakeholder support and commitment; it is also about understanding how decisions are made, who the gatekeepers are, who has access to the resources we need and when we are ourselves the target of political game playing.

Being organizationally intelligent demonstrates a professional and personal maturity. It enables you to move and work easily and confidently across all areas of the organization, to build influence and support at all levels of the organization, from the C-suite to operational levels, and to be able to 'read' the situation and make it work to your own and your project's advantage.

9.7.1   NETWORKING AND ORGANIZATIONAL NETWORKING

Projects always herald change. They create disturbances at personal, departmental and organizational levels so there will always be unexpected realignments to be negotiated and tried out. Some people will lose out, some will resist and some will change easily but there will always be a complex web of new or different relationship patterns to be unravelled if the project is to be successfully implemented and adopted with sustained impact.

Hastings (1993) describes the purpose of networking as breaking down boundaries and creating quick and open person-to-person communications. Just as networking helps to develop mutual support and collaboration for an individual, organizational networking helps to break down barriers and develop collaboration between individuals and functional and other groups, both inside and outside the organization.

Experience and research suggest that increasing the range, scope and volume of collaboration between individuals at different levels, across different functions and across organizational boundaries brings great advantage. An important feature of projects is that they form, dissolve and reform, bringing together people preferably because of what they can contribute, rather than because of who they are. Organizational networking is about removing boundaries and barriers, creating a web of links and contacts between individuals in order to get things done, so supporting these project dynamics.

At a time when organizations are increasingly driving productivity improvements, much of the effort has resulted in leaner and flatter organizations. This means that more emphasis is being placed on collaboration and matrix working across functions and divisions. Matrix working, multifunctional and multi-located teams hold no surprises for those of us who have worked for many years in project environments; however, it does highlight the need to build relationships, recognize and use our bases of power, exercise influence, collaborate and build alliances with others to achieve results.

9.7.2   POWER AND POLITICS

Power and politics within organizations and how they impact projects are rarely talked about. They often carry negative connotations and are considered predatory, unsavoury and focused on self-interest (Coleman, 2013), but at the same time we recognize the benefit of someone who understands and can use organizational politics and power structures effectively for the success of the project. Pfeffer (1993) describes politics as the 'art of using influence, authority and power to achieve goals' and, in its crudest form, 'power' is defined as the ability to get someone to do something you want done, or the ability to make things happen in the way you want.

However you view them, they are a part of organizational life and strongly impact the way projects operate, since many of the important decisions in organizations involve the allocation of scarce resources (typically personnel, expertise, budget, technology and capital equipment). As such, this again puts the spotlight on the project leader's ability to build relationships, recognize and use their bases of power, use influence, and collaborate and build alliances with others to achieve results not just within their own organization, but also in the client's and suppliers' organizations.

If you cannot avoid involvement in the politics and power plays that projects will set in motion, you need to understand how you currently react to these and how you might respond differently to give you more advantage. Pinto (1996) identified three positions that people typically take when faced with organizational politics: the Naïve, the Political Sensible and the Shark. Each of these has its own view, intent, techniques and favourite tactics (see Table 9.3).

Table 9.3   Three political positions and their view, intent, techniques and favourite tactics

Characteristics	Naïve	Sensible	Shark
Underlying attitude: 'Politics is ... '	Unpleasant	Necessary	An opportunity
Intent	Avoid at all costs	Used to further the team's, project's and department's goals	Self-serving and predatory
Techniques	Tell it like it is	Network, expand connections, use system to give and receive favours	Manipulation, use of fraud and deceit when necessary
Favourite tactics	None, the truth will win out	Negotiation, bargaining	Bullying, misuse of information, cultivate and use 'friends' and other contacts

Source: Reproduced with kind permission of Jeffrey K. Pinto

Of the three positions, the Political Sensible is the one that understands that political behaviour is necessary at times: 'Politically sensible individuals use politics as a way of making contacts, cutting deals, and gaining power and resources for their departments or projects in order to further corporate, rather than entirely personal, ends' (Pinto, 1996). The Political Sensible deliberately uses politics to the benefit of their project so avoiding being a victim of politics themselves and avoiding using politics for their own self-serving ambitions.

9.7.3   ABILITY TO READ POLITICAL DYNAMICS

Baddeley and James (1987) identified guidelines on some aspects of political behaviour (see Figure 9.3). The horizontal dimension (politically aware/lack of political awareness) describes an individual's ability to read the political dynamics of their organization or situation. So, how clearly do you understand and appreciate:

- How informally things are done?
- What decisions are made or avoided?
- What really matters, despite what is publicly said?
- What happens in practice: why do events turn out in a particular way?
- What patterns of behaviour, resisting or enabling, are repeated?
- What are the taboo subjects and undiscussable topics?
- Who are the most powerful or influential voices in the organization?

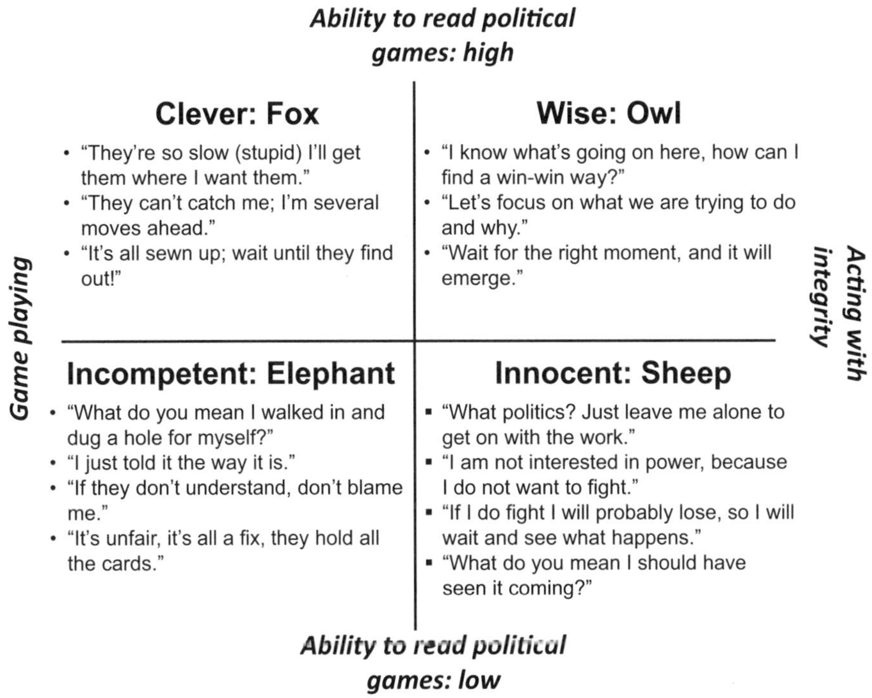

Ability to read political games: high

Clever: Fox

- "They're so slow (stupid) I'll get them where I want them."
- "They can't catch me; I'm several moves ahead."
- "It's all sewn up; wait until they find out!"

Wise: Owl

- "I know what's going on here, how can I find a win-win way?"
- "Let's focus on what we are trying to do and why."
- "Wait for the right moment, and it will emerge."

Incompetent: Elephant

- "What do you mean I walked in and dug a hole for myself?"
- "I just told it the way it is."
- "If they don't understand, don't blame me."
- "It's unfair, it's all a fix, they hold all the cards."

Innocent: Sheep

- "What politics? Just leave me alone to get on with the work."
- "I am not interested in power, because I do not want to fight."
- "If I do fight I will probably lose, so I will wait and see what happens."
- "What do you mean I should have seen it coming?"

Game playing

Acting with integrity

Ability to read political games: low

Figure 9.3   Nature of political dynamics
Source: Adapted from Baddeley and James (1987)

Every organization has its own distinctive answers to these questions. If you are well tuned-in to these dynamics and see what occurs as part of a repeated pattern, not just a chance event aimed randomly at you, then you are in a better position to work out what to do.

The vertical dimension (psychological game playing/acting with integrity) is based on the level of integrity: are you working for the common good of the project, or purely for yourself?

As a result, Baddeley and James identified four distinct political behaviours (Clever, Wise, Incompetent and Innocent), each with its own characteristics and set of behaviours that we might adopt in different situations. We can use this model to reflect on our own behaviour in an organizational context and we can also use it to read the behaviour of others. It is worth noting that these are behaviours and not fixed traits. Why is this important? Simply because it means it is possible to develop 'wise' behaviour by understanding the situation and adapting our reaction to it. So which are you nearest to: the Sheep, Elephant, Fox or Owl (see Table 9.4 opposite)?

9.7.4   IMPROVING YOUR POWER BASE

Typically the project leader's power base is focused on two main sources (French and Raven, 1959; Hersey and Blanchard, 1982):

- Personal power: your relationship with others in the organization.
- Positional power: your position within the organization and hierarchy, providing formal channels of authority within the organization.

As a project leader you will typically have to rely on the former, rather than the latter. So how can you improve your power base? We've already talked extensively about the need to connect with others, to cultivate and continually review good working relationships based on respect, perceived need, obligation and mutuality. Keeping abreast of current thought and good practice in project leadership, project management and your sector will also enable you to build your expertise and so personal credibility and profile within the organization and externally. Find ways to market and promote your project so that team members and stakeholders actively want to be associated with it. Be loud and clear about how and why your project is aligned with the organization's Vision and strategy, so how it benefits the organization. This can put you into a good position to bargain and negotiate for resources and support; it can also provide you the opportunity to promote yourself by establishing a credible reputation and track record.

Table 9.4   Typical behaviours of Sheep, Elephant, Fox or Owl

	Typical behaviour
Sheep: **Innocent**	• Listens but does not hear • Capacity for friendship and loyalty • Open and shares information • Tends to rely on hierarchy and authority • Doesn't network, doesn't build support for own position or team/project • Sticks to ethical, organizational and professional rules • Literal: believes you are powerful if you are right
Elephant: **Incompetent**	• Doesn't listen to others • Sees things as 'either – or' • Not skilled interpersonally: low EI • Inner-goal oriented • Doesn't recognize 'direction', doesn't appreciate political purpose • Plays psychological games but doesn't read those of others • Concerned with own feelings to the exclusion of others'
Fox: **Clever**	• Controlling and manipulative • Interested in power and with associating with focus of power • Unprincipled, inner-goal oriented, not ethical • Likes games involving winners and losers • Aggressive but well-masked: charming manner
Owl: **Wise**	• Aware of purpose • Open, shares information • Negotiates, cooperates and gets support • Not defensive, learns from mistakes, reflects on events • Can cope with being disliked, good interpersonal skills • Excellent listener, aware of others' viewpoints • Sees realities, knows how the formal processes work • Likes win–win situations • In tune with the grapevine

Source: Adapted from Baddeley and James (1987)

As a final word, we don't always recognize our own power or strength in a professional relationship. This is one of the ways in which we unknowingly give away power to someone else. Start looking at what you bring to the organization and project team, and what you bring to the relationships with your key stakeholders.

9.7.5   COLLABORATION

Whereas leadership has traditionally focused on the individual as a leader, leadership is now progressively moving towards the collective efforts of a team. Project leaders will come across new challenges for which they have no experience on which to base decisions. They will look to the specialists in the project team and to their professional networks inside and outside the organization in order to help make the best decision. This means they need to build support across groups, be open to ideas and accept that they won't always have the answer. Successful project leaders recognize that one of their strengths needs to be the ability to integrate their own and others' strengths and capabilities to the full. This is not just about being able to collaborate on a personal level, but also to foster collaboration across the project.

This also means the ability to collaborate across multiple disciplines, the ability to collaborate virtually and multiculturally, and the ability to collaborate across geography and across hierarchy levels to develop a 'cross party constituency of support'. This isn't limited to the immediate project team. It should also extend to the client organization and to delivery partners in order to share knowledge and experience, and to make good decisions. It is generally recognized now that collaborative relationships also lead to better cost and risk management, as well as levels of innovation not normally achieved in a typical client–supplier relationship. Successful relationship-building is key to this.

Conclusion

Stakeholders, and ranking stakeholders according to various attributes, are important to the project leader because of the role they play and the support they can provide throughout the life of the project. Stakeholder relationships are dynamic and, as such, they need review, reappraisal and renegotiation throughout the life of the project. This is about identifying the right stakeholders for the right time of the project lifecycle. Key players are the sponsor, the client and the project team and the successful project leader will prioritize these and actively build collaborative working relationships.

Projects cause change and stimulate power plays and political activity within the organization. This is natural, so the project leader has to learn to read the power and political patterns of the organization, understand their own style and how they respond, as well as being able to use this knowledge in order to negotiate, persuade and network on behalf of the project.

Key Questions

We suggest you run through your current project and ask:

- Stakeholders:
  - Who stands to gain most from this project, and who stands to lose most?
  - How do you currently prioritize your stakeholders and how might you do this in the future to greater benefit?
- Relationship-building: How would you describe your relationship with your:
  - project sponsor;
  - client;
  - project team.
  How would they describe their relationship with you?
- Project sponsor:
  - How does your organization develop and support its own project sponsorship capability?
  - What kinds of projects within your organization are provided with project sponsors?
  - How does your organization measure the success of the role, and of the individual within the role?
  - Can you identify a 'safe' scenario early on in the project that you can use to test the response from the sponsor and those whose support is critical to you and the project's success?
- Organizational intelligence:
  - How would you rate your own organizational intelligence?
  - How well do you recognize the organization intelligence of others? Who do you know who is organizationally intelligent and what can you learn from them that would help you with your own position?
  - Which are you nearest to: the Sheep, Elephant, Fox or Owl? In which situations?
  - How would you describe your personal and positional power? How can you improve your personal and positional power within your organization in order to improve outcomes for a) yourself, b) your project?
  - How do you regard organizational politics? Would others describe you as a Shark, as a Political Sensible or as a Naïve?

References

Baddeley, S. and James, K (1987) *Political Skills Model: Reading and Carrying* Office for Public Management and Ashridge, London, UK.

Cameron, K. and Lavine, M (2006) *Making the Impossible Possible* Berrett-Koehler Publishers Inc, San Francisco, CA.

Coleman, S. (2013) 'Dealing with power and politics', in *Business Analysis and Leadership: Influencing Change*, Pullen, P. and Archer, J. (eds), Kogan Page.

French, J.R.P. and Raven, B (1959) 'The bases of social power', in *Group Dynamics*, Cartwright, D. and Zander, A. (eds), Harper & Row, New York.

French, W.A. and Granrose, J. (1995) *Practical Business Ethics* Prentice Hall, Englewood Cliffs, NJ.

Hastings, C. (1993) *The New Organization: Growing the Culture of Organizational Networking* McGraw-Hill International (UK) Limited, Maidenhead, UK.

Hersey, P. and Blanchard, K.H. (1982) *Management of Organizational Behaviour*, 4th *edition*, Prentice Hall, Upper Saddle River, NJ.

James, V., Rosenhead, R. and Taylor, P. (2013) *Strategies for Project Sponsorship* Management Concepts Press, Tysons Corner, VA.

Maylor, H. and Johnson, M. (2009) *How's Your Outsourcing? The Role of the Intelligent Client in Programme Success* ICPM, Cranfield University, Bedford, UK.

Pfeffer, J. (1993) *Managing with Power: Politics and Influence in Organizations* Harvard Business School Press, Boston, MA.

Pinto, J.K. (1996) *Power & Politics in Project Management* Project Management Institute, Newtown Square, PA.

The Standish Group (2012) *The Year of the Executive Sponsor.*

Communication and Engagement

If you talk to a man in a language he understands, that goes to his head. If you talk to him in his language, it goes to his heart.

Nelson Mandela

Introduction

In Chapter 10 we look at communication and engagement with stakeholders. Project management research and literature continues to tell us that providing a strong narrative, clear articulation of relevant messages through appropriate channels, and welcoming and acting on feedback all help to build understanding of the Vision, Big Picture and benefit of projects in order to align understanding, support and commitment. Yet many project teams still regard communication as peripheral to their role and it is often not planned beyond the launch or start-up activity. It is seen as the tactical 'sending information and stuff out' rather than as a strategic way to ensure common understanding and to manage the image of the project and of the organization; a 'nice to have' if time and the budget permit.

The impact of social media and digital technology on communication and engagement has been transformational not just for multinationals, but for small and medium-sized enterprises, and their project teams. The variety and wealth of traditional and non-traditional channels of communication has expanded to enable us to communicate easily and effectively and to share information real-time across continents.

We also look at project branding and marketing in order to gain support and build credibility for the project, the project team and the project leader.

10.1   Project Leadership, Communication and Engagement

Project leadership is primarily a contact sport: be there and be visible. This is leadership by walking about (apologies to Tom Peters), not being closed away in an office. Even as a project leader sited away from parts of your multi-located team, you don't have to be or need to be remote, especially with the technology currently available.

Your project team, your stakeholders, your client: everyone is watching you and taking their cue from you so be a positive role model. Communication is not just about the content and language we use, it is also about how we say things and convey messages. The benefits of good communication are well understood, particularly when it leads to engagement and active support and commitment. Sinickas (2007) identifies ways of measuring the effectiveness of communication, and of providing evidence of return on investment for communication activities. These can include tracking and monitoring:

- communication activities (messages and channels);
- audience perceptions (knowledge and attitudes);
- changes in behaviours;
- direct financial impact on organizational goals.

However, our typical experience is that much project communication is sparse, often emailing out curt progress updates rather than a way of keeping the project visible and high on the agenda to build trust and confidence, and to raise support. The challenge is that project leaders aren't typically skilled in this area and few projects recognize the benefit of securing sufficient resources to support a communications specialist throughout the life of the project. 'Pushing out information and stuff' is often only a one-way flow, and you ignore or restrict feedback at your peril. This, then, is the difference between broadcasting and dialogue.

10.2   The Value of Communication and Engagement

Communication is as important to the success of projects as it is to the success of day-to-day business, both inside and outside the organization. It is also one of the primary ways to build relationships, engagement and commitment, and it covers a spectrum of ways of getting your message out there. Communication works for the project at both the strategic and the tactical levels:

- Strategic: able to articulate the relevance of the project to the organization's own Vision and strategy; speaks the language of business so is able to position the project within the commercial mindset; is a way of developing awareness, credibility and support for the project at senior level so building advocacy for the project and storing up support in times of challenge, crisis, conflict and so on.
- Tactical: day-to-day operational communication for continued interest and motivation; progress reporting; team meetings; video talking heads; in-house news updates and so on.

As project leaders, we use communication for a variety of reasons within our projects. These reasons can be to:

- ensure stakeholders understand project's aims and achievements;
- win support from specific stakeholders for specific purposes;
- increase knowledge and understanding of the project;
- overcome resistance from particular stakeholders, clients, end users;
- enable transparency of what is happening within the project;
- ensure relevant and timely status reporting at all project levels;
- provide visibility of governance and leadership to the project team and stakeholders;
- change attitudes and perceptions about the project;
- actively manage the image of the project;
- provide a call to action;
- share knowledge and experience;
- facilitate collaboration;
- build engagement, credibility and commitment;
- help us negotiate and bargain for resources;
- keep the project team motivated.

> We once proposed a communications strategy to a blue chip multinational who was about to roll-out a global business transformation programme. We were turned down in favour of a tactical schedule of emailing personnel random snippets of information at those times the project team had any 'spare moments'. The lack of a communication and engagement strategy appropriate to the scale and importance of the programme was later cited as one of a range of factors contributing to its failure.

Repetition and familiarity are important in keeping our attention so communication must be planned to ensure that the appropriate messages are directed to each stakeholder group with appropriate frequency and that feedback is understood for its own messages and impact on the project.

10.2.1   COMMUNICATION AND THE VIRTUAL PROJECT TEAM

Communicating with virtual teams can often be problematic due to multiple locations, geographic distance, different cultures and different functional focuses. Traditional and direct communication channels won't always work as effectively for these groups but there is a huge variety of technology available to help bridge the gap. These include web and video conferencing, instant messaging/chat, email, podcasts, shared access sites for project documentation and project team forums, online collaboration tools and social media.

From a technical viewpoint we have the tools we need to do our jobs and to share information from most anywhere we choose. Cloud computing has made information sharing and remote access easy. Mobile phones, tablets and laptops have better functionality and are more robust than ever. Organizations are increasingly adopting information-sharing tools as well as social-collaboration tools as enablers for remote working. These have significantly changed the way we interact with each other while working so that we can both communicate rapidly and feel that sense of team, whether we sit in the same building or on opposite sides of the globe.

> One of the project leaders we have talked with from the defence industry developed some key principles to increase the effectiveness of remote working. He describes frequent contact (for example, daily calls, emails, video conferencing), face-to-face visits (at least once a quarter) and team meetings (not just for progress reporting but also including a socializing element). He suggested that the fundamental principle of successful remote working is that project team members need to be integrated, properly led and suitably motivated so that he recognized he needed to put effort into building relationships within the team and to get 'serious on communication'. This meant he needed to ensure that team members were fully trained in the use of the technology identified to support effective communication, even to the level of smartphone apps. As he explained, 'It is the continued communication which feeds involvement and motivation for the project. I lead a geographically dispersed team, so we just need to be smarter about how we communicate.'

Whether you are able to include a communications expert or marketing expert within the project team, it is also worth remembering that the project team members are also part of the advocacy and championing: do your project team members see project marketing as part of their role? As project leader you can help the project team to articulate the project and its benefits to their own contacts and networks to influence and develop support. We encourage project leaders we work with to develop a simple set of benefits which can be used as an 'elevator pitch' for all members of the team.

10.2.2   ESCALATING COMMUNICATION

Communication is part of the process of engaging your stakeholders. Mapping the type and level of communication to the different types of stakeholder is important. In some cases building awareness and understanding in your stakeholders is all you require; in others you need your stakeholders on board as champions (see Figure 10.1).

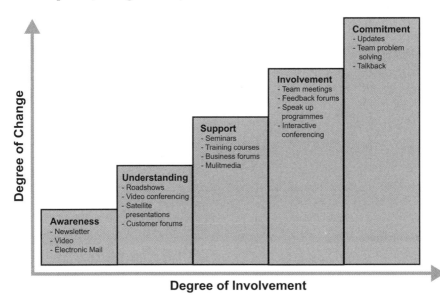

Figure 10.1   The communication escalator
Source: Quirke, 2008

Using this tailored approach, we can focus our resources particularly on those stakeholders who we have prioritized, knowing we are making best use of our resources for:

- keeping informed;
- maintaining interest;
- actively consulting;
- promoting strong buy-in from key players.

Figure 10.2 illustrates how you might categorize stakeholders in terms of communication using the example of introducing a new outsourcing initiative for medical management within the healthcare sector.

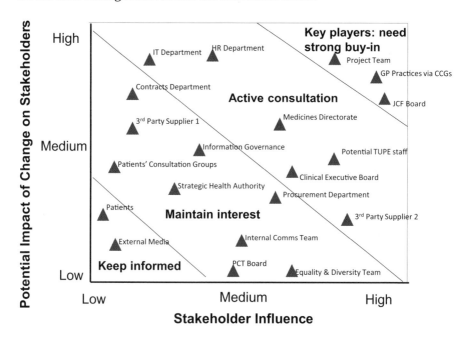

Figure 10.2   Mapping impact and influence for healthcare stakeholders
Source: © The Business Evolution Business Ltd. Reproduced with permission

10.3   From Providing Information to Storytelling

Excellent leaders help their people connect with the Vision and understand the Big Picture by enabling them to appreciate what the journey is going to look like and feel like. They do this by talking to the heart positively and empathically in order to engage the emotions. They use language that can be clearly understood by everyone across the organization and at all levels from the post room to the R&D specialists: language that is simple, understandable and repeatable. They also have a conversational style that is appealing and engages the interest, rather than a formal or directive presentational style. Increasingly, leaders are explaining their projects and their impact through storytelling and dialogue. As well as their obvious entertainment value quotes, strong images, stories and metaphors can help the messages stick long after the telling. Of the five roles described by Sparrow (2012) for successfully developing organizational culture to support growth and drive performance, the Prophet and the Storyteller are the two that inspire and bring the journey to a future state to life using rich language to align and direct action.

Using storytelling inspires and draws in commitment. Do you use target and information-orientated language or perhaps a more subtle weave of imagery and Vision to inspire and motivate? Excellent leaders speak to their wide audiences in terms of Vision, whereas business and project speak used to convey progress and achievement is often dry and stark lacking depth, expression and emotion. A good Vision story weaves peoples' struggles and frustrations into hope for the future. Good storytelling vocabulary is vivid and imagination capturing. It snares the senses and stays with the listener long after the conversation has finished.

Good communication and good storytelling can be seen as a performance, the 'theatre of business'. Just as any other theatre performance, there needs to be congruence and harmony between the words, the vocal and the visual. Olivier and Janni (2004) look at Shakespeare's *Henry V's* poignant and captivating speech 'Once more unto the breach, dear friends, once more, or close the wall up with our English dead!' (Act 3, Scene 1) which lead with emotion and heart, then compare this with a more traditional project management communication:

In our experience, most Warrior managers in Henry's position would probably say something on the lines of:

> Good morning troops. Now you all know why I had to call another briefing. I did set you a very simple strategic target – 91 days ago – to take this small town of Harfleur in one week. That means you are currently running 84 days behind schedule. This is going to have severe budget implications for the rest of the campaign, I can assure you. And that's not all; latest figures from the sick bay indicate there are now 3,000 of you claiming sick leave, while a recent communiqué from the morgue informs me there are currently 2,000 of you ... .dead.

Source: © Olivier and Janni 2004. Reproduced with kind permission of the authors.

10.4   Feedback

Effective communication is a two-way process: the meaning of your communication is the response you get. You carry the responsibility of ensuring your messages are clear and are received in the way in which you intended. If you aren't clear about what you mean and what your intention is, the recipient can easily (and sometimes deliberately) misinterpret. Feedback helps us to complete the communication loop so set up easy to access and easy to use feedback mechanisms for the communications you send out.

Feedback allows the project leader to understand how particular communication and messages have landed with the range of stakeholders, and so what they may need to address further. Table 10.1 outlines ways of facilitating direct and indirect feedback through the use of both qualitative (understanding ideas and concerns) and quantitative (understanding the strength of response) measures:

Table 10.1   Direct and indirect feedback

	Direct feedback	Indirect feedback
What:	• Face to face • Qualitative (for example, conversation and dialogue) • Quantitative (for example, conversation and dialogue)	• Remote • Qualitative (for example free text, comments) • Quantitative (for example Likert scale)
How:	• Visits • Direct observation • Networking • Interviews • Focus groups • Telephone helplines • Summarizing, reflecting back, repeating and paraphrasing • Using clarifying and open questions	• Email and online questionnaires • Managed online forums • Smart phone apps

In short, ensure information is framed clearly and objectively; give it the requisite context and colour to help the receiver understand or make a decision (if one is required). You are inviting feedback for different reasons:

• to ensure messages have landed well;
• to build support, trust and confidence in you as the project leader, the project and team;
• to move stakeholders to particular action.

10.5   Framing Communication

We see spin doctors in action, especially in politics. We all see companies and the way they exaggerate their products' benefits in marketing campaigns or the way in which they try to colour the way they are perceived in the market. Similarly, you could make outrageous claims about the project and the way it is run. Naturally you want to provide a positive image of the project and progress. We recognize there is a temptation to put everything in the best possible light, but don't overplay your hand. If you choose to set a tone of uncompromisingly sunny communication and positive messages when the reality is that the project is not going well this can jeopardize your credibility, and the support and goodwill you have built up will fade. Those 'moments of truth', the informal networks, project team member discussions with colleagues over a coffee or after work colour the perception of what is happening. A balance needs to be struck: at one end of the spectrum is the naked truth and at the other complete fiction. If there are challenges, it is much better to acknowledge them and provide a way forward rather than trying to gloss over them. We acknowledge it can be difficult to 'speak truth to power', especially if you know your reputation and job is on the line, but there are ways of using appropriate language and presenting possible solutions as well as difficulties. As project leader you are expected to meet these challenges.

10.6   Project Branding and Marketing

Although the concept of communicating within projects is mainstream, even if it is not designed and executed for all projects, the idea of branding and marketing a project is a little more unusual for the project management community. The benefit of branding, marketing and communicating the project well is that together they reinforce the messages about the project; they help build advocacy and commitment for the project and influence the way conflict between projects is resolved. Together and done well they are a benefit to the project: the good reputation of the project is established, long-term support is built and resistance is decreased.

'Branding' is a way by which companies give personality and imbibe their products and services with human values. For a business, it is often called the business's 'identity' since it not only embodies what it looks like, but also what the business is and its values. Consider some brands past and present: Coca Cola, Harley-Davidson, Barclays, Citroen, Tata, Lehman Brothers, Rolls Royce,

Mastercard, Trinity College Dublin, Virgin, Toyota, Aeroflot, Apple, Chanel, DeLorien, the Springboks, Hotel Chocolat, David Beckham, Woolworths. Just saying the name of these brands sparks visual images as well as associations, perceptions and memories of particular experiences, not all of which may have been positive.

Transfer this idea into a project setting and you can understand why the concept of project branding may be attractive and beneficial. Brands promise something. As long as they deliver on that promise they have continued engagement, confidence and support. So what do we mean by 'brand'? In its most basic form a brand is a 'set of associations that a person (or group of people) makes with a company, product, service, individual or organisation' (www.designcouncil.org.uk). Therefore project branding offers a coherent identity to the project and helps to differentiate it from others that might challenge it for resources and support. Your project may be unique in terms of quality, Vision, reliability, new ways of working, change, collaboration and partnership, opening up new markets, the use of leading-edge technology, health and safety, innovative design and engineering, or for other reasons.

Think about:

- What are the values you want stakeholders to associate with your project? Have a look at your benefit statements and see what these suggest.
- Why should people want to work on your project (aside from being delegated to do so)? One interim project leader we spoke with recently explained why he had chosen a contract to work on the transformation of a major UK utility over the transformation of a top-end retailer. The top-end retailer had a high-profile and instantly recognizable brand; however, it was the transformation of the major UK utility that the project leader chose to get involved with because, in his words, '... (it) touches pretty much every person in the UK'.
- What are the stories you want people to tell when the project is finished and delivered.

A fundamental rule of branding is to keep it simple; the more clearly defined and compact, the better. One way of branding the project is through its name. Other ways of branding the project are through consistency of message and tone, and the intelligent use of communication. Although branding is thought of as an external-facing form of communication since it focuses primarily on projecting out an image, it also has an important role to play in creating the internal culture for the project team.

MacNicol (2014) developed a simple and effective four-stage project branding process shown below in Table 10.2:

Table 10.2   Four-stage project branding process

Stage	Purpose	Key activities
Opportunity	Identify what you wish to achieve and with whom	• Review the project objectives • Identify who you wish to influence • Identify the desirable change in behaviour • Identify the benefits
Discovery	Identify the project attributes to build into an engaging brand	• Identify the existing project attributes • Be creative – identify potential project attributes • Choose the project attributes • Define the project brand
Implementation	Build the project brand into the DNA of your project	• Identify the changes on the project • Build into the DNA • Communicate to your market • Model the behaviours and way of working
Benefits	Monitor the achievement of benefits	• Put in place measures to monitor the benefits • Monitor the benefits • Identify enhancements • Learn lessons and apply

Source: © Team Animation Ltd. Produced with permission

What does marketing offer? Marketing in the context of a project is concerned with raising the profile so building attention and traction for the project, the project team and the project leader. The primary value in marketing your project is to communicate the project's value. The key questions are:

- How does it provide value to the organization (for example, will it free up cash flow? Improve service levels? Increase profitability?)
- How does it tie in with the organization's strategy (for example, will it help move the organization into new markets? Demonstrate new capability?)
- What will customers, users or stakeholders be able to do once the project is delivered?
- What can the organization expect to see as a result?
- What can the client expect to see as a result?

In the past, we have borrowed unashamedly some of the concepts from mainstream marketing to help clients develop branding, marketing campaigns and communication plans. Why have we done this? Because marketers look to understand their products and services: the benefits, how they would be used, why they would be used and by whom. They identify their market and segment it carefully, identifying what is important to each group. For each market segment they build a profile of the perceived benefits, their way of life and their values. They design their campaigns and communications to fit this profile. Advertisements will only appear in selected places, the message will be angled accordingly and the expectations will be accurately set. When they get it right, buying is easy, there is little resistance, and the good reputation of their product or service is established.

10.7   From Stakeholders to Customers

It helps if we think of end users, suppliers, contractors and other stakeholders as customers. What is the difference? It is a question of attitude. For instance, users are a passive breed who have to take what they are given. They are a faceless, anonymous lot who are at the end of a chain of complex tasks. They should be grateful for what they get. Customers, on the other hand, have a choice. They are individuals who need to be encouraged to buy. They can be seen as purchasers who should want to continue to support a product or a service. They are worthy of continuous effort, thought and planning; they are certainly not an afterthought.

Many people experience difficulties in seeing people who are fellow employees within the same organization as customers, mainly because there is no choice: 'you will have this system', 'this is the building you will work in', 'these are the policies and procedures that will be implemented'. Often this is true, choice *is* limited. But what may be unlimited is the willingness and enthusiasm of people in taking on something new, implementing it and using it to its full capacity. So the question is how to make people positively want and welcome what you are providing as a result of your project.

10.8   Planning Project Marketing

As we've said, we own up to borrowing some of the concepts from mainstream marketing to help clients develop branding, marketing and communication plans. The generic model outlined in Table 10.3 has been used and refined with a variety of clients. It provides a robust structure to cover both internal and external marketing, helping to tailor plans and activities to engage and hold interest.

Table 10.3   Project marketing plan model

Question	Description
What is the project?	What are the particular features, advantages, differentiators and benefits of the project? How is it aligned with the Vision and strategy of the organization?
Where are we starting from?	Use tools and techniques such as appreciate enquiry, performance indicators and success criteria to identify and rate your communication activities to date: • How effective have they been? • What has worked well previously for you/your team members/ your former projects/other projects within the organization?
Who do we need to communicate to?	Identify and prioritize internal and external stakeholders, groups and key players. Acknowledge virtual, multi-located and multicultural team environments: • Understand power, attitude, influence, interest, urgency and proximity • Understand expectations of the project and notions of 'success' • Decide who *wants* vs. who *needs* to know what

Why are we communicating?	What are the objectives for communication for each of the stakeholders identified above:
	• Clarify what we are trying to achieve with our communications;
	• Define key objectives and success criteria by linking communications activities to the aims of the project
	• Do we want to do any or all of the following:
	  ○ Increase awareness, knowledge and understanding of the project?
	  ○ Change attitudes and perceptions about the project?
	  ○ Have our stakeholders commit to a specific action?
	  ○ Actively manage the image of the project?

What are we communicating?	What are the relevant messages we want to get to these various stakeholders? These messages will help stakeholders understand how the project is relevant to them and how it will impact them:
	• How are the particular features, advantages, differentiators and benefits of the project important for each of these stakeholders?
	• What content do we need to create?
	  ○ Formal progress reporting, summary dashboard, tailored vs. generic communication messages
	  ○ Clear content that has impact: easy-to-read and understand, avoid jargon, establish the appropriate tone of the content, keep it short and simple
	  ○ Professional: get it proofread and, if necessary, engage a copywriter

Table 10.3   Project marketing plan model (*concluded*)

Question	Description
How will we communicate?	Identify the range of media and channels you can use which are relevant to your stakeholders. Which channels have the most impact for which set of stakeholders? What are the costs and production timescales associated with each channel? Appropriate channels might be: • Face to face (those 'moments of truth'): one to one interactions, team meetings, 'Town Hall' meetings, conferences, (facilitated) workshops, seminars, presentations, site visits, Back to the Floor, road shows, and so on • Printed: newsletters, bulletins, infographics, pamphlets and brochures, staff magazine/ newspaper, printed flyers, posters, FAQs, and so on • Multimedia: conference and audio calls, e-bulletins, text messaging, business radio, apps, video conferencing, email, podcasts, webinars, video talking heads, and so on • Online: internet, intranet, shared workspaces, ezines, blogs, emails, extranet, and so on
When will we communicate?	Develop and implement an ongoing schedule of activities and tasks. The frequency of communication may differ according to the stakeholders being targeted. Communicating the messages once is not enough: consider the frequency with which businesses market their products and services. This is not a one-off, but a sequence of messages over the project lifecycle, so create and develop a tactical plan allocating budget, timing, resources and ownership Will the schedule of communications be based on the calendar, on specific events or on particular points in the project lifecycle?
Who is going to do what?	Who is going to be responsible for which parts of the plan? What skills are needed to deliver?
How is this going to happen?	How are we going to deliver this plan in a consistent and quality way? What operational processes do we need?
What's the evidence?	Monitor, measure, review: • How will we know we have got it right? Which success criteria have we met? • Have our branding, marketing, communications been received in the way we anticipated? • What feedback mechanisms have we put in place to understand how our branding, marketing, communications have been received? • Analyse the impact of the communications to understand when we have got it right, and also to understand when and where it needs modifying.

Source: © The Business Evolution Business Ltd. Reproduced with permission

We strongly believe that internal marketing is as important as external. We do see projects that think that internal customers are not 'real' customers, so they do not need to be targeted with the same rigour or with specially designed and frequent communication; it is often regarded as wasting valuable time and money on internal people. However, we also frequently hear disappointed project leaders and their sponsors saying: 'I don't understand why they are so resistant and can't see the benefits.'

Pilkington (2013) suggests that the way communication content is developed and then distributed will change as the project progresses. In the early days, the focus will be on the project sponsor and governance structure; later in the project, the focus will shift to the end users who will use the new product or service. At the same time, the style of communication will shift from targeted to include a more 'broadcast' style approach, which is designed to reach larger groups of people (see Figure 10.3).

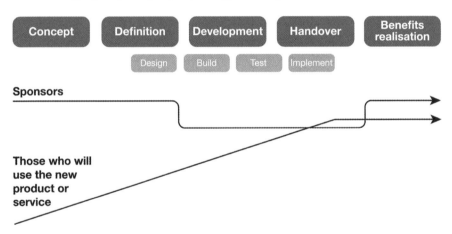

Figure 10.3   The shifting focus of communication between stakeholder groups during the life of the project
Source: Pilkington, 2013

10.9   Informal Communication and Marketing

The team, as well as the project leader, market the project informally: collectively, in what they do and how they do it, they create the image that the project presents to stakeholders and the outside world. You as the project leader are in a position to manage that image. How stakeholders experience their 'moments of truth' relates directly to how they rate the project. This may be unfair, but unfortunately that is how it is, so informal communication is going on whether you plan it or not. The team's image can be managed actively, and informal marketing or networking can be harnessed to your advantage if you do it consciously. Two of the most obvious ways of managing the team's image is through:

- team culture;
- networking and informal contacts.

10.9.1   TEAM CULTURE

One of the questions to be answered by the project leader during the start-up phase is, 'What sort of team culture is necessary for the project?' So how will the project team work together? How will the team communicate with each other and stakeholders? Will you be assertive, available, easily contactable? Will you only let problems emerge so that the guilty can be hunted and blamed? In your marketing plan, you can design the image you want to present and you can plan what you need to do to realize that image. Unfortunately, having plans is not enough. You must also establish behavioural ground rules such as how quickly the team responds to new requests and even to the detail about how team members will pass on telephone messages if they answer each other's telephones. To complete the loop you need to monitor whether those behavioural standards are met, and how stakeholders perceive them.

10.9.2   NETWORKING AND INFORMAL CONTACTS

Formal communications are official and therefore important but they are heavily supported by informal contact. We tend to take more notice of informal communication, because it is *personal*. It is communication directly with us, we are engaged in it and can respond directly to what is said and who has said it. It is alive and immediate.

Spending time and energy building support informally and flushing out what is often labelled as 'resistance' is a hidden part of internal marketing. There are a variety of roles and their particular focus of activity that belong under the label 'networking'. These roles concern energy, which means gaining organizational attention, movement and building critical mass for the project and the organizational issues that it raises. These roles are described in Table 10.4.

Table 10.4   Networking roles

Animateur	Attracts and radiates energy by talking informally to a wide range of people about the Vision, the potential business impact
Integrator	Radiates and transfers energy by connecting together different points of view, representing the balances and dilemmas that have to be resolved, often putting the right people in touch with each other at the right moment
Mentor	Transfers energy by tuning market segments into the project culture, usually making explicit how the project culture works, why, and what the ground rules are in practice
Broker	Boosts everything by using his/her own and other people's networks, running meetings or workshops that demonstrably put stakeholders in touch with each other so that they can exchange know-how and understand differences
Disseminator	Amplifies energy by being the communications centre or anchor, knowing what is happening and willingly and regularly letting others know; the spider in the web: he/she 'thinks' communications
Investigator	Amplifies energy by being curious and excited by what others are doing or thinking, acting as a detective who is aware of resources, know-how and experience in non-traditional places
Developer	Creates energy in others by being good at coaching, giving positive feedback, facilitating learning between people, designing workshops, giving advice or ideas on how to transfer skills and expertise
Counterpart	Attracts energy by being specifically linked to another stakeholder, so a team member may be the link person who works with and maintains the relationship within a market segment

Internal marketing needs to be energized, so how can you use some of these ideas to continuously stimulate the informal network around your project? You cannot do it all alone, so who is good at what in your team? Do they see internal marketing as part of their job as a team member?

10.10 Branding and Marketing the Project Leader

As project leader you will be highly visible throughout the project lifecycle and to stakeholders. This visibility is as much about you as it is about the project. Many eyes will be on you as you navigate your way through the project and rating how you handle particular challenges along the way. How will you manage your image? What do you want this project to say about you?

Certainly, leading a high-visibility or major project can leave project leaders feeling exposed and vulnerable. Building a high profile for yourself, your team and your project can ensure you can command the attention and support necessary, particularly when you find yourself having to bargain, influence or negotiate for resources against other projects.

Conclusion

Developing engagement, commitment and support all have their roots in effective two-way communication. This means understanding your audience and what, how and when they need to know information about the project. Being able to bring in an experienced communications or marketing expert will clearly benefit your communications, but even without this it is possible for you and the project team to make a positive difference through branding, formal and informal project marketing, and through your networks and contacts.

Communication has progressed from the tactical 'sending information and stuff out' level to a strategic way to manage the image of the project and actively build engagement. Effective framing of communication can reinforce a positive reputation for being effective, so helping to secure official and unofficial resources. The technology available also has developed significantly, providing new communication channels. This means not only is there a wider choice about how you provide messages and information to your stakeholders, but also how you keep distant project team members close.

The benefit of branding, marketing and communicating the project well is that together they help build awareness, engagement, clarity and advocacy for the project. Branding, then, is a way of defining and articulating the identity of your project to the team and other stakeholders. Developing a marketing plan helps to make communication activities required for the project visible, resourced and budgeted for.

Key Questions

We suggest you run through your current project and ask:

- How is your project communication currently benefiting your project? How could it work better for you?
- How will you brand your project to help build support and commitment from your stakeholders?
- What marketing plans have you developed for your project to raise the profile of your project and build support and commitment?
- Do your project team members understand how they informally communicate and market the project to their own networks and contacts, and how might this be improved?
- As the project leader, how are you developing your own image and profile? What do you hope to achieve with this?

References

MacNicol, D. (2014) 'How to brand' in *Project Branding, Winning Both the Hearts and Minds of Your Stakeholders*, Taylor, P. (ed.), RMC Publications, Inc., Minnetonka, MN.

Olivier, R. and Janni, N. (2004) *Peak Performance Presentations: How to Present with Passion and Purpose* Articulate Press.

Pilkington, A. (2013) Communicating Projects Gower Publishing Limited, Farnham, UK.

Quirke, B. (2008) *Making the Connections: Using Internal Communication to Turn Strategy into Action* Gower Publishing Limited, Farnham, UK.

Sinickas, A. (2007) *How to Measure Your Communication Programs* Sinickas Communications Publishing, Lake Forest, CA.

Sparrow, J. (2012) *The Culture Builders* Gower Publishing Limited, Farnham, UK.

PART 4
BUILDING PERSONAL AND ORGANIZATIONAL CAPABILITY

Tell me and I forget
Teach me and I remember
Involve me and I learn.

Benjamin Franklin

So far we have identified the importance of the role of the project leader and of the activity of project leadership through the project lifecycle. It is often assumed that anointing an individual with the title 'project leader' automatically confers on them a mantle of ability to burst through blockages, rustle up resources and play the politics successfully. Well, it doesn't. At the individual level and at the organizational level much consideration needs to be given to developing the project leadership role, the project leader and the organization itself to actively support these.

From our experience of working with a broad range of project leaders, we fully concur with Kouzes and Posner (2007) that 'leadership is a set of skills and abilities'. They found that leaders who devote more time and energy to learning, regardless of their style of learning, are higher-performing leaders. There are many ways to learn to be better but they believe the most important ingredient is that you do it often. Simply put, those leaders who practise more often and put in more time for learning are better at leading, in our case learning from working on the right projects at the right time. Furthermore, their data was pretty clear that learning comes before leading. Therefore you should ask yourself: 'Am I devoting sufficient time and energy to learning in order to get better at leading?' and 'Am I making use of all the opportunities offered to me?'

In parallel, every organization should also be reflecting, considering and creating their own leadership strategy, asking themselves what type of and how many leaders it needs to help realize its Vision, strategy and ambitions – not only those who can run the business but also those who can deliver the change necessary to ensure future success. Further, every organization needs to clarify what type of project leadership skills and behaviours are required to help move forward.

Part 4 is about achieving what the first three parts of the book have described: how you become an effective project leader and exhibit effective project leadership. Depending on who you are may change the way you use Part 4:

- Are you an individual who wishes to develop your own project leadership capability?
- Are you the person responsible for, or with an interest in, the development of your organization's project management community and capability?

In Part 4

- Chapter 11 focuses on the individual and how you can take control of your own development and the course of your career, navigating your way through the multiplicity of development options. It also identifies the options available to the organization's learning and development team to assist them when developing project leaders within the organization.
- Chapter 12 identifies the many ways that organizations can assist the individual to develop their leadership capability, providing not only the structures and materials but also the reason and motivation to excel. This chapter also provides a diagnostic to identify what your organization is doing to assist in developing and supporting project leadership capability. As an individual, you may find this particularly useful when discussing what assistance your organization can provide.
- Chapter 13 describes what many project leaders and organizations desire to have in place: an idealized project leadership development programme for:
  - those individuals already in the role who wish to enhance their capabilities;
  - for those individuals who aspire to become an effective project leader;
  - for those organizations that recognize that developing their project leadership capacity and capability will allow them to move forward with their vision and ambitions.

The structure and success criteria for a successful development programme are described to allow your organization to assess against this what it currently offers, and how it can improve.

References

Kouzes, J.M. and Posner, B.Z. (2007) *The Leadership Challenge,* 4th *Edition* Jossey-Bass, San Francisco, CA.

CHAPTER 11

Building Personal Capability

Ability is what you're capable of doing.
Motivation determines what you do.
Attitude determines how well you do it.

Lout Holtz

Introduction

Similar to other professions, project leaders need to take responsibility for continuing to train and adding to their skills. Project leadership development is about self-development. Chapter 11 is about how, as a project leader, you can take control of your own development by viewing your career as a project and applying the same principles as you would to any other project:

- define what you want to achieve and why;
- set the direction you want to take;
- identify and build those relationships that will help support your ambitions and aspirations;
- find the necessary resources to achieve it;
- honestly review progress and modify the plan as your personal circumstances or ambitions change.

The concept of self-learning and career responsibility is becoming more commonplace as individuals are given greater freedom in developing their careers, complemented by understanding what type of development will be of most benefit to you and the responsibility for making it happen.

In this chapter we introduce a simple stepped approach (shown in Figure 11.1), answering four questions in turn that will help you to build and enhance your personal capability as a project leader. You can choose how rigorously you wish to follow the suggested approach but it should ideally be aligned to, and supported by, your organization. Chapter 12 looks at the types of support that may be available and that you may wish to ask for from the organization.

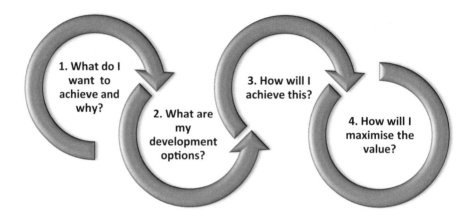

Figure 11.1   Four-step personal development process

11.1   Step 1 – What Do I Want to Achieve and Why?

'Development' generally begins with an understanding of current or future need and the motivation to do something about it. This might be gained through an assessment of some form or as a result of a trigger: feedback following a mistake or because you have identified a new challenge that you haven't tackled before. We encourage you to take the time to consider why you want to develop and what you may achieve, hopefully before you have the opportunity to learn from failure. So let's look at drivers and motivation first and then discuss what needs to be done:

- *What made me decide to lead projects?* Was this a conscious choice or were you focused in this direction?
- *What do I enjoy about leading a project?* Think about the times when you felt most energized and proud of your achievement: when was that and what was the trigger for you having these feelings?
- *What do I find challenging and what would I rather not have to do?* For many this may be easier to answer! Don't think about just the incident which may have been unpleasant or stressful, but the things which were the trigger.
- *What are my strengths?* Never an easy one to answer but can be informed by asking peers and colleagues for honest feedback and by using psychometric profiling or similar tools.
- *Do I make enough of my strengths and is there a way I could develop them further and make more use of them?* Life can be so much more pleasant

if we can find a way to maximize what we are good at complemented by a team providing other key capabilities.

- *What are my weaknesses?* Look at this from the perspective of a so-called weakness being a strength that we misapply (inappropriately) or overdo (with, of course, the best intentions). What are your misapplied or overdone strengths?
- *What is it I think I will gain from developing my project leadership capability?* This final question is the one that will provide you with the greatest value. Examples might include:
  - being able to take advantage of more challenging roles;
  - the desire to progress your career in this specific direction;
  - to improve your effectiveness in the role;
  - a personal desire for development and fulfilment.

If you're not able to answer this final 'what' question, the 'when', 'where' and 'how' will become immaterial.

Now take some time to reflect on what aspects of your project leadership capability need to be developed. There are many ways to do this, but we have found the following categories particularly helpful:

- Knowledge: what you know. For example, understanding the technologies and methodologies deployed, tools and techniques.
- Skills: what you do. The ability that you have to apply this knowledge in what you do on a day-to-day basis, carrying out the technical aspects of the project leader role.
- Competencies: how you do it.

Unsurprisingly, we urge you to focus on competencies, as defined earlier in the book, balanced with knowledge and skills. Parts 1, 2 and 3 of the book have already hopefully made the case for the importance of how you lead the project, not just what you do.

Now consider timescale. In order to gain clarity around what you want to achieve, we suggest you work through the following steps using Figure 11.2. A five-year horizon is a reasonable timeframe on the understanding that things do change regarding your own circumstances, the organization and the wider environment:

- Reflect on what kind of leader you are now. Consider your current role and context as well as understanding your own strengths, needs and preferences. Your current position represents the bull's eye in the middle of the concentric circles.

- Reflect on what kind of leader you would like to be in five years' time. What role will you have, on what types of project, what focus will you have, what will be important to you? This reflection represents the outer most of the concentric circles: where do you want to be in five years' time?

- Think about the roles, opportunities and development you need to take advantage of in order to achieve this over the five-year horizon.

- For each of the five years, be specific about the changes you will make over each successive 12-month period and consider what you need to do to achieve these changes. We will talk later about creating your Project Leadership Development Plan and the following sections will help to inform the content. Apply the principles of rolling-wave planning: planning in detail only as far as is sensible and required and using milestones for future activities or events.

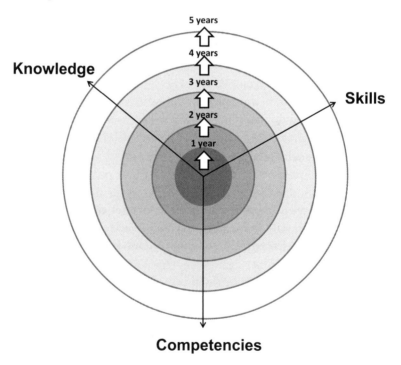

Figure 11.2   Development of personal capability through knowledge, skills and competencies

11.2   Step 2 – What Are My Development Options?

In this step we will help you to understand the choice of development options available and what will work best for you. This also includes an insight into how we learn best, since this can help us gain the maximum value from any investment in time or resources.

11.2.1   HOW WE LEARN BEST

There are some statistics that might be useful to clarify which of these development options will be of most benefit. The 70/20/10 model for learning and development (Lombardo and Eichinger, 1996) suggests that if you wish to develop new skills then:

> *Development generally begins with a realization of current or future need and the motivation to do something about it. This might come from feedback, a mistake, watching other people's reactions, failing or not being up to a task – in other words, from experience. The odds are that development will be about 70% from on-the-job experiences, working on tasks and problems; about 20% from feedback and working around good and bad examples of the need, and 10% from courses and reading.*

This is not to say that 'courses' or other means of gaining insights and knowledge are not important; it is just that without people to work with to develop your thinking and an opportunity to use your new skills in real-life, developing knowledge can end up only as an academic exercise. If you consider the average retention rates from 'traditional passive' approaches of lecturing (5 per cent) through reading (10 per cent), audio–visual (20 per cent) and demonstration (30 per cent) against the 'active' approaches of discussion groups (50 per cent), practice by doing (75 per cent) and teaching others/ immediate use (90 per cent) (Source: National Training Laboratories Institute) you begin to appreciate that truly effective development comes from the meaningful application of new knowledge in the workplace soon after acquiring the new knowledge, and gaining the feedback necessary to identify the value achieved. There must also be opportunities to discuss with peers the challenges to applying this knowledge, something we will expand on in Chapter 13 when discussing an idealized development programme.

People need to learn how to learn in order to gain the maximum value from any investment in time or resources. Different models exist to help you reflect on how you learn. The Experiential Learning Cycle (Kolb, 1984) identifies the typical cycle of learning. The cycle is subtly different for each person, with a difference in preference which any development activity should take account of:

*   reflect on experience;
*   assimilate and conceptualize;
*   experiment and practise;
*   plan for application.

It can also be of value to consider individual learning styles. A popular model developed by Honey and Mumford (1982), based upon the work of Kolb, identified four distinct learning styles or preferences:

*   Activist
*   Theorist
*   Pragmatist
*   Reflector.

As a result of their research, Honey and Mumford recommend that in order to maximize a leader's learning they should understand their preferred learning style and seek out opportunities to learn using that style. This makes learning more focused, easier and more enjoyable. It also helps to expand the ways in which individuals learn, from formal to informal and planned to spontaneous. Do you know what your learning style is? To be an effective learner you should also develop the ability to learn in other styles, to take advantage of opportunities that may be presented and to learn to be flexible – a key attribute of a project leader.

The characteristics of the four learning styles are summarized in Table 11.1 below, along with some hints as to how a project leader with that particular learning style can best develop.

We discussed insights into brain sciences, as they are commonly referred to, in Chapter 1. Why are these important? Together with other associated fields, they provide further insights into how we learn, the challenges to learning and what we can do to become more effective.

Table 11.1   Effective developmental activities for different learning styles

Learning style	Description	Effective project leader developmental activities
Activists – learn by doing	Activists need to get their hands dirty on projects and get direct experience. They typically have an open-minded approach to learning, involving themselves fully and trying new experiences	• Problem solving with project team members, possibly using brainstorming or similar techniques • Role-plays where learning points can be experienced • All forms of interactive learning • Group work opportunities
Theorists – like to understand the theory behind the actions	Theorists need models, concepts and facts in order to engage in their particular learning process. They prefer to analyse new information and experiences, develop a theory that they then test and then apply in new project situations	• Concentrate on concepts and theories presented in a variety of ways • Opportunity to apply the theories and then discuss in Implementation Groups or as part of the community • Like to debate and consider different angles to test their theory • Models backed up by objective data • Hearing stories and having the opportunity to discuss
Pragmatists – need to be able to see how to put the learning into practice in the real world	Application to projects is critical since abstract concepts are of limited use unless the individual can see a way to put the ideas into action on their projects. Enjoy trying out new ideas, theories and techniques to see if they work in practice	• Intense and comprehensive briefings on a topic can be provided as long as they are interactive • Case studies, building on these and solving problems can be very effective • Application on live projects is the most important mechanism • Need time to think about how to apply the learning on the project
Reflectors – learn by observing and thinking about what has happened	Prefer to stand back, initially watch from the sidelines and view experiences from a number of different perspectives. Collect data and take the time to work towards a conclusion that they can then apply on their projects	• Content should be presented from a variety of perspectives • Develop through problem-based learning and paired discussions • Benefit from self-analysis/personality questionnaires • Require time-out to process and reflect after observing activities • Implementation Groups can be an effective means of learning • Welcome feedback from others and can gain considerable value from coaching/mentoring

11.2.2   DEVELOPMENT OPTIONS

There are many ways in which you can develop project leadership skills. Key interventions are identified in Table 11.2 opposite. We often find organizations are uncertain how to best develop their project leader community so we have created a comprehensive development framework to provide organizations with an approach that can be modified to suit their specific needs. This framework can also be used by individuals to understand the range of development options they might take advantage of. These interventions are different in nature, not mutually exclusive and will be of greatest value if blended to meet your particular objectives and context. The names given to each are used widely but may be known differently between organizations and cultures; for example, coaching is a term used widely but interpreted in varying ways.

Think of the variety of interventions as the ingredients that go into your personal recipe for development. The list is neither mutually exclusive nor collectively exhaustive. It will be your choice to specify which ingredients, how much of each, when they are added and how much energy you will add to the mix! The choice you make is dependent on:

- your personal preferences;
- the context in which you find yourself: for example, the availability of and ease of access to each type of intervention;
- your developmental needs; for example, what developmental needs have you identified from Figure 11.2.

For each type of intervention you can ask four questions:

- Is this readily available to me?
- Is this of interest to me?
- Will it benefit me directly?
- Will it benefit the projects I work on and the organization?

Any development work that may impact on the effective delivery of your role must be carefully considered, regardless of whether you are full-time employed by an organization or an interim contractor. For example, a Community Investment Initiative may require a considerable investment in time over a prolonged period of time. If you do commit to this, you should plan for possible clashes with your primary role in your organization and even your personal life.

Table 11.2   Key interventions for personal development

Activity	Description
Self-reflection Creating the space and time to reflect on your actions and reactions to events, and what you can learn from your experiences	This is a high-value activity shown to increase self-awareness and that distinguishes high performers. Requires only time and commitment to perform it until it becomes a habit. This is becoming mainstream through areas such as meditation, mindfulness.
Reflective journal Documenting your reflections to facilitate identification and embedding of insights and understanding	Capturing what is important, interesting and instructive to the individual in note form, diagrams and mind maps. Documenting the interplay between the content of a development programme, experience and personal learning helps to crystallize independent and critical thought, understanding and follow-up.
Personal performance management Gaining insight on your performance	Understanding your performance in relation to the project and the organization's expectations. Gaining this insight may be a result of formal 360-degree appraisals, discussions with peers, seniors, coach or mentor, or informal discussions with your network. However, these are only a means to better understanding and should be used as the basis on which to plan your further development to improve personal performance.
Project experience Working on live projects to apply what has been learned and gain critical experience	This can be a primary source of development if the project offers the correct blend and level of challenge, and the necessary environment and support for learning to take place.
Self-study Personally instigated and directed exploration and learning in topics of interest and value	The internet has made available a vast array of materials, in particular video, which provides easy access and engagement with relevant subject matter. The range of research and of printed and e-books cover many specialized project management areas of knowledge is also increasing and being continuously updated.
Feedback Requesting and obtaining insight on personal performance	From different perspectives such as peers, colleagues, mentors, coaches, line managers, project team members, clients, suppliers. Often people are delighted to provide informal feedback as well as providing more formal feedback through 360 appraisals, but you must be sure you want it and are ready for potentially uncomfortable messages. Positive feedback is always uplifting and reassuring, but often it is the negative and challenging feedback that helps us most. Another way often used to gain feedback is the use of psychometric profiling tools such as those discussed in Part 1.

Table 11.2   Key interventions for personal development (*continued*)

Activity	Description
*Coaching Helping to work through particular concerns or to improve performance on a one-to-one focused basis	Coaching is one of the most powerful development options, which works on a one-to-one basis focused on a specific personal area. Provided by a qualified internal or external coach who will help you work through a particular challenge. In the past it was seen as an indication of poor performance, but increasingly coaching is being used at all levels of the organization including the C-suite to help develop individuals achieve the best performance possible.
*Mentoring Formal or informal mentoring providing advice and support from the mentor's own experiences	Mentoring is typically provided by someone senior in experience who has similar experience of a role or responsibility within the organization or industry. Their own experience of a similar issue or situation can help you work through your own issue or situation. Mentoring can be one to one, or one to many. Mentoring is especially useful for individuals new to an organization, to a particular experience or for individuals wanting to develop their career in a particular way.
*Buddying Informal supportive relationship typically with a peer or colleague	Buddying provides an opportunity to share and compare approaches and experiences with others, typically to provide mutual support through a close association. It can be an organized activity or something you initiate yourself with specific individuals for specific reasons, and might extend over days, weeks or months. Buddying is especially effective for individuals new to a project or organization.
*Shadowing Gaining insight from observing other project leaders	Job or work shadowing allows interaction with, and observation of, a variety of individuals and activities. It can be an organized activity or something you initiate yourself with specific individuals for specific reasons. It is temporary but might extend over days, weeks or months. Shadowing is effective for individuals moving into a new role, needing to understand more about something specific or developing particular expertise.
Secondments Gaining experience in new environments, either internal or external to the organization	Secondments are where an individual temporarily transfers to another role, team, office or organization for a *defined* period of time typically to exchange experiences or skills, so working to the mutual benefit of all parties. Secondments are based on a set of clear objectives, valuable experience and fresh perspectives. New expertise can be applied back in the original role at the end of the agreed period.
*Training Gaining knowledge and skills through formal training	Training covers diverse learning activities, typically formalized. Increasingly training is being delivered using a blended mix of activities through different channels to meet individual needs for ease and flexibility of access to learning. There are a multiplicity of options available from the traditional face-to-face 'classroom'-based training, through to part-time training, distance and e-learning, simulation and gamification.

Table 11.2 Key interventions for personal development (*continued*)

Activity	Description
*Storytelling Actively seeking out those who have specific insights and knowledge	Seeking opportunities to listen to others who have met and overcome particular challenges and so who have specific insights and knowledge which may be beneficial to your own position. These storytellers may be peers or leaders in your own organization, networks or industry sector.
Communities of Interest Joining and participating in communities and groups	Communities of Interest are also known as Communities of Practice. These communities are groups of individuals who share an interest in something and look to share experience, knowledge, skills and learning in order to do this better. These Communities of Interest can be: • Internal or external to the organization • Face to face or virtual/online • Formalized through professional bodies or informal.
Professional body membership Participating in the wider profession	Belonging to an appropriate professional body provides access to policy makers, researchers, relevant and current knowledge and to networks of contacts. Membership provides recognition for your knowledge, understanding and practice. Developing your membership to senior levels also demonstrates commitment to your career, development and accomplishments. Many professional bodies now actively encourage Continuing Professional Development, provide access to mentoring schemes, provide online forums for discussions and knowledge sharing, and work to raise the understanding and value of their members' contribution to business and the economy.
Professional body qualifications and accreditation Appropriate development opportunities to gain formal qualifications and accreditation	Choosing to benefit from the range of qualifications and accreditations from a relevant professional body demonstrates your skill and commitment, increases your value to your organization and enhances your career prospects
Community investment initiatives Investing the time and energy to contribute to the wider community and society	This may be instigated by the organization under the typical headings of 'Corporate Social Responsibility' or 'Business in the Community', or it may be a result of your involvement in a Community of Interest. Regardless, these are opportunities for personal development and recognition. For example, researching and producing guidance for the community on a topic in which you wish to develop your own capability such as Stakeholder Engagement.
Organizational investment task Investing the time and energy to contribute to the wider organization	Involvement in organizational initiatives outside your immediate area and remit are opportunities for personal development, networking and recognition within the organization. This might include involvement in particular internal initiatives, research or briefings.

Table 11.2　Key interventions for personal development (*concluded*)

Activity	Description
Networking Interacting with others to exchange information and knowledge, and to develop professional contacts	Actively building networks inside and outside the organization for contacts, relationships and collaboration. Helps to broaden your horizon and exposure to different experience, people and ways of working. 　At best, networking represents opportunities to gain information and knowledge, and to explore role models, mentors and career opportunities. In short, it is an excellent way to develop your own professional network to support your future career.
Undergraduate academic qualification Gaining the foundation knowledge and accreditation in an appropriate subject	There are an increasing number of undergraduate qualifications directly and indirectly around leading projects, typically focused on a particular sector or function. 　Often this type of development opportunity represents high financial and time investment to the individual and organization, so it is important to demonstrate how this is aligned to your career plan.
Postgraduate academic qualification Obtaining advanced knowledge and skills to assist in more challenging projects and situations	There are a diverse range of options now available to graduates and non-graduates including MBAs and MScs focused on providing specialized development, typically for more complex projects and for more experienced practitioners wishing to enhance their own knowledge or experience. 　Often this type of development opportunity represents high financial and time investment to the individual and organization, so it is important to demonstrate how this is aligned to your career plan.
*Conferences, seminars and expos Being exposed to new offerings and thinking	The opportunity to hear a variety of practitioners' and researchers' own experience and findings; also, taking the opportunity to present your own experience and research.

* For each above there is considerable value in reciprocating what you have received. So if you are able to take advantage of coaching, mentoring, storytelling, research and training can you provide the same to others within your organization, professional body or network? As an example, if you deliver training you must thoroughly understand the subject and be ready and willing to be challenged about what you are saying.

In our experience, and backed up by development industry guidance, self-reflection is likely one of the most powerful, underrated and least used activities. Bennis and Thomas (2002) describe them as the 'crucibles' of leadership, typically severe tests or trials. These crucibles are intense, often traumatic and nearly always unplanned, and leaders find meaning in, and learn from, the most negative events. Bennis and Thomas suggest that the ability to identify the challenges/successes you are facing, the reasons for these, the actions taken and the outcomes achieved can provide extremely valuable insights that can help the individual to continuously develop without the need for external resources of input.

Learning by doing is extremely powerful. It can be challenging to begin with, but it is ultimately very beneficial and rewarding. Research into the ways different individuals learn has helped us understand that a blended mix of development interventions as shown in Table 11.2 and delivery channels as shown in Table 11.3 helps individuals to retain learning and to embed new behaviours.

Table 11.3   Channels for personal development activities

Channel	Description
Face-to-face	A face-to-face session or event is a live meeting among participants and trainers, instructors or facilitators. This is the more traditional channel for learning and development, and covers one-to-one and one-to-many scenarios. They can also help to break down barriers and provide real cross-cultural experiences and networking opportunities, so facilitating the building of relationships and encouraging the sharing of knowledge. For example: formal training, workshops, conferences, seminars, Action Learning Groups, Peer-to-Peer Learning. This can also cover face-to-face support for learning and development such as coaching and mentoring.
E-learning	E-Learning is a type of distance learning conducted via electronic media, typically on the internet. For example: podcasts, webinars, videos, apps, remote learning and development through higher education institutions or particular businesses.
Social media	Social media is increasingly being used as a channel for the dissemination of knowledge, ideas, insight, inspiration and discussion, as well as for views and opinions. Some social media is recognized at being a better source of information and knowledge sharing than others, but it is generally a useful way to gain exposure to the stream of new information and thinking. For example: LinkedIn, Niume, Twitter.
Remote support	Remote support is a type of distance support for learning and development conducted via the telephone, email, video conferencing. It is often used for coaching and mentoring to support learning and development.

Given the above suggestions about interventions and channels, the key questions to consider are:

- Which activities are available to me immediately or through some form of investment either in terms of time or resources?
- Given my objectives for the next 12 months, which of these activities would be most beneficial?
- Which channels are available to/will work best for me?

11.2.3   IDENTIFYING YOUR PERSONAL DEVELOPMENT PREFERENCES

After considering your learning style in 11.2.1, now consider which of the development options identified above will work best for you. For example, if you are looking at undergraduate or post-graduate academic qualifications, is your preference to do this remotely via distance or e-learning, or to physically attend lectures and action-learning groups? Figure 11.3 represents a model to which a number of the interventions in Table 11.2 have been mapped. The two axes are:

- Involvement of others. The level of intervention and interaction you prefer when gaining new knowledge or skills.
- Use of materials. The quantity and level of materials you prefer when gaining new knowledge or skills.

Firstly, identify the quadrant you are most comfortable in and typically focus on when developing yourself. Then consider other quadrants and options and which may be helpful in achieving your development goals. Given the need for project leaders to be adaptable and resourceful, you should consider all options in the pursuit of your own development.

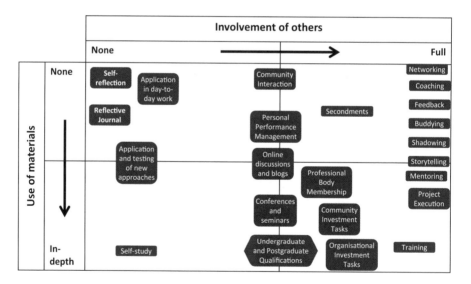

Figure 11.3   Identifying your personal development preferences
Source: © Team Animation Ltd. All rights reserved. Reproduced with permission

11.3   Step 3 – How Will I Achieve This?

Step 3 looks at planning and taking action. From Steps 1 and 2 you will have gained insight and knowledge about what you want to achieve and what your options for development are, but now you need to make it happen in order to realize the value. From our experience of working with multiple project communities, we have found the following simple 3Es development model in Figure 11.4 a helpful way of considering the three broad interrelated activities that are required to develop effectively.

A description of each activity is included in Table 11.4, identifying its importance and providing an explanation:

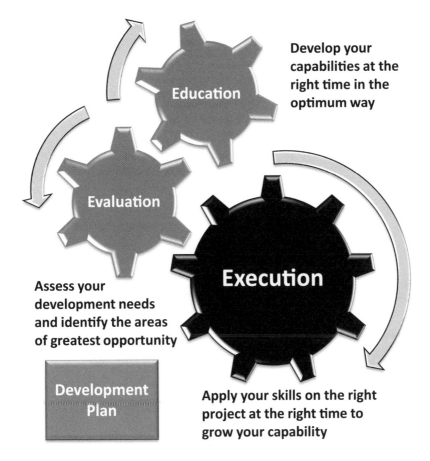

Figure 11.4   3Es development model

Table 11.4   Describing the 3Es development model

	Importance and key considerations
Experience Apply your skills on the right project at the right time to grow your capability	• *'Learning by doing'* represents the highest retention of knowledge (National Training Laboratories Institute) • If a structured approach is not in place for allocating people to projects based, at least in part, on their development needs then you will need to identify alternative ways • Proactively seek opportunities by speaking to resource managers, sponsors and peers, making them aware of your development needs, requirements and availability
Evaluation Assess your development needs and identify the areas of greatest opportunity	• There are a range of ways in which you can gain the necessary insight, some of which are freely available to you and others which come from your organization • Professional project management bodies have career frameworks and underlying competency models which individuals can use to assess development and qualification opportunities • The organization you work for may have their own job families and career frameworks which you can use to assess development and promotion opportunities • Your organization may have performance management processes which will provide feedback • Psychometric profiling tools such as those discussed in Chapter 2 can be of great value • Also consider asking peers and colleagues for feedback on which intervention options have worked best for them and why
Education Gain the knowledge and skills necessary to be successful	• Earlier sections of Chapter 11 describe the many ways in which you can obtain development opportunities • Chapter 13 describes an idealized project leader development programme that will also be of value to consider

The above model provides an excellent framework against which you can consider the broad strands of your development. Focus on balancing all three areas so that you avoid solely relying on your project-based experience while not obtaining any fresh ideas or skills (Education) or feedback on how well you are performing and providing context to your development (Evaluation).

From a practical perspective, this step is also about developing your plans, and also making these plans happen. Consider the following four key activities as described in Table 11.5. These should be very familiar to you since they are closely aligned to project activities:

- creating your Project Leadership Development Plan;
- identifying and engaging your development team;
- taking control and planning your steps;
- keeping on track.

Table 11.5   Activities to ensure your development happens

	Activities necessary to make your development happen
Creating your Project Leadership Development Plan	Now is the time to write your development plan. The key to a successful plan is to strike a balance between two opposing forces. It needs to be comprehensive enough to ensure you have included everything you have worked on throughout this guide, but not too long that you can't remember what's in it. Ideally keep it to one page so that you can easily reference it and also discuss with your own line manager or sponsor. It is suggested that you use the 3Es as a structure and then identify what is planned against each and what actions you need to take.
Identifying and engaging your development team	Just as projects need the involvement of a variety of people, skills and expertise to be successful so it is with development. Look to identify and engage your 'development team': the collection of individuals who can provide you with development, signposting, networks, coaches, mentors. Key relationships will typically be with your direct manager who will act as your sponsor to ensure you obtain the support necessary; as such, you will both need to agree what must be achieved. You might also have a functional manager, the person to whom you report on a daily basis. Secondary relationships include other colleagues and communities you are part of. Each can play an important role for your development and learning if these relationships are planned and if the individuals are suitably informed and motivated to help.
Taking control and planning your steps	Organizations are now encouraging their employees to take greater responsibility for their own development and career paths. This, then, is a great opportunity to apply the planning, control and monitoring activities to your 'project career' that you apply to your projects for their success. Linking your career aspirations and development plan into your organization's own career and development processes can help you take advantage of the different types of interventions that your organization supports. Plan your development activities and goals over the five-year period we described in Section 11.1.
Keeping on track	Will it go as planned? Not always. Does it matter? Not entirely. The key thing is that you are taking positive steps and development is rarely wasted. Opportunities have a habit of appearing when you least expect them but you will need to keep your eyes and mind open to them. To help opportunities appear, start to consider the branding and marketing for yourself in the same way that you have provided for your project. Talk to your sponsor, peers and colleagues about the types of opportunities you are on the lookout for so that they can alert you to them when they appear. Like any good plan, once produced it is only as good as the effort that goes in to adapting it to suit the changing world we find ourselves in. We would suggest reviewing it in outline every three months and in full every year, or as your situation within the organization or personal aspirations change. Further, those skills and competencies that the organization values as it adapts itself to changing external pressures may also influence your development plan. Here, being adaptable is key. You have your plan; now consider how you will get the most out of it.

11.4   Step 4 – How Will I Maximize the Value?

Gaining the value from any development activity or career progression requires us to shift behaviours and ways of doing things; in other words, to transition. Making these transitions requires a number of fundamental shifts to be made by the individual making the change. Project leaders are typically promoted on the basis of their technical ability and few make the transition necessary into a senior position that requires a skill set that is focused differently. So while their positions become bigger, more prestigious and more influential, the individual may not undertake the change required in how they manage their work and relationships. There is also the danger that simply because of an individual's age and experience, they are promoted into a project leader role when they have changed little about what they do or how they do it. This issue is exacerbated by anointing an individual with the title of 'Senior' or 'Director' at which point it is often assumed that they suddenly take on a mantle of relevant and appropriate skills, knowledge and competencies. So it is not infrequent to find a project leader enthusiastically assisting a project team member to do the tasks they once did. In other words, they are continuing to do what they are comfortable doing, rather than what the leadership role demands. The temptation is to go back to what you were doing previously and had undoubtedly been successful in. Here, an important responsibility of the organization is to support a new project leader in making the transition easily and in a timely fashion, especially since it often takes between six and 12 months to be effective in a new role.

The project leader must not only make the personal shift but also help others to identify and relate to the transition they are making. Transition is not a matter of doing more of what was done before; rather it is about doing things differently. Some of the key changes that you will need to make involve:

- Review and modify your values. On the basis that what you believe is important is what you put your energy into, project leaders must change what they believe from their individual contribution and hence what they do. For example, as a project leader takes on more challenging projects or gains promotion, the benefit they can add is more about how they enable others and not what they personally deliver. So if delivering a quality product and being an expert in a particular area is important to the person and has stood them in good stead in their career, becoming a project leader may be challenging as their role will demand that they focus on developing others and developing the environment for their success.

- Gaining new skills. This involves leaving behind the familiar and being challenged to do new things in new ways. Inevitably this will bring some degree of discomfort. You must accept that when undertaking new things you will need time to learn and put these new things into practice effectively. You cannot expect to be fully effective immediately.
- Time. Two changes of perspective are needed around how you relate to and deal with time, namely:
  - What you spend your time doing. As a project manager, a lot of what occupies your time can be around the completion of tasks to ensure you maintain progress and momentum. Moving into more senior positions, such as the project leadership role, shifts your focus increasingly to enabling others to do what they need to do, understanding how the project fits into the respective strategy and vision of the organization and client.
  - The horizon over which you are looking. An early entry project leader is focused predominantly on the end of task or workstream (timeline: days, weeks or months) while an experienced project leader is looking to the end of the project (timeline: months, quarters or even years ahead). Your timeline must change, the aim being to look as far out as is appropriate.

You must accept that when transitioning it is quite usual to feel uncomfortable as you are doing things differently. Support is critical when you make these transitions; you will not instantly gain these new capabilities and may need the space to fail. Some key points to note when making personal change are:

- It takes approximately three weeks to break a simple habit so if you typically go for a week without speaking to all key project team members you will have to consciously remind yourself to be in communication, using prompts and reminders.
- Your project team, colleagues and peers will not be aware that you are looking to make these changes unless you tell them. They may simply put it down to unusual behaviour, so discuss this with them to gain their understanding and support.
- In taking on a new role, it can take six months or more to become effective. The lesson here is: don't expect to be effective immediately and discuss this with your manager to ensure you have common expectations.

- Often people moving into a new role are expected to be performing effectively within three months, putting on the pressure to add value as soon as possible. If they cannot do this easily and quickly in their new role they may revert back to their old role. This means they may end up doing what they used to do for part of the time but in a new, typically more senior position. Transitions are not successful where newly promoted managers continue to focus on managing rather than leading.

Ultimately, to make a successful transition you need to make changes in what you do as shown in Figure 11.5. In turn this means that you need to:

- apply the new skills and knowledge;
- enhance what you do to be more effective;
- learn to empower others and delegate work to allow you time and space;
- stop doing certain activities even though this brings a degree of discomfort.

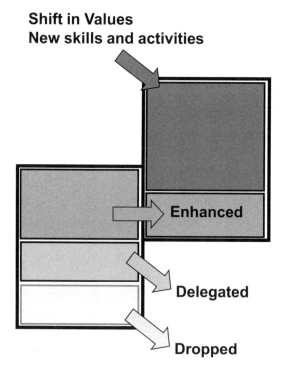

Figure 11.5   Transitioning options

> *Completing the Eight Lookings Diagnostic will help you identify gaps in your skills, knowledge and competencies and will help you develop your Personal Development Plan.*

Conclusion

Increasingly organizations are encouraging their staff to take responsibility for their own development and career path. A simple stepped approach can help you build and enhance your project leadership capability. If you approach your personal development as a project, there is a greater chance of achieving success. This will also provide you with a sound basis against which to modify your plan as circumstances change, which they inevitably will. An understanding of the ways in which you learn and develop best will also help you to distinguish those development options which will be most effective for you. Do also consider other options and don't simply continue to do what you have always done: developing new capabilities may require new approaches. Finally, consider whether your career path aligns with your own personal values.

Key questions

- Do I know where I am heading and what I need to do to get there?
- What is important to me about what I do and how I do it?
- What are my strengths and how can I best play to these?
- What are my development needs and how will I know I have achieved them?
- What am I going to start doing, stop doing, continue doing and learn to do better?

We recommend you work through the four-step development process and have any necessary conversations with your organization.

References

Association for Project Management (www.apm.org.uk).

Bennis, W.G. and Thomas, R.J. (2002) 'Crucibles of leadership' *Harvard Business Review*, September 2002.

Honey, P. and Mumford, A. (1982) *Manual of Learning Styles* P Honey, London.

International Project Management Association (www.ipma.ch).

Kolb, D.A., Boyatzis, R.E. and Mainemelis, C. (2001) 'Experiential learning theory: Previous research and new directions', in *Perspective on Learning, Thinking and Cognitive Styles*, Sternberg, R.J and Zhang, L-F (eds) Laurence Erlbaum Associates, New York.

Lombardo, M.M. and Eichinger, R.W. (1996) *The Career Architect Development Planner*, 1st edition Lominger, Minneapolis, MN.

National Training Laboratories Institute (www.ntl.org).

Project Management Institute (www.pmi.org).

CHAPTER 12

Building Organizational Capability

Developing expertise depends essentially on quality and speed of feedback, as well as on sufficient opportunity to practice.

Daniel Kahneman

Introduction

Chapter 11 focused on what you as an individual can do to develop your project leadership capability. This chapter is primarily aimed at development professionals: those individuals responsible for developing the capability of the project management community within the organization. You will find this chapter useful as it provides a framework against which you can compare your current approach to help develop project leadership talent. It is equally useful for project leaders who wish to understand what organizational support can be provided to them, putting them in an informed position when discussing development options with their manager.

Hemel (2012) and others are starting to challenge the structure and way of working within organizations, provoking a rethink about the role of hierarchy and management within organizations. Project management provides many lessons for working outside hierarchy, for collaborative and cross-functional working, and for self-organizing teams who actively push the organization forward. Project leadership also provides lessons about leaders who are held accountable for their own roles and contribute equally to the success of the entire unit.

The fundamental question for those appointing, supporting or developing project leaders should be, 'Is the organization making it easy for them to do their job and providing them with the necessary support?' From our own experience of designing, developing and delivering development programmes to help organizations achieve the capacity and capability they want in line with their

Vision, this is not always the case. We recognize it is critical that the organization does everything that is appropriate and practical to support development.

12.1   Clarifying the Organization's Future Capability Needs and Priorities

Organizations are constantly changing. It therefore makes sense that if you wish to improve your organization's capability you should be basing this on future needs. It will take time for the changes to happen; with of course an acceptance of any short-term needs which must be prioritized. A key question is how do you assess the future leadership capabilities that are important to your organization?

Figure 12.1 illustrates a model that can assist project leaders and organizations to identify what capabilities are important in the future. The aim is to use all four perspectives to identify the 'sweet spot' of future capabilities.

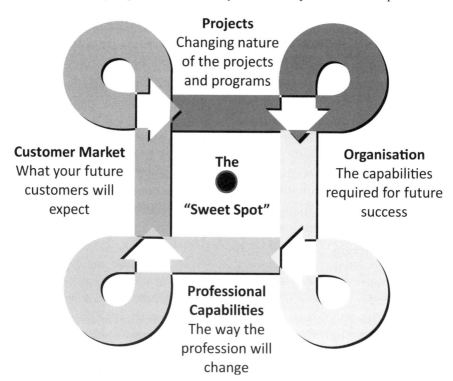

Figure 12.1   Identifying the organization's future capability needs

Table 12.1 captures some of the relevant questions that both the project leader and the organization should ask to hit this sweet spot. It is probable that the answers provided by the project leader will not match those answers provided by the organization, but it is better to be clear about gaps in perception sooner rather than later to allow you to plan accordingly. The considerations are described in order of influence from the project leader's perspective.

Table 12.1 The questions to ask to identify future capability needs

Consideration	Influence	Questions the project leader should ask	Questions the organization should ask
Organization The capabilities required for future success and translated to project leadership requirements	↓	• What does the organization require of its future project leaders and does this meet my own aspirations?	• Based on our business strategy and where we want to be as a business, what are the capabilities that will be critical to our success? • **What are the benefits of us having these requirements as we need them?**
Projects Changing nature of the projects		• What types of projects do I want to lead in the future?	• In the future and given the knowledge we have, what type of projects will we require? • **What benefits would we achieve from successful delivery?**
Professional capabilities The way the profession will change		• Am I clear about what the profession will require of a project leader in the future?	• Given the impact of professional bodies and key influencers, how might the role of the project leader change? • **What would be the benefits of our project leader community aligning to these changes?**
Customer market What your future customers will expect		• For the type of customers I wish to work with, how might their expectations change my role?	• Given our understanding of the market and customers, what will be the expectations on the organization and in turn the project leaders? • **What benefits would we achieve from meeting future customer expectations?**

From this analysis, future capabilities will be identified which may not necessarily be radically different from current capabilities, but which may show a different focus and importance. The outcomes from this exercise will identify the future areas of focus for development and talent planning.

It is then important to identify relative priorities since not all development requirements can be delivered at the same time. The following approach, as shown in Figure 12.2, can be helpful in assisting the organization to prioritize in these circumstances. Current Capability is mapped against Future Importance to help identify which areas of capability should be prioritized. The Low > High axes are deliberately changed to identify areas of low priority in the bottom left and high priority in the top right, which is how we normally present such information.

Often by developing one particular capability you can influence others. So for example. by primarily focusing on Vision and Objectives you will help develop knowledge of Benefits Management. A similar approach can be used for the leadership behaviours expected by individuals (discussed in detail in Chapter 1). In this case, you might focus development on Negotiation Skills which will in turn impact Decision Making.

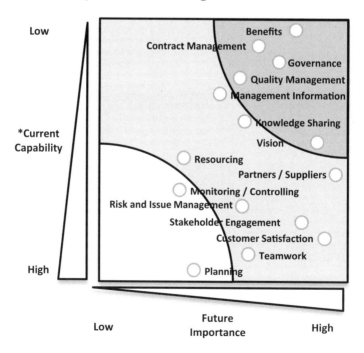

Figure 12.2   Prioritization of future capabilities

12.2   Assessing the Organization's Support for Project Leaders and Project Leadership

Below is a framework that we have created through working with organizations to identify the multiple elements that must be in place to fully support the development and sustained success of project leaders. The framework is made up of elements that are neither mutually exclusive nor collectively exhaustive. It is focused on the individual and on the collective capability of the organization to lead projects. We've represented this framework as a honeycomb (see Figure 12.3), since in reality each element is interrelated and supports other elements.

The elements will be of differing importance and priority for each organization and may well be combined. We have used this framework as a diagnostic tool to help organizations to identify what is most important to focus on, and then plan to make the necessary changes to support project leaders.

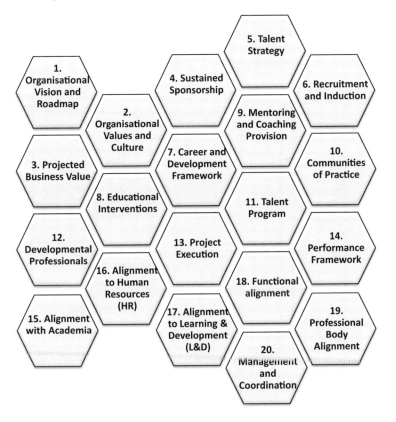

Figure 12.3   Honeycomb Project Leadership Development Framework™

The framework can be used in two ways:

1. by the organizational leader and development professional to assess the organization's support to help identify gaps and plan for improvement;
2. by the project leader as a checklist for discussion with your manager or Learning and Development function regarding what support can be provided and the areas of greatest need for you personally.

We will look at the above framework from the point of view of the person responsible for, or with an interest in, the development of their organization's project leadership capability and community.

From our experience the primary requirement is to demonstrate a clear link between organizational objectives and project leadership development. This link will be unique to the organization, influenced by factors including but not limited to its client base, products and services, culture, size and maturity. Without it, the value will not be perceived and therefore support will be limited or short lived. Table 12.2 below illustrates the Project Leadership Development Diagnostic™. This is a framework to help this assessment, prompting key questions to the organization.

Table 12.2   Project Leadership Development Diagnostic™

Area and overview	Description and questions the organizational representative should ask	✓
1. Organizational Vision and Roadmap Clarity over where the organization is going, what it needs to be successful and the part project leaders play in achieving this	Without clarity here there is no purpose or direction to any leadership development. Any development should align with agreed business objectives. The causes of poor performance and capability gaps should be identified, then development plans for project leaders identified. For example, a greater focus on supporting innovation and cross-functional collaboration. **Question:** What are the leadership capabilities that are critical to support the delivery of the organizations strategy? **Note:** See Figure 12.1 for the factors that must be taken into account when identifying the critical future capabilities.	
2. Organizational Values and Culture What is important to the organization and the manner in which it works	We need to understand the values (or equivalent) of the organization, clarifying the 'how' which can be more important than the 'what'. This then provides clarity to the project leader regarding the expectation on their personal behaviours and the way they lead the project. For example, to align to its values an organization may take an ethical stance when working with suppliers or insist on a zero tolerance safety culture. **Question:** Can the organization clearly articulate its values to allow the project leader to orientate themselves when making decisions?	

Table 12.2   Project Leadership Development Diagnostic™ (*continued*)

Area and overview	Description and questions the organizational representative should ask	
3. Projected Business Value Clear demonstration of how any investment in development will benefit the organization	Each organization has a different way in which it objectively or subjectively makes decisions regarding its investment decisions. As a basis for sustained support to the development of project leaders, the organization must clearly articulate how this value can be measured. For some organizations there is a need to define business metrics, assess the impact of any intervention and adjust the strategy accordingly.	
	Question: Are we clear about the value we wish to achieve? Do we have a method in place to assess what has been achieved and the expected return?	
4. Sustained Sponsorship Ongoing commitment and approval of resources by senior managers	Sponsorship, as we have stressed throughout the book, is critical to any endeavour – the ongoing support and commitment by senior managers to ensure success and long-term value for the organization. Building and sustaining a high-value project leadership capability has the same requirement.	
	Question: Do we have the sponsorship necessary to provide the resources and support to the project leaders to perform effectively and develop their capability?	
5. Talent Strategy A clear and robust strategy that covers how the organization will identify and grow the talent of tomorrow	Building and maintaining a pool of capable project leaders requires planning and sustained effort. The strategy should describe: • the future capabilities required; • the approach to identifying talent; • how this talent should be developed (in the case of project leaders this might be primarily through the projects they work on); • the way that this will be managed.	
	Question: Is there a talent strategy, with associated implementation plan, in place and understood by key stakeholders describing how we develop and maintain a capable pool of project leaders?	
6. Recruitment and Induction Processes to identify project leaders and effectively on-board them into the organization	When the organization's capabilities need cannot be fulfilled internally in the short term, it will typically rely on recruiting in the types and numbers of project leaders required for future success. This might be through the use of contractors and interims, as well as permanent employees. Again, the decisions made should be aligned to the organization's strategy.	
	Question: Do we have the necessary processes and information to allow us to on-board the correct type of project leader when we need them?	

Table 12.2   Project Leadership Development Diagnostic™ (continued)

Area and overview	Description and questions the organizational representative should ask	
7. Career and Development Framework Communicates what is expected of an individual, how they can develop and be supported, and how progress will be assessed and rewarded	This will typically include: • job families and associated role descriptions (often using a structure specific to the organization); • clear definition not only of what a person should do (tasks), and knowledge they should have (skills) but also how they should do it (competencies); • specified career path and how transition will happen • associated developmental path to support career progression • recruitment, induction, reward and recognition, and retention strategy. **Question:** Do we have a career framework that clearly defines how a project leader is chosen, developed and progresses from a career perspective?	
8. Educational Interventions Design and maintenance of educational resources to support flexible individual and group development	The organization must ensure that there is sufficient breadth (in terms of topics) and depth (in terms of options for delivering) together with the commitment and resources to sustain this. Flexibility is key to ensure that people of different needs, learning styles and situations have equal opportunities to support their development. **Question:** Do we have a suite of educational interventions that can help support the development of project leaders with any necessary required new skills?	
9. Mentoring and Coaching Provision Commitment and support from those with the wisdom and skills to develop leadership capabilities	Coaching and mentoring are powerful development options based on a good relationship between the project leader and the coach and/or mentor. Coaching was historically seen as an indication of poor performance, but increasingly coaching is being used to help accelerate personal and professional development. Mentoring is typically provided internally by someone with greater experience within the organization or industry. **Question:** Do we have the structures and mentors/coaches in place to provide one-to-one or one-to-many support for project leaders?	
10. Communities of Practice Sharing knowledge and interest with peers inside, and external to, the organization	Communities of Practice are groups of people who share a common interest, in this case leading projects. Sharing knowledge and good practice supports development and provides insight into different ways of working. Communities of Practice are primarily community-driven but can be designed to take account of the organization's structure and culture. Roles within the community can be defined if this is helpful. **Question:** Is there a supportive network of project leaders and associated roles that come together as a community to support their collective development? This might be within the organization, or externally through professional bodies or similar.	

Table 12.2   Project Leadership Development Diagnostic™ (continued)

Area and overview	Description and questions the organizational representative should ask	
11. Talent Programme An intense and focused developmental programme geared to providing the organization with the project leaders it needs for its success	This is a Project Leader Development Programme, geared to the needs of the organization and flexible in the way it is delivered to meet individual needs and learning styles. This is described in detail in Chapter 11. **Question:** Does the organization have a talent programme with the primary aim of developing the next generation of project leaders?	
12. Developmental Professionals Professional instructors and facilitators who can develop the project leaders	These may be development professionals or practitioners who have been identified and deployed to maximize support to project leaders. **Question:** Do we have the structures and people in place to identify, support and manage the best trainers and facilitators to develop our future project leaders?	
13. Project Execution Critical process to identify appropriate project opportunities to support the individual's development	An individual's personal development is influenced primarily by what they can learn from applying new knowledge on programmes and projects (see the 70/20/10 model). It is critical therefore that individuals work on the right projects at the optimum time to develop their capability. It will not always be possible but with careful planning this can slowly be optimized for the whole community. This requires a broader control of the portfolio of projects – information regarding future demand/ capacity and community capability. **Question:** Do we have the processes in place and information available to allow us to identify appropriate project opportunities to develop the individual project leader?	
14. Performance Framework To provide the necessary objective feedback to allow project leaders to know where to focus their developmental effort	Typically separate 'career/development' and 'performance' to ensure the community is clear about the distinction. In addition, individual performance should be assessed against a broad set of factors, which includes but is not exclusive to project performance. So, project leaders will typically be assessed using the overall organization's HR performance framework although adaptations may be appropriate. **Question:** Is there a performance framework in place which aims to provide the project leader with the insights necessary to support their development?	

Table 12.2   Project Leadership Development Diagnostic™ (continued)

Area and overview	Description and questions the organizational representative should ask	
15. Alignment with Academia Utilizing the resources and opportunities provided by academic and research bodies to support the development of project leaders	It can be important to build relationships with academia to gain access to what is often leading-edge thinking, new insights and research. It is helpful to identify the best and most usable academic research applicable to the organization's sector and business, and distil it into ready-to-apply knowledge. **Question:** Do we have relationships in place with academic bodies that can provide knowledge, insights and new thinking to support our project leaders?	
16. Alignment to Human Resources (HR) Support which can be provided by HR to maximize the effectiveness of project leaders	Dependent on the relative maturity of HR and its purpose within the organization. For example, within some organizations the HR function sponsors and controls all development programmes; in others, it is left to the business units and HR focuses on compensation, incentives, promotion and succession planning. HR may assist in running Development and Assessment centres if required. Their primary focus can come in developing and assisting in the delivery of a *talent* strategy and development programmes. They can also play an important part in making available project resources by the effective sourcing and on-boarding of project team members. **Question:** Do we have the support of HR to maximize the effectiveness of our project leaders?	
17. Alignment to Learning and Development (L&D) The particular processes and practices within HR that align with education and training of personnel	In some organizations this is a separate function from HR. It is important that their expertise and resources are used in any development strategy. L&D can assist in commissioning and delivery of educational interventions and also provide support in the way of a Virtual Learning Environment or similar. There can often be challenges when L&D do not fully understand the often-unique development needs of project leaders. **Question:** Do we have the support of L&D in the development of our project leaders?	
18. Functional Alignment Alignment of the multiple organizational functions including Finance, Marketing, Internal Comms to support the project leader	It is important to have alignment and support from all functions within the organization to ensure that project leaders have the minimum level of internal friction when delivering projects, thereby improving the outcome and also their own development. It should be made clear what resources and support are required from different functional areas. **Question:** How aligned are the multiple functions within the organization to support project leaders to deliver success?	

Table 12.2   Project Leadership Development Diagnostic™ (concluded)

Area and overview	Description and questions the organizational representative should ask	✓
19. Professional Body Alignment Utilizing the resources that professional bodies can provide to support the development and performance of project leaders	Building relationships with the different areas within professional bodies (such as knowledge sharing, events, communities) to maximize the value the organization and project leaders can gain. The organization's talent strategy may be aligned to different professional bodies. **Question**: Do we have relationships in place with professional bodies that can provide access to knowledge, qualifications and accreditation to support our project leaders?	
20. Management and Coordination Critical processes to ensure that each element is managed and resources prioritized to best support project leaders' performance	There are multiple elements that go into developing and supporting the delivery of projects, as identified above. It is important that there is sufficient design, management, monitoring and controlling of each to maximize the value of any investment in time or resources by the organization. Without this coordination, support will be fragmented and likely of little value. **Question**: Do we have the governance and planning in place to effectively manage the multiple elements identified above to deliver the support and development opportunities to our project leaders?	

We have worked with a range of organizations that have used similar frameworks to help them grasp the multiple influences at play and to assess objectively where effort should be directed to achieve maximum benefit. An example is shown in Figure 12.4, which identifies the profile for an organization using a scale of 0 (Unaware) to 5 (Optimized) for each area. Within the full diagnostic we have identified a series of questions that help an assessment to be made.

The challenge faced by most if not all organizations to some degree is defining the nature of the project leader's role and how this fits with typical structures such as job families, career frameworks, leadership framework and competencies.

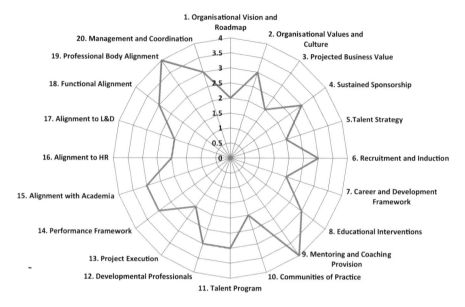

Figure 12.4   Project Leadership Development Diagnostic™ output

12.3   The Project Leader's View

Whatever shape and content of support is provided, from the project leader's perspective it must be kept simple in terms of what is presented to them and how they need to work with it. Accessibility and immediate relevance are also important. Figure 12.5 opposite is a suggested structure that can be used as a front end to present to project leaders.

We have used a similar model with a large technology company to assist its project leaders to focus on only the most important aspects when working on their development. The Development Plan summarizes activities in each area and acts as a point of focus and reference throughout the year.

Conclusion

Project leaders play an important role in supporting organizations to execute their strategy and meet their ambitions. Therefore it is important that every effort is made to support them and their development. The organization should be clear about what it requires from its future project leaders and how it can

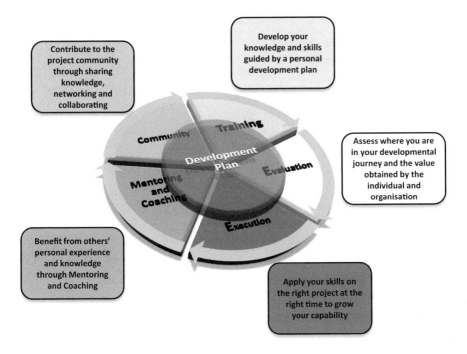

Contribute to the project community through sharing knowledge, networking and collaborating

Develop your knowledge and skills guided by a personal development plan

Community

Training

Development Plan

Evaluation

Mentoring and Coaching

Execution

Assess where you are in your developmental journey and the value obtained by the individual and organisation

Benefit from others' personal experience and knowledge through Mentoring and Coaching

Apply your skills on the right project at the right time to grow your capability

Figure 12.5   Project leaders' development model

support them to deliver what can be a challenging role. From a project leader's perspective they are looking for certainty and clarity to allow them to plan their career and development.

Key Questions

- How does the organization assess the future leadership capabilities that are important to achieve their strategy and ambitions?
- What project leadership capabilities does the organization need in the future to be successful?
- What are the key priorities for the organization to invest in?
- How does the organization provide clarity about their learning and development priorities to their project leadership community? What support does the organization give to their project leaders to provide opportunities to develop?

Reference

Hamel, G. (2012) *What Matters Now* Jossey-Bass, San Francisco, CA.

CHAPTER 13

An Idealized Project Leadership Development Programme

…. nobody can teach you leadership. It is something you have to learn.

John Adair

Introduction

In Chapters 11 and 12 we looked at building project leadership capability from the perspective of the individual and support offered by the organization. This chapter identifies the key characteristics of an 'ideal' project leadership development programme. We use the term "ideal" because what we are presenting here is a blueprint incorporating good practice from a range of assignments we have worked on and from in-depth research of such programs. As such, this blueprint can be modified and customized to the needs of any particular organization and their community of project leaders. To be truly effective, the programme must draw on all of the resources available to provide a comprehensive and flexible experience for those it wishes to develop. Realistically, there may be resource implications that impact the ambition of the organization, whether this implication is financial, support and commitment from key stakeholders, or the ability of the organization to deliver.

From our own experiences of designing, developing and delivering development programmes we are able to offer here a framework for an 'ideal' project leadership development programme which can then be modified by the organization. We share this with you in order to provide a basis from which to understand and start the conversation around the scale of the task, the elements involved, the blend of content and delivery channels, the commitment necessary for investing in your project management community, more specifically in your project leadership capability.

13.1   Can Project Leadership Skills be Taught?

Perhaps surprisingly, the answer is no, at least in part. Traditional competency training provides the building blocks by teaching 'what' needs to be done. It misses the subtlety of the 'how'. We have discussed previously that it is the 'how' that differentiates the best leaders since training the traditional skills on their own simply cannot impact the required leadership skills. Unlike technical skills, these leadership competencies are more art than science and are undertaken in individual ways by every leader. Our experience and research has shown that project leaders can be enabled to emerge, but that this requires an entirely new learning process and focus. Given the unique context within which each organization operates, any developmental programme must be aligned to equip participants with the necessary development opportunities to best deal with these challenges. Further, creating a cadre of leadership requires cross-functional planning within the organization to link such elements as career planning, resource management (including capacity/demand management and assignment management), appraisal, recognition and rewards.

For any effective development to occur, those talented individuals with the potential to become leaders must first be identified. Then the skills so pertinent to leadership must be developed in ways that enable the new project leader to demonstrably change how they work. The flexible framework presented later in this chapter provides a focus for discussion within your organization.

13.2   Why Leadership Development Programmes Fail

Gurdjian, Halbeisen and Lane (2012) suggested that, in order to overcome the four common mistakes they identified in leadership development, organizations need to:

- focus on context, so matching specific leadership skills and traits to the current context;
- present different perspectives and values, so adjusting the mindsets that underpin behaviour;
- tie leadership development to organizational projects, so embedding leadership development in relevant work of real value to the organization;
- monitor the impact, so ensuring the development programme provides tangible benefits to the organization and provides a return on investment.

We will pick up on each of these points in the following development programme description. Our own experience and research also shows that other significant challenges include:

- Designing, developing and delivering across diverse locations and different cultures and languages requires flexibility around what is provided, how and where (while still maintaining a sound foundation).
- Scalability and buy-in issues where there may be a successful pilot but the roll-out to a wider community may encounter challenges around quality and resources, or around buy-in from different business units or regions.
- Challenges engaging individual learners who have particular issues such as:
  - availability – it is not unusual for some learners to have more work to do than time available. In these cases it is about providing 'bite-sized' learning at times and in ways that suit them best;
  - some learners, especially those at senior levels, feel that they don't need to learn, effectively being 'too cool for school'. In these cases, it is about directly linking the learning to personal and organizational outcomes;
  - some managers are reticent about allowing senior and well-paid personnel time out for development. Often the feeling here is that these individuals got to where they are *because* of their knowledge and experience, therefore there are few areas left for them to develop. In these cases, it is again about directly linking the learning to personal and organizational outcomes. It can also be about renaming the development programme altogether and using instead the more general title of 'updates' or 'information briefings'.

The most ineffective kinds of development programmes are those that are often classed as 'sheep dipping' exercises, where everyone goes through the same short, intense development regardless of what they need individually, their experience, expertise, learning styles (discussed in Chapter 11), strengths and development needs. There is little warning that you are about to be dunked and no towel to dry you when you get out! Some development programmes we know of rely on an intensive programme focused on one type of intervention, typically exclusively face-to-face workshops or exclusively e-learning. We advocate a blended approach of discussion, the practical, the presentation of current thought and practice and so on, using a number of channels over several months and ideally longer than a year. This has the benefit of providing a variety of delivery channels, including as many different ways of learning as possible, and over an extended time period, so helping to embed new behaviours and allowing sufficient time and space for reflection and practice. We also advocate that development is backed up by coaching or mentoring, so providing delegates with that all important non-judgmental and objective time-out to discuss issues which are important to them but which they won't share with peers because they believe it would demonstrate weakness or ignorance.

Other development programmes don't gain senior-level support or sufficient budget so fizzle out after one or two modules, leaving a very jaundiced view of the organization itself and its willingness to invest in its personnel. We have experienced this exact situation with a multinational firm wishing to improve the capability and thereby performance of their large project management community. Various issues led to the halting of the programme, including a change of senior sponsor, insufficient budget to allow reasonable momentum to be created, complex organizational politics and demanding customer roles for those on the programme, making it difficult for them to fully commit to the programme. Additionally, the fact that there was not a clear enough link between the individual and organizational challenges, the purpose of the programme and its ability to deliver value also presented an internal issue about the viability of the programme.

13.3　Planning for Success

Designed, developed and delivered properly, this type of development programme is a significant investment for any organization in terms of time, commitment and finance. Understandably, organizations want to evaluate the impact and return on investment. That is why success criteria for the programme should be identified and agreed upfront in just the same way as we described for any project in Chapter 8. In this way, the evaluation process for both the individual and organization is designed into the system itself, development programme reviews can be scheduled at key points throughout and a formal evaluation of the organization's expectations can be assessed at the conclusion of the programme.

An effective evaluation process (see Chapter 12, Table 12.2 Project Leadership Development Diagnostic™ as a basis for this) will build on an organization's existing appraisal system.

So how do you define success for those involved? When working with a major international infrastructure consultancy we developed, and obtained agreement from all stakeholders, a set of success criteria. Further work was done to identify, where possible, appropriate metrics against which the programme performance could be monitored. Table 13.1 identifies some of the success criteria from four different perspectives. Your organization will potentially have a different set of stakeholders and of course success criteria.

Table 13.1   Example success criteria for a leadership development programme

Customer	The programme: • Does not negatively impact project performance • Provides benefit to client projects through application of new tools and approaches, and knowledge transfer, with a measureable performance improvement
Programme	The programme: • Results in cost effective personal/leadership development • Helps to develop the organization's knowledge library • Is aligned (content, timing, and so on) to other group development programmes. For example, senior management team and leadership programmes • Ensures coaching and mentoring are effective techniques and have a demonstrably positive impact on participant's performance and development • Is tailored to participant's development needs • Allows participants to share their learning with others in the community • Provides clarity over the selection process for participants so that regions and staff feel the process is fair and transparent • Is inspirational and highly engaging for participants • Provides a strong and lasting network for each cohort of participants • Uses work assignments to consolidate learning and drive development
Organization	• The value/impact of the programme contributes to delivering the organization's strategy • Participants want to develop their careers within the organization • The programme has a positive and measurable return on investment • Regions and functions understand the value and actively support the programme (financially, time and internal promotion) • Existing and potential clients have a positive perception of the programme
Participants	• I will learn something new which will be relevant to my current and future project roles • The commitment required (time, activity and effort) is clear and manageable • The impact on those I interact with (work and personal life) is clear and manageable • Being part of the programme will accelerate my career development • The value I will receive from the programme is worth the time and effort I will need to invest in it • The programme will be inspiring, engaging and exciting throughout – not just in learning sessions • I will be put into relevant roles, enabling me to apply, embed and develop what I have learned • My project team and sponsor understand and buy into my involvement in the programme • I am allowed the necessary time to engage fully in the programme

13.4   What Does an Ideal Project Leadership Development Programme Look Like?

To achieve what has been set out previously as a 'blended approach' over a period of months requires flexibility of delivery and ongoing support to successfully embed new learning and behaviour in participants. This blended approach can include:

- face-to-face facilitator-led workshops using a mix of discussion, practical exercises, role playing and presentation of current thinking and good practice;
- residential and non-residential development;
- e-learning support via podcasts, web conferencing facilities, social and mobile media, online indicators and analytical tools and reports;
- one-to-one coaching;
- one-to-one or one-to-many tutorials and workshop discussions;
- action learning groups with other cohort members or within projects;
- other support, for example telephone and email coaching support plus access to a website with a variety of articles, resources and contacts providing an ongoing community of interest;
- individual reflective journals.

Many of the above approaches were discussed in Chapter 11. The benefit of this 'blended approach' is the variety of delivery channels and approaches to learning, mirroring the variety of participants' own learning styles.

A further dimension of the ideal Project Leader Development Programme is the extended timescale, allowing participants to develop over a period of time. Dedicated development and learning time is interspersed with the opportunity to translate the knowledge gained into practice back in the workplace, so helping embed new learnings and behaviours.

Assuming all of the elements are in place, the organization has the opportunity to robustly and successfully develop their project leaders. Figure 13.1 shows the core elements of an Ideal Project Leader Development Programme.

Table 13.2 provides a description of the various considerations and elements of the framework based on a comprehensive understanding of the needs of the organization and the needs and requirements of each participant, as discussed earlier. It is a topic worthy of considerably more discussion but the following should provide a good initial briefing to allow you to have an informed conversation within your organization.

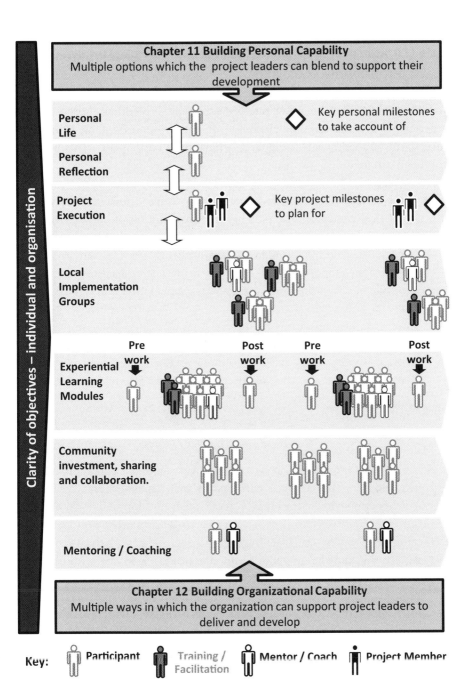

Figure 13.1   Core elements of a Project Leader Development Programme

Table 13.2   Considerations and elements of an ideal Project Leadership Development Programme

Consideration and key question	Points/ questions to consider for each aspect of a Project Leader Development Programme
Clarity of Objectives What are we aiming to achieve?	• The first and most important. Is it clear what will be achieved from the investment including the changes in behaviours of those participating?
Participants Who should be on the programme?	• Typically 'High Potentials' (similar development programmes are often referred to as HiPo programmes)
	• Typically only run for those who have the potential to take on leadership roles, but there is considerable value in running these development programmes for a broader spectrum of participants to maximize the skill depth of the community
	• There should be a positive decision by the participants to be part of the programme. To be beneficial the programme needs to stretch and challenge participates, but not to stress them. Therefore it is desirable for participants to *positively say no* to participating; in our experience this typically occurs when the personal commitment is fully understood
Timescale How long it should last and how should it be phased?	• Programmes should last around 18 months. Shorter timeframes are unlikely to provide any lasting results as new behaviours may not yet have become habits
	• On the grounds of cost and available time, organizations often make a false economy by choosing a single day or half-day isolated session in terms of learning content. The most these types of short session can effectively achieve is to heighten the sense of awareness that there are other choices, skills and behaviours from which participants can benefit. It is only by providing a longer-term, blended and multidimensional development programme that organizations start to see a real change
Structure How should it be structured in terms of the number of modules and type of interventions?	• 'Experiential learning modules' are the most visible aspect of most programmes. It is important therefore to consider how many such modules are required, for what length and at what time intervals. Since the primary source of learning comes from the projects the leader works on, there must be sufficient time allowed between each module for application, testing, discussion, retesting and so on of the knowledge gained
	• Running multiple cohorts (or groups) of participants in parallel provides greater flexibility in terms of catching up on modules for those participants who have availability or scheduling issues

Table 13.2 Considerations and elements of an ideal Project Leadership Development Programme (*continued*)

Consideration and key question	Points/ questions to consider for each aspect of a Project Leader Development Programme
Module Topics What experiences, topics and materials should be included?	• It is important that the experiential workshops encourage reflection during and after each new discussion. This enables individuals to consider how they might change the way they do things, and to consider different options and choices of behaviour • Varied interventions should be designed into the programme to best support a change in behaviours. This multi-pronged approach greatly increases the chance of behavioural change since individuals have different learning styles • External speakers, site visits, multi-location running, changing facilitators and so on should all be considered in this approach since again this supports different learning styles • Using an appropriate set of tools such as psychometric profiling provides participants with insights about themselves and how they interact with others. Choosing the right tool for the job will depend on the objectives of the programme • Ensure the programme adds to what has already been invested in by the organization • Requiring participants to complete pre-module and post-module work ensures that maximum value is gained. This should ideally be built into the 'Implementation Groups' that will be discussed below
Module Facilitation How should they be designed, run and facilitated?	• Initial modules are typically designed and facilitated by external parties who can bring experience and knowledge from other programmes and industries • To meet the community's needs and to allow them to feel a sense of ownership the cohort should then start to adapt what is planned for the remainder of the programme. They are being asked to demonstrate what the programme aims to develop – leadership • Participants will therefore start to research and present elements of modules, requiring them to consolidate and embed knowledge that they have gained in the process • Control therefore changes as you move through the programme – modelling the principles of leadership by moving from follower to leader • Leaders want to choose their own path and method for achieving this so the programme must be flexible enough to accommodate different personal styles, motivations and circumstances

Table 13.2   Considerations and elements of an ideal Project Leadership Development Programme (*continued*)

Consideration and key question	Points/ questions to consider for each aspect of a Project Leader Development Programme

Implementation Groups How should participants benefit between modules from interaction with fellow cohort members?	• Ideally local cohort members should meet face to face where possible, otherwise utilizing social media technologies to get together and work virtually
	• Action Learning Groups or Peer Learning Groups should be a key part of the programme since these groups provide peer support and forums for discussions. The greatest learning will come from working through issues, challenges and successes with peers. These groups are typically set up with three to four members. Groups should be facilitated, at least initially, by an experienced team coach with the aim of meeting at least twice between modules. These meetings can be used to:
	  ○ Challenge and support participants to implement what they have learnt; also to encourage them to model a mentoring approach to facilitate the flow of learning into their own teams
	  ○ Create a peer group that is a power house of new project management initiatives for the organization. Groups can support Community of Practice initiatives such as cascading of knowledge across the community to share learning and experiences. This ensures the maximum number of people gain from the exercise and it openly demonstrates the organization's commitment to development
	• To focus on 'how' they are operating and implementing their learning and not just talking about operating differently. This creates a high-calibre group of project leaders

Mentoring and/or Coaching What one-to-one support is required for individual participants to accelerate their development?	• Coaching and mentoring are often talked about as one and the same thing, but there are subtle differences that are worth exploring since they will impact the support provided and so the benefit received. They must be distinguished as such in the organization and within the programme • Interventions should be fundamentally mentoring/ coaching (individual and team)-based and focus on how they work rather than what they do. This provides support to the individuals in the most effective way possible and models their move into leadership • Growing bodies of evidence suggest that the key differentiator of successful project leaders is the quality of their relationships: particularly relationships with key stakeholders. Coaching and mentoring is recognized as the ideal way to learn these skills because it takes place through the relationship with the mentor/coach. Primary objectives are to: ○ Ensure the areas covered elsewhere in the development programme are transferred into working practices and behaviours

Table 13.2   Considerations and elements of an ideal Project Leadership Development Programme (*continued*)

Consideration and key question	Points/ questions to consider for each aspect of a Project Leader Development Programme
Mentoring and/or Coaching (*continued*)	○ Discuss what has worked for the participant ○ Provide positive challenge to the participant ○ Identify what has not gone well, why and how to recover the situation ○ Help the participant find other choices about how they might do things and to look at different perspectives • We have found Structured Coaching to be particularly successful. This combines personally focused development with key project leadership content aligned to the organization's objectives. Content, number of sessions and feedback can all be shaped to fit the context. This appeals to both the participant and organization as it provides a pre-defined structure to work through. It provides: ○ Coaching to accelerate participants' leadership skills, capability and performance ○ Content designed to challenge participants to focus on the key aspects of project success ○ Focus on outcomes to ensure less prevarication and more action • Organizational fitness for purpose is designed into the process by first establishing the organization's requirements and, within this, the participant's needs
Project Execution How do we ensure there are on-the-job opportunities to apply the knowledge and embed the learning?	• Research continually shows that the most effective means of learning is through doing, and leadership development is no exception. Translating learning into doing is most easily and readily done in the work place. This not only provides experiential challenge, it also provides a range of opportunities: ○ For the individual to put into practice those things introduced through the development programme and get to get immediate feedback from peers and colleagues ○ For the organization to gain directly from a highly motivated group of individuals tackling a particular issue or area of the organization, and to make the development programme real and relevant for both the individual and for the organization • Key to this is a robust approach towards the balancing of resource capability, demand and capacity and the needs of individuals to develop their careers. A process must be in place to regularly monitor and make decisions that not only meet the needs of the development programme but also the organization and the participants • The participant must plan their development around the project they are provided as part of the development programme

Table 13.2 Considerations and elements of an ideal Project Leadership Development Programme (*concluded*)

Consideration and key question	Points/questions to consider for each aspect of a Project Leader Development Programme
Community Engagement What value can be achieved for the participant, and in return from the community, by contributing time and knowledge?	• If the organization has a supportive Community of Practice (a group of people who share a concern or a passion for something they do and learn how to do it better as they interact regularly) this can be highly supportive to the participants • A Community of Practice is focused on developing the skills and capability and is designed to use the expertise and enthusiasm of project management champions who will take ownership of key areas of knowledge • Programme participants may engage in joint activities and discussions with other community members, help each other, and share information thereby building relationships that may be useful in the future. These informal networks that are developed have been shown to be as powerful as the formal networks enabling them to learn from each other. Also community members are themselves practitioners and together they develop a shared repertoire of resources: experiences, stories, tools, ways of addressing recurring problems – in short a shared practice. This takes time and sustained interaction
Personal Life How can personal, customer and talent programme needs be balanced?	• The development program, like work, must fit with a participant's personal life. A strange perspective, perhaps, but as well as identifying individuals for the programme the organization should ensure the participant can give the programme the time and energy it requires, so that the individual's personal circumstances, commitments and responsibilities must be factored in
Personal Reflection How can the space be created to ensure that learning is efficiently and properly processed and internalized?	• It is critical that the participant has the time to reflect on what has been learned and experienced, and look to embed this in their way of working • Reflection is key to obtaining the value from development programmes. If the time is not provided, the participant may not identify the lessons • Participants may have to be encouraged to do this as a prescribed task as part of the programme, if it is not a habit from which they already benefit

13.5 What Single Thing Makes the Biggest Difference in Embedding the Learning?

It may seem strange to pick out what appears to be a single aspect of personal development, but in our opinion reflection is the least used and most valuable.

Multiple studies have shown that having the ability to reflect and learn from experiences is critical to any leader. Some individuals require a highly structured approach to this to ensure that it is done, but others require only a prompt and request for feedback to ensure it is effective.

We've long made use of reflective journals as an integral part of our development programmes to help our participants' critical reflective practice. This is the point we prompt participants to consider the interplay between the content of the development programme and their learning from it, how they learn best and any course of further action they need to take. Documenting this in a journal in note form, diagrams, mind maps, colour-coded (in fact, in whatever form is most relevant to the individual) helps to crystallize independent and critical thought, understanding and follow-up. Typically, participants fill the reflective journal with thoughts and reflections, ideas and new bits of knowledge gained, things they have enjoyed and the things they continue to grapple with. It's theirs, it is personal to them and it contains whatever is important to them. Typically, the following are some of the things that participants consider:

- What did I learn during this last development session?
- What did I contribute?
- How would I best describe where I currently am and what I am feeling about it?
- What happened when I tried something new? Why did I succeed or fail?
- Did I have an 'aha' moment?
- Why am I having a déjà vu moment?
- Did I consider an alternative perspective? Why or why not?
- What have I learned so far that is causing me to do things differently or think about things differently?
- What new behaviours and/or ways of doing things do I prefer to keep to myself and why?
- What research / readings have I have done to support my development?
- What new technological or specialist skills do I need to develop and how will I use them?
- What are my personal feelings about the development programme and how I am benefitting from it?
- What are my plans for the next week?

One healthcare project leader told us: 'I use the reflective journal to rant and let off steam. By the end of writing I feel more informed about my emotional state and usually have one or two questions or issues which I will reflect on further. I also have a rule where I am not allowed to cross anything out or remove anything from the journal, which can be quite insightful.'

Conclusion

Evidence from our experience and research across multiple projects, project management communities and industry sectors demonstrates it is how project leaders engage with individuals, teams and organizations that is the real differentiator of success. Any project leadership development programme needs to be able to configure this to the specific context of the organization, not just for the current situation, but for the future.

There are many reasons why development programmes fail, primarily around a lack of alignment to the organization's objectives. This typically results in inadequate support, which in turn leads to the slow death of the programme. This frustrates not only those who have put their energies into conceiving and initiating the development programme but more importantly the project leaders who are left demotivated and questioning the organization's commitment to them and the real value of their role to the organization.

We have offered here an ideal project leadership development programme framework, not as a definitive approach but as a way of helping start the conversation within the organization about:

- developing project leaders;
- the many facets of an ideal project leadership development programme;
- understanding the commitment required by the participants and by the organization;
- the adaptations required to meet the organization's needs.

Key Questions

- Is there a development programme currently in place in your organization?
- If so:
  - Is it seen as adding value?
  - How does it compare in composition to the ideal development programme described?

  - What elements could be added to enhance what is already in place?
- If not, what would be the benefits to:
  - Me?
  - My fellow project leaders?
  - The organization?

References

Gurdjian, P., Halbeisen, T. and Lane, K. (2012) 'Why leadership-development programmes fail', January, McKinsey & Company.

Appendix:
The Eight Lookings Diagnostic

The diagnostic overleaf provides an indication of the focus you have for a particular looking. It is not a measure of quality or performance, and does not rely on the perception of others such as the project team. It also provides you with an indication of your project leadership style. We suggest you complete the diagnostic on a current project if you believe this is representative of your typical approach. The output of the diagnostic is to provide you with:

- insights into your current project leadership style;
- a basis for self-reflection on your approach;
- a basis for discussion about your professional development.

To what extent are each of these statements true? Try to make your judgment honestly and put a cross at what you consider is the appropriate point on the scale from 'Not at all true' to 'Very true'.

	Not at all true				Very true

A.

1	I clearly demonstrate to my sponsor and senior management that I understand the full impact of the project on the organization	1	2	3	4	5
2	I understand the client's vision and how delivery of the project will help them to achieve this	1	2	3	4	5
3	I ensure that my project has appropriate mechanisms for controlling, monitoring and measuring progress	1	2	3	4	5
4	I provide individual team members with all the support they need to enable them to do their jobs to the best of their ability	1	2	3	4	5
5	I can confidently say that I keep the client fully informed about project progress	1	2	3	4	5
6	I understand the vision of the project and its relevance to the organization in achieving its vision	1	2	3	4	5
7	I and all members of the team are very clear about our targets	1	2	3	4	5
8	I regularly take time out to reflect on events and what can be learned from them	1	2	3	4	5

B.

1	I am honest with myself about my own performance as a leader	1	2	3	4	5
2	I feel confident my sponsor will act appropriately to my requests for support or guidance	1	2	3	4	5
3	I understand how the project will impact the client	1	2	3	4	5
4	I ensure that we are good at providing timely and accurate progress and performance updates	1	2	3	4	5
5	I review individual performance and progress with team members regularly	1	2	3	4	5
6	I genuinely regard the client and their team as part of the project team	1	2	3	4	5
7	I understand how the project is aligned with the organization's strategy	1	2	3	4	5

C.

1	I ensure that team members share with me the responsibility for planning and anticipating	1	2	3	4	5
2	I actively invite feedback on my performance as project leader from a range of sources	1	2	3	4	5
3	I help my sponsor to help me by keeping them fully informed	1	2	3	4	5

		Not at all true				Very true
4	I am confident of the plans made with the client for making the changes to deliver the benefits	1	2	3	4	5
5	When things go wrong, we are good at taking effective action to put things right quickly	1	2	3	4	5
6	I put time and effort into developing our effectiveness in working as a high-performing team	1	2	3	4	5
7	I have a clearly developed strategy for marketing the project within the client organization	1	2	3	4	5
8	I understand the benefits to the organization of delivering the project	1	2	3	4	5

D.

1	I understand how this project fits with other projects and initiatives	1	2	3	4	5
2	I am constantly trying to anticipate the problems that might lie over the horizon	1	2	3	4	5
3	I take active steps to manage my stress to ensure that I remain a successful leader	1	2	3	4	5
4	I fully understand the expectations of the project's internal key stakeholders.	1	2	3	4	5
5	I work with the client on any challenges to delivery within their organization	1	2	3	4	5
6	I ensure that my project team never repeats the same mistake	1	2	3	4	5
7	I am aware of the strengths and weaknesses of my key team members	1	2	3	4	5
8	Team members share with me the responsibility for managing important external relationships with the client	1	2	3	4	5

E.

1	I am successful at persuading the client to provide the resources needed from their organization	1	2	3	4	5
2	I understand and act on any organizational challenges to successful delivery	1	2	3	4	5
3	Much of my information for planning comes from members of the team, peer reviews or even outsiders with relevant experience and expertise	1	2	3	4	5
4	I make conscious decisions about changing my priorities and, if required, approach at each stage of the project lifecycle	1	2	3	4	5
5	I believe myself to be organizationally and politically intelligent and understand how decisions impacting my project are made	1	2	3	4	5

		Not at all true				Very true
6	I ensure the team has the same level of understanding of the client as I do	1	2	3	4	5
7	I ensure that team members share with me the responsibility for keeping things on track	1	2	3	4	5
8	I actively foster collaboration and good working relationships between team members	1	2	3	4	5
F.						
1	I bring members of the team together regularly to build relationships and trust	1	2	3	4	5
2	I actively build and maintain relationships with key and primary external stakeholders	1	2	3	4	5
3	I actively manage resources and secure them from the organization for delivery	1	2	3	4	5
4	I am seldom caught out by unforeseen events	1	2	3	4	5
5	I seek regular feedback from others about how to improve my performance as project leader	1	2	3	4	5
6	I have built the necessary support and commitment within the organization for the project	1	2	3	4	5
7	The client and I have agreed and clarified each other's roles and responsibilities	1	2	3	4	5
8	I ensure that success is celebrated when we pass an important landmark in the project	1	2	3	4	5
G.						
1	I ensure that we have reliable sources of feedback about how we're doing	1	2	3	4	5
2	I ensure that my project team members are clear about the performance I expect of them	1	2	3	4	5
3	I understand the political and cultural challenges that the client has within their organization	1	2	3	4	5
4	I ensure the team has the same level of understanding of the organization as I do	1	2	3	4	5
5	I am good at imagining what might happen in the future and the risks this may cause	1	2	3	4	5
6	I take time out to think about how effectively I am leading the project and the impact I am having	1	2	3	4	5
7	I feel confident in confronting and trying to resolve disagreements at a senior level that affect the project.	1	2	3	4	5
8	I understand my own role as an intelligent client for the project's contractors	1	2	3	4	5

On the following table, record the score you assigned for each of the statements using the 1-5 scale. So, for example, if you scored yourself as 4 on Statement A6 then record 4 against A6 below, and so on. Once you have completed the table, add up your score for each group. Consider what these scores are telling you: what are your strengths and how can you share these to help develop others? What particular areas do you need to develop further, and how might you do this?

Looking Upwards	Looking Outwards
A1	A5
B2	B6
C3	C7
D4	D8
E5	E1
F6	F2
G7	F3
Total	Total
Looking Internally	**Looking Externally**
A6	A2
B7	B3
C8	C4
D1	D5
E2	E6
F3	F7
G4	G8
Total	Total
Looking Backwards	**Looking Forwards**
A3	A7
B4	B8
C5	C1
D6	D2
E7	E3
F8	F4
G1	G5
Total	Total

Looking Inwards	Looking Downwards
A8	A4
B1	B5
C2	C6
D3	D7
E4	E8
F5	F1
G6	G2
Total	**Total**

Index